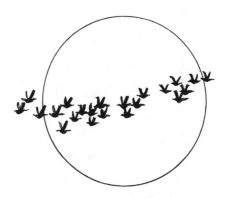

PRACTICAL
WILDLIFE
MANAGEMENT

PRACTICAL
WILDLIFE
MANAGEMENT

DR. GEORGE V. BURGER

WINCHESTER PRESS

To Jeannine, whose encouragement and assistance made it possible.

Library of Congress Catalog Card No. 72-96090
ISBN 0-87691-099-1
Published by Winchester Press
460 Park Avenue, New York 10022
Printed in the United States of America

Contents

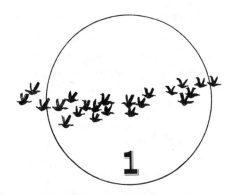

WHAT'S IT ALL ABOUT?

Never before has mankind been so concerned about a healthy environment—or so in need of it. The relentless growth of our population and the industries that support it destroy the air, soil, and water upon which present and future depend. With this increasingly publicized specter haunting us, and with social, political, racial, and "generation-gap" tensions mounting, can anyone justify a concern for wildlife?

You and I must think so, or I wouldn't be writing this, and you wouldn't be reading it. Yet many people would disagree, and I, for one, have had qualms about devoting time to birds and fish when people are in such trouble. So, if for no other reason than to reassure ourselves, let's look briefly at the value of wildlife in today's world.

In an era when pollsters sample populations and statisticians feed endless figures to computers to forecast everything from economic trends to the potential for a new breakfast food, any key indicators of change have great importance. Through TV coverage of elections, for example, we have become familiar with the prediction—often surprisingly accurate—of the outcome of a presidential race based on early returns from a few picked voting precincts.

For a far more important area of concern—our basic environment—wildlife serves as an indicator or barometer, quietly reflect-

2　ing the changes man makes in his world and the potential effects of these changes on man himself.

The toxic effects of hard pesticides, mercury, oil spills, water pollution, and many other agents of destruction to man were first revealed when songbirds twitched spasmodically on lawns or fish rolled belly-up in the shallows. It is nothing new. The fertile prairie states have seen the prairie chicken all but disappear, to be replaced by the pheasant, which now in its turn is declining—mute testimony to changing land use. My children catch carp and bullheads in the same streams where, at their age, I caught bluegills and an occasional largemouth bass, and where my father caught smallmouth bass and once in a while a walleye.

All this should tell us something, and it looks as if we are beginning to listen. It is no advantage to a brown pelican or a bald eagle to be more sensitive than man to pollutants, but it is a considerable break for us—perhaps more of a break than we deserve. In any event, as a barometer of environmental changes that can affect our lives and our comforts, wildlife is literally a lifesaver.

Conceivably, of course, architects, engineers, and scientists might devise elaborate concrete warrens with triply filtered air and reconditioned water to ensure our survival without great concern for a "natural" environment. Our survival, perhaps, but what of our sanity? As tensions mount in a crowded, problem-filled world, there is an increasing need to escape—even briefly—from crowds and offices and apartments, polluted or air-conditioned air, filthy or chlorinated water, to some contact with nature.

The need is relative. To the city dweller, "escape" may be a tiny park with a tree and twenty feet of grass—or ten feet of elbow room at a city fishing lagoon. To a busy housewife, it can be a shaded back yard and a bird feeder. To the more affluent, it is more frequently becoming a second home, on a lake or in a rural setting. To some, it is a wilderness pack trip. For nearly all, however, it is "wildlife" that makes the setting complete, whether it be a house sparrow in the park, a chickadee at the feeder, a brood of ducks at the cabin pier, or an osprey over the trail.

It is really not my intention to catalog the "uses" and "values" of wildlife, much less to explain why man seems inherently more content in settings that also contain other creatures. The continuing sale of millions of hunting and fishing licenses, the burgeoning industries devoted to camping and off-the-road vehicles, and the soaring use of national parks and public lands are ample proof that wildlife is valuable to man.

What I hope to point out is that there are basic ideas you can explore, things you can do, and sources of help and information you can turn to if you are interested in wildlife, for whatever reason. And it is well to understand that a variety of reasons do exist. Those who enjoy hunting and fishing are naturally concerned with improving their sport; bird-watchers are eager to increase their viewing opportunities by enhancing songbird habitat. Farmers and rural landowners consider supplementing their income by improving wildlife populations to attract fee-hunting or camping parties. City and suburban park planners and landscape architects are interested in the greater value—both monetary and less tangible—of developments and landscapes that retain or attract wildlife.

Just as motives for improving conditions for wildlife differ, so do opportunities. Obviously, if you own a big chunk of land, there is a lot you can do physically, on your own. I have been lucky enough to help manage two large tracts of land—one in Maryland and one in Illinois—that were originally purchased by well-to-do individuals and converted from semibarren crop and pastureland into virtual paradises for a variety of wildlife. Here, ample funds, plenty of land with good, natural features, and good-sized work crews were involved. But I have seen equally impressive results on a thirty-acre Wisconsin "farm" where the owner wanted better hunting and fishing for himself and his son, and in the half-acre suburban back yard of an amateur naturalist.

While it is an advantage, obviously, to own land on which you want to improve conditions for wildlife, it is not a necessity. Many a sportsmen's group, formally organized as a club or simply a collection of friends, has worked out an agreement with farmers to cooperate for better hunting. There is no reason why bird-watchers and others with like interests cannot also work out lease agreements or less formal arrangements with rural landowners to improve wildlife habitat to mutual advantage. And there is no city, suburb, or small town I know whose parks and other public properties would not benefit from improvements for wildlife, worked for and sponsored by interested and informed citizens' groups. What it boils down to is that there are many reasons, places, and opportunities to improve this land of ours for wildlife, whether you own property or not, whether you live in the city or the country, on a small lot or a thousand acres.

But aren't there conflicts in all this? Take motives, for example. Doesn't management primarily for better hunting work directly against efforts to increase all species—game and nongame? Can

4   there possibly be a relationship between improving wildlife in a back yard or city park and on a big country estate? And if we want to preserve wildlife and a natural setting, how can we talk of "management"?

To help understand the answers to these and other questions, and as background to the chapters that follow, it is essential to explain some of the principles and ideas behind wildlife management programs.

ANIMAL SPECIES AND NATURAL COMMUNITIES

As the result of at least one and a half billion years of evolution, more than 1,089,000 different species of plants and animals live today on this earth. The individual members of any one species are not found scattered evenly over the earth's surface. Deer are not distributed in equal packages in each county of Michigan, for example, or in each state in the United States. Neither are robins, bark beetles, or white pines.

Instead, members of one species tend to occur in units or groups in irregular fashion. They appear, in general, in all areas they have been able to reach by migration, dispersal, or other movements over the years, and where conditions favor their existence. Such units, or *populations,* have obvious advantages. For example, no self-respecting animal can last long if it has to search worldwide for a mate every breeding season. Populations have survival advantages over single individuals in defense, in feeding, and in many other areas. So, when we talk about a species, we are usually talking about a living population, composed of different age groups, and not a zoo specimen.

Just as single individuals of a species rarely live alone and isolated, a population of any one species does not exist independent of other living organisms and populations. Instead, around the world, we find certain groupings of populations of plants and animals living together. These assemblages of plant and animal populations sharing the same living space are called natural *communities.* Communities in nature may be large or small. A cavity in a hollow tree in Wisconsin's Mississippi River bottoms contains fungi—small plants living on rotting tree tissues. A population of tiny mites feeds on the fungi; various beetles, ants, and spiders subsist on the mites and in turn fall prey to tree frogs. If the tree cavity collects rainwater, other fungi and the larvae or young of several other insects thrive in the tiny pool. This is a community, and at the same time it

is a part of a larger river floodplain community composed of species
populations of characteristic trees, birds, mammals, and insects, covering parts of several states.

Hard-and-fast, highly precise definitions and rules rarely apply to nature. But, in general, a community consists of a number of species populations, plant and animal, living in the same area (large or small) and dependent upon one another directly or indirectly.

What determines the boundaries, structure, and make-up of a natural community, flexible as it may be? The "environment"—an all-embracing word that means every single factor affecting that community. Obviously, this includes physical features—sunlight, temperature, humidity, wind, and rain. Perhaps not so obviously, the environment of any community and of each of its component species populations consists of all living things, plant and animal, in their relationships with one another.

The end result of evolution is to fit an organism to its environment. Each species fits into and occupies a certain place—a *niche*—in the community, in relationship to both physical factors and to other species. It is nowhere near as simple as it sounds. First, the physical factors provide the stage effects. They are never the same—light, wind, humidity, all can change daily and minute by minute. Seasons come and go, causing changes in day lengths, precipitation, and temperature. Longer range cycles—of rainfall or sunspots, for example—are at work. And the physical factors interact; a passing cloud mass, obstructing sunlight, causes a temperature change, which in turn alters humidity. These shifting patterns of weather and climate play over a stage set that may vary from steep, rocky slopes to flatlands, on a substrate of water, sand, rockhard clay, fertile soil, or mud. Here again interaction goes on. Rainfall changes a firm substrate to mud; temperature changes convert water to ice, creating a physical barrier for some animals, removing a barrier for others. So even the physical background of the environment is never stable, but consists of a shifting, changing, interwoven setting into which a species must fit and adapt, or vanish from the community.

Clothing the stage are the plants. As food, as shelter, and in many other ways, they are the basis of all animal life. This will become more obvious as—further along—we look at ways to attract and increase wildlife. Time and again, whether we are dealing with robins or pheasants, cottontails or deer, ducks or grosbeaks, wildlife and wildlife management hinges upon plants and their manipulation.

All living things require and use energy to perform their life functions. The ultimate source of all this energy is the sun. Green plants, through the process of photosynthesis, capture sunlight energy and bind it in the form of sugars and other materials, thus making it available to animals, who are incapable of directly utilizing sunlight energy themselves. Plant-eating animals, or *herbivores,* like the cottontail rabbit, in turn become the energy source for *carnivores,* or meat-eaters, such as the red fox. Thus, directly or indirectly, sooner or later, all animals depend upon plants—the food base of the living community—for life. The energy relationships that result are the threads tying populations together in the fabric of the community.

In this way, the pattern of plant distribution, in a township or across a continent, tends to determine the distribution of animals. Among the herbivores—the plant-eaters—are those that feed upon only one species of plant or one type of plant food. Crossbills, attractive birds of the north, have specially adapted bills, for which they are named, for extracting seeds from the cones of pines and other coniferous trees. Thus they are unlikely to be found far from mature stands of conifers. Other herbivores, such as deer and the cottontail rabbit, feed on a variety of plants and consequently are much less restricted in range. Even here, however, certain special relationships exist. The blacktail deer of California will eat upward of forty different kinds of plants, but seem to thrive and reproduce best where one species of buckbrush is common.

In addition to their role as trappers and suppliers of energy, plants furnish essential shelter to animals. This function of "cover," offering protection from weather and predators, and providing choice sites for nesting, loafing, and other activities, is one we will explore in detail. Besides providing shelter from a passing storm or a circling hawk, plants have a great effect upon the physical features and even the climate in which animal communities exist. The sunlight reaching the ground, and ground-dwelling animals, in a dense forest may be only 1 percent of the amount in the open. Shade and evaporation of water from plants provide natural climate control in heavily vegetated areas, preventing temperature extremes that can be detrimental to many animals.

In very real ways, then, the presence or absence of plants, their distribution as species, and growth forms—grasses, shrubs, trees—provide the key to animal abundance and distribution. Often it is a two-way street. The smaller members of the animal community—bees, butterflies, other insects, and even birds, bats, and snails—are

the primary vehicles for the pollination of plants, the process in
which the sperm, carried in the pollen grain, is transferred to the
egg-bearing portion of the plant. Fertilization and seed formation,
the aftermath of pollination, help guarantee the continuation of
flowering plants. The lovely flowers and sweet perfume we find so
attractive in many plants are really devices for enticing animals
whose visits ensure pollination. Animals participate even further in
providing assists to plant distribution. Those "stick-tights" and
burrs that cling fiendishly to your clothes after a walk in the woods
and fields cling to the fur of passing mammals just as well. Brushed
off, the seeds they hold can form a new colony of plants many feet,
yards, or miles from the parent plants.

Equally intricate are the relationships between animal populations themselves. In fact, the presence and degree of success of
any one animal species in a community often depends upon the
presence, or absence, of others. This is obvious in the case of para-
sitic animals and their hosts. But there are other, less obvious situations in which dependencies have evolved through time. The little
burrowing owl of the plains, for example, nests underground in burrows dug by prairie dogs. Like other animal species closely associated with prairie-dog towns, the small owl's fortunes are closely related to the ups and downs of prairie-dog populations. The cattle
egret, a white heronlike bird of the Old World that has become successfully established in the United States in recent years, is closely
linked with cattle, feeding primarily on insects attracted to or
flushed up by feeding herds. Cottontail rabbits seem to be more
abundant, and their populations often show fewer fluctuations from
year to year, where there are good numbers of woodchucks or
groundhogs, whose burrows provide shelter for the rabbits against
predators, as well as against hunters and weather.

A number of animals have developed similar close relationships with man. The rat and the house mouse come to mind first,
but there are other examples. The opossum, with his naked ears and
tail, is not well adapted to cold. That his range has expanded north-
ward in recent years, even into Canada, seems partly due to the
presence of man's buildings, under which Bre'r Possum can shelter
from the winter winds.

This leads us to realize that the impact one animal population
makes on the environment in a community can profoundly affect
the lives and distribution of others. The reintroduction and sub-
sequent prospering of beaver colonies in many states has resulted in
numerous dammed-up streams and beaver ponds. Where beaver es-

tablish a pond, some fish and smaller organisms that require fast-running water disappear, and flooded shrubs and trees die. But other plants and other aquatic organisms thrive, and waterfowl and wading birds may find usable habitat where none existed before. The most sweeping changes worked on community environments by one animal to the benefit or detriment of others are those wrought by man, of course—first with ax, plow, fire, and drain tiles, and now with pollutants.

Not so obvious among the relationships of animals, but perhaps most important of all in the long view, is competition—for food, for shelter, for space itself. No bloody, spectacular, fang-and-claw affair, competition in a natural environment is slow, quiet, and complex, involving all species in a community whose food and habitat requirements overlap. Because their size and life span make them easier to study, small organisms have been used to work out some of the subtleties of competition. One example comes from five species of small beetles that live on stored grain. When populations of beetle species A and B were placed on grain together in a lab study, A always prospered while B sooner or later disappeared. Both ate grain and both were similar in size, but individuals of A survived, as young and adults, at a slightly higher rate—possibly because of better food utilization. Regardless of the relative numbers at the start, the end result was always the same.

When populations of species C and D were tested together, C survived and D gradually died out. In this case, bettle C was larger, and, though normally a grain-eater, ate D's eggs whenever possible. When populations of the "champs"—A and C—from these two individual "matches" were brought together in grain, C (the larger) fed on A's eggs as it had on D's, but A, unlike D, was able to survive in reduced numbers. When C and E were combined in the same environment, the eventual survivor depended entirely on which was most numerous at the start. When A, C, and D populations were all mixed, the only change was a reduction in number of A beetles. The presence of A served as a buffer between C and D, so that D, unable to survive alone with C, could exist when A was present.

Here, in microcosm, are demonstrated some of the many sides of competition constantly at work in any community. As a result of such studies and many other observations, we learn that no two related species can occupy exactly the same niche—use the same food supply in the same fashion, for example—in a natural area without competition sooner or later eliminating one. Where such close competition exists, the surviving species is the one best adapted and

most efficient in energy utilization, food seeking, reproduction, or
other ways. Successful adaptation to a new niche, through evolution, is the sole hope for the displaced species.

Through this slow, endless process over millions of years, the community develops until thousands of species populations of animals large and small, can co-exist on the grasslands, or in the forest, with food and shelter requirements that may overlap but are never identical. The great herds of hoofed animals of the African grasslands and scrub are a good example. Dozens of species of antelope and others use the same space, look much alike, are all plant-eaters working over the same range of vegetation, but each species depends primarily upon specific plants not heavily used by others.

Of all the relationships between members of a natural community, food—energy—is the common bond that gives the community its shape and structure. In an oak-hickory woods in the northern Midwest, for instance, the fertile loam soil supports an oak tree whose acorns feed a gray squirrel on which a red fox dines. This simplified "food chain" can be expanded almost endlessly. One dead branch on the oak supports a population of wood-boring beetle larvae on which a woodpecker feeds before its capture by a circling hawk. The same hawk later kills and carries to its young a snake, sluggish from dining on a toad whose stomach contains spiders attracted to insects feeding on the leaves of the oak. The single food chain thus is part of a "web," and these simple examples merely hint at the larger complexity of relationships in the food webs of a mature community.

The structure of the community as regards food can be illustrated in another way, revealing something of predator and prey. Size of eater and of eaten tend to set limits on one another (ignoring scavengers, for the moment). A predator must depend on prey small enough to catch and eat, yet large enough (or present in sufficient quantity) to more than replace the energy expended in the chase and capture. A weasel cannot prey on lions, nor can a lion sustain life on weasels. From this principle comes the *pyramid of numbers* or *food pyramid* concept of food relationships. Here the community is viewed as a broad base of very numerous, small organisms (sustained by plants with the entirety based on the soil) supporting progressively smaller numbers of progressively larger animals. An old study of a grassland community in Arizona, for example, showed a population of various mice and other small rodents estimated at 25,628 individuals per square mile. The same plants and insects feeding these rodents also supplied some 180 rabbits and quail. Together, the rodents, quail, and rabbits of a square mile sustained on the average four hawks and owls and one coyote. "Each hill has but one tiger," say the Chinese.

It is easy to misinterpret this picture of food relationships. For example, since the meat-eaters of each level prey upon the smaller animals of lower levels, it might be falsely concluded that the number of prey are controlled by predators. However, in a self-sustaining natural community, all else being equal, the population size of each animal species depends primarily upon the quantity and quality of food available. Man's influence on the environment has distorted this relationship in too many instances, as we shall point out later, but in nearly all except the most disturbed communities this relationship is still at work. Wildlife biologists studying relatively natural areas in the mountains of Mexico found forests of yellow pine with a thriving undergrowth of buckbrush, a prime deer browse. Occasional uncontrolled wild fires kept the buckbrush—which resprouts vigorously after burning—young, tender, and abundant. Whitetail deer were plentiful, and so were wolves and mountain lions. Despite unchecked predation, deer remained extremely common until the encroachment of man led to large-scale clearing and brush removal. Their food supply gone, deer numbers nosedived; with their prey dwindling, populations of the large predators in turn melted away.

In these examples of food relationships, we have seen only the most direct and easily understood liaisons. A hint of the real complexity of the food "chains," "webs," and "pyramids" may be suggested by the awareness that the position of one species often does not remain the same. Role may vary with age. The adult wood duck gleaning acorns on the forest floor lives largely on vegetable material, but as a duckling he depended upon a diet of almost 100 percent animal material—primarily insects. The ruffed grouse "budding" in an aspen grove, and the cock pheasant searching for seeds in a cornfield, likewise began life dependent on high-protein insect diets. Many species, like the black bear and the raccoon, are *omnivores*, changing their diet day to day, or seasonally, from plants to animals. Animals that depend upon insects or green plant parts must hibernate in winter, or migrate south, if they are in northern climes; in tropical areas where long dry seasons occur, resident animals often "aestivate" or become inactive, until the rains return. As food requirements and choices change with age, by season, or from day to day, relative positions in the food web and in the energy relationships of the community shift and vary.

All of these factors—physical conditions, soil, weather, terrain,
relationships of plant-to-plant, animal-to-plant, and animal-to-animal—determine the nature of the living community and actually
constitute its environment. *Ecology,* that much used and abused
word, is the study of these relationships within the living community. If there are any overriding rules that ecologists have learned,
they are these: That what affects one species in a community affects
all, eventually, so closely interdependent have the living components of the community become through evolution. And that the
environment and the community are never the same, from place to
place or minute to minute. A storm flattens a section of forest, a fire
sweeps over miles of grassland, a woodchuck digs a burrow, a leaping squirrel dislodges a dead branch, a breeze in the treetops ripples
the leaves and alters, briefly, the sun-flecks on the forest floor—and
lives large and small, or whole populations, are changed for seconds
or centuries. Nothing is stable in nature; nothing is exactly the same
twice. A "balance of nature" may exist, but never long at the same
point or with the same weights and measures.

VARIATIONS IN WILDLIFE POPULATIONS

Through the remainder of this book we shall be dealing chiefly
with methods of increasing populations of certain animal species,
so let us look a bit further into how these populations function. We
can ask two basic questions. First, what determines where a species
can exist and where it cannot? We have tried to answer this in the
preceding exploration of a "community"; briefly, the answer is a
suitable environment in terms of food, shelter, climate, and neighbors. Second, what establishes the size of the population of a given
species where it can and does exist—what limits its numbers?

As we explore management for wildlife, we shall find that
sometimes, with luck and under the right circumstances, we can fulfill the requirements of the first question, and create an environment
suitable to induce new species to move into and prosper in the area.
More often, our efforts will have a better chance of success if aimed
toward increasing populations already present in the habitat we can
influence. So the second question—what controls population size—
will often arise. It is not hard to see that wildlife populations change
from year to year, both in numbers and individuals. Twenty mallards may pass your blind this fall, or two robins nest in your yard.
There may have been twenty-four mallards last fall and sixteen

next—or four robins and one. And the mallards or robins you see one year may or may not be the same individuals next season. These changes are true of all animal populations and occur as the result of two decisive forces—reproduction and mortality or, simply, life and death.

Aldo Leopold, in his classic book *Game Management,* clearly stated how these forces interact for wildlife populations. He pointed out that each animal species has a *breeding potential*—a built-in maximum capacity to reproduce under ideal conditions—which is inherited and just as characteristic of that species as its tooth pattern or skull shape. Bobwhite quail, for instance, are normally monogamous, breed when a year old, and nest once a year with an average of fourteen eggs. With no problems of any kind, a pair of bobwhite can thus increase to sixteen at the end of one year, to 128 the following year, and to 1024 the third year.

This breeding potential varies with the species. California's blacktail deer normally takes two years before it is capable of reproduction. A two-year-old doe, under ideal conditions, will give birth to twins. Starting with a pair of adults, an increase to four blacktails could result at the end of one year. But the yearlings will not reproduce, so at the end of the second year the total will be six deer—the original pair, their two fawns, and their two yearlings. By the end of the third year there will be ten blacktails—a far cry from 1,024 bobwhite. Different as they are, these examples do not begin to express the extremes that exist. The blue crab of the western Atlantic may carry nearly two million eggs at one time, while a cow elephant begins to breed at the age of thirty, and averages six young—if all goes well—in a lifetime.

This variation in breeding potential is caused mainly by inherent limits characteristic of the species, including the minimum breeding age or age when reproduction is first possible (one year in the bobwhite and two in the blacktail, for example), and the maximum breeding age beyond which individuals are too old to reproduce successfully. Of equal and obvious importance is the number of young a female can have in a year—not only how many per brood or litter, but how many broods or litters can be produced each season. A ringnecked pheasant ideally turns out one brood of ten to twelve young a year. A cottontail, however, while averaging only four to seven young in a litter, may produce three or four litters in one season.

Large or small, it is evident that the breeding potential, or maximum production rate, of any species would, if maintained, sooner or later put us knee-deep in quail or roof-deep in elephants. That this doesn't happen is due to a number of *reproductive factors* which work to reduce the rate of production, and to various *decimating factors* which kill off some of the individuals that are produced.

Let us look at the reproductive factors first. They include such things as the balance between sexes in a population. Many species, such as the Canada goose, are monogamous—one male mates with one female. Any departure from a one-to-one sex ratio in a flock of Canadas means the surplus birds will be nonproductive. In polygamous species, such as the ringnecked pheasant, a single male usually breeds with a harem of several hens. Here, excess roosters are also nonessential dead weight. This is the biological basis for "cocks only" hunting regulations for pheasants, since a large proportion of the male birds can be removed without affecting the next year's production.

Environmental conditions, including weather, are also determinants in reproduction. During periodic dry springs in the Colorado and Mojave deserts, California and Gambel quail may not nest at all. In the desert, no rain means no new, green vegetation, and the absence of greens from the menu apparently interferes with the production of hormones that normally trigger breeding behavior in the quail.

An adequate diet, in quantity and quality, may be the most critical, though often least obvious, influence in productivity for most wildlife. Numerous field studies, from New York to California, have shown that deer herds on some ranges achieve excellent production—90 percent or more of the does are pregnant, a large percentage of these produce twin fawns, and a third or more even breed as yearlings. But in herds on other ranges in the same states, few if any yearlings breed, less than 75 percent of the adult does are pregnant, and most of these bear only one fawn.

Such differences, commonly occurring among plant-eating animals, can be traced to the amount and nutritional value of available plant foods. Plants reflect—in density and in the nutrients they contain—soil fertility. Deer-browse plants on the thin, rocky soils of parts of Canada and the northern portions of many New England and Lake states are more scattered, grow more slowly, and may contain smaller quantities of essential nutrients than do their counterparts further south. This influence is apparent to deer hunters, who know that farmland bucks, taken on fertile agricultural areas of a state, normally are heavier and have bigger racks than all but a few

14 backwoods animals. What they may not know is that farmland does, for the same reason (availability of better, more abundant browse owing to fertile soil) normally come closer to reaching breeding potential than do their cousins on less fertile North Woods ranges. Diet affects reproductive rates among meat-eating animals in similar ways; when prey is abundant, carnivores produce and successfully raise more young than when prey is scarce.

For these reasons—sex and age ratios in the population, weather, nutrition—and others, few species anywhere maintain their full breeding potential for long. Despite such curbs, vast numbers of young are hatched or born, more than enough to overrun the earth if all survived. We are not tripping over rabbits, or inundated by a tide of titmice, because many forces, which biologists call decimating factors, are constantly whittling away. Predation is the first to come to mind—nearly every animal species has another that preys upon it. Starvation, disease, and parasites are also instrumental, not so often killing animals directly, but weakening them to the point where they become easy victims for predators. Accidents play no small part in the process of elimination. Migrating land birds are forced down at sea by storms. Young partridge are immobilized by mudballs forming on their feet after rains on clay soil. A tree nest is blown down by wind. Fires destroy dwelling places, and the young and unwary.

Man has added his share of decimating factors—not just the gun, but such others as oil slicks that trap sea birds and mammals, skyscrapers against which night-flying migrant birds crash, and pesticides that kill outright or reduce breeding ability.

Losses attributable to any one cause are seldom the same year after year. Accidents and weather may take only a very slight toll for a decade and then, in a major fire or severe winter, wreak havoc. A series of mild winters in southwestern Wisconsin can lead to some of the finest quail coveys anywhere, yet in the spring following a single hard winter with deep, crusted snow, you are lucky to hear one bobwhite whistle in a township. Moreover, like all features of an animal's environment, causes of death interact. The drought or deep snow that renders food scarce may kill a few birds or mammals directly by starvation, but in addition many more are weakened and become easier victims of disease, parasites, and predators—and the exhausted survivors may produce fewer young in the spring.

Breeding potential is often compared to a strong, flat spring constantly trying to shoot upward. Conditions in the population and

its environment—the reproductive and decimating factors—combine
to hold the spring down, checking its surge upward by preventing
some young from being produced and pruning away at those that
are.

For any animal species, hummingbird or blue whale, and for
the community of which it is a part, the crucial question is where
the balance—the point of equilibrium between life and death (for
the population, not the individual)—will strike. If the factors that reduce production and kill living individuals depress the spring below the point where reproduction no longer outpaces mortality, extinction—in a local community or as a species—is inevitable.
Countless species, like the dinosaurs, have gone this route. But for
most living animals, the balance is struck at a point of survival. The
question is, how many? Will the species be abundant or rare? Will
it increase, decline, or remain stable?

Since our interest here is in managing land for more wildlife,
our chief concern is with what determines this balance between life
and death, what fixes the population level of a given species in a
given place at a given time. Bascially, we can consider that how
"well" a species "does" depends on the degree to which the area it
inhabits, or is introduced to, supplies the basic necessities of life.
This is not as simple as it sounds, if you recall the endless inter-
relationships of a natural community.

Regarding these necessities, food is the most obvious one. Sus-
tenance must be appropriate, animal or vegetable, and be present at
the proper stage in life of the animal, at the right season, in sufficient quantity, and adequately nutritious to support life and reproductive ability. Water is also essential, either freely available in
ponds, streams, and lakes, or as dewdrops, or in the form of succulent plant parts. Cover is equally important, including shelter from
weather for individuals, adequate protection of nests from both
weather and predation, a spot in which to loaf at midday or to sleep
securely at night. The implications of the term "cover" are almost
infinite. For the woodchuck and ground squirrel the cover requirement is soil texture that permits digging a burrow that won't cave
in. The wood duck and bluebird demand a hollow tree with certain
limits on the size of the opening and the depth of the cavity. A secure spot in which to roost for the night is a necessity for most
birds, and this single type of cover, aside from all the other different
cover needs of other animals, exists in such variety as to mean a
very special kind of tree for a wild turkey, and a certain combination of ground plants for a pheasant.

Most animals have certain additional, special, idiosyncratic requirements of their habitat. Many birds, lacking teeth, must have access to grit—rock fragments of the right size and texture which, when swallowed, will grind up tough plant food into digestible form. Caribou prosper only amid open, windswept terrain that allows relief from maddening fly swarms in northern summers. Prairie chickens fail to survive in the absence of suitable "booming grounds" where they can display to potential mates.

Not only is each requirement for food, water, cover, and special needs that a species demands from its surroundings both critical and complicated in itself, but the immediate location of these with relationship to one another is equally vital. I recall a winter spent in southeastern Wisconsin working with pheasants. My study area included a tamarack swamp which furnished ringnecks with good protection from both predators and hunters in winter. We left some rows of corn standing in cultivated fields 50 to 100 yards from this swamp as supplementary winter food for the pheasants. Three winters out of the four that I spent there, all went well. There were the usual snows and thaws; pheasants wintered in the swamp and in several other places, and the swamp birds ranged out to feed on the corn. But throughout that fourth winter, from late November to mid-February, there was seldom less than 24 inches of snow on the level. As soon as it warmed to a thaw there would be more snow, and then more bitter cold in a vicious cycle, week after week.

Those pheasants that could make it left the "poorer" winter cover (perfectly adequate three years out of four) and moved to the tamaracks. There was still fair protection from predators here in thickets of dogwood, poison sumac, meadowsweet, and willow, and the hunters had long since traded guns for sacks of corn to lug into the swamp. But natural food sources, and the supplementary feed hunters toted in, were soon covered by fresh snow or exhausted by the unusual concentration of pheasants.

The standing rows of field corn were still there, as in the previous winters. But the 50 to 100 yards of space between the bog and the corn, usually clothed in grass and goldenrod, was now a white blanket, and the standing cornstalks, with their inviting, full ears, protruded from the same stark background. The cold and snow had brought in an unusual number of hawks that winter, especially Cooper's hawks. Ringnecks that tried to or did reach the corn strips were perfect targets on a white background, and a number were taken by hawks. Before long, few pheasants ventured the trip, and I found many frozen to death in the swamp.

I have always thought of that winter as one of the most pointed instances in my experience of the dependence of an animal population on the conditions of its habitat—not just on the presence of basic necessities, but on how advantageously they are blended. The swamp furnished ample cover and water in the form of snow. But due to extraordinary weather, normally adequate food supplies in the sheltered area were exhausted or buried, and the same weather rendered the usually available supplementary food source—the corn strips—a deathtrap. Had the corn immediately adjoined the swamp, or if the intervening space had supported brush or evergreens—in short, if food and cover had been better mixed—many more pheasants might have survived the winter.

"Edge," achieved by the interspersion of different species and growth forms of vegetation, is a fundamental principle of wildlife management. Perennial grasses, annual sorghums, and trees meet here to furnish food, shelter, and nesting cover in one small area.

18   I emphasize the point because it is fundamental. Population levels are set not just by the amount and quality of food, water, cover, and so forth, but by how and where these necessities are situated in relation to one another. A good food supply may be located on the same section of land as good cover, but it must be safely accessible. This principle of interspersion, as wildlife biologists call it, is one you have probably come to appreciate if you have spent time in the outdoors. If you are a bird-watcher, you learn that the best chance to see a variety of birds is at the edge of a woodland, not in its center. Where woodland, marsh, and grassy uplands meet, you will do even better. As a hunter, too, you work your pointer, or take your stand for deer, at the margins of field and brush or forest.

The mixture of food and cover for wildlife on the land in the foreground contrasts sharply with huge single-crop fields in the distance.

Wildlife, by and large, is dependent on *edges*. The necessities of
life are more apt to occur where two or more types of cover meet
than in the center of any single type. This is the reason why large,
modern farms, with huge fields of a uniform crop, support less wildlife than the old-fashioned farm with its small fields and diverse
plantings—here oats, there corn or hay, yonder a pasture, and usually a woodlot. This iq the reason that extensive stands of second-
growth timber, all the same age, that now clothe much of the Northeast and northern Midwest have less wildlife than existed when
there were still a few scattered farms and openings. The single-age,
single-species stands, characteristic of many commercial timber-
producing tree farms, by no means offer wildlife all that their advertising would have us believe.

On the whole, the better the mixture of cover and habitat, the
more numerous the edges, and the wider the variety of characteristics in a given unit of land, then the more plentiful and divergent
the wildlife populations will be.

The amount, availability, and distribution of food, cover, water,
and a host of special requirements tend to determine the general
population level where the reproductive "spring" is balanced by
mortality. This level is often called the *carrying capacity* of a given
unit of land for a given wildlife species. As the breeding rate of the
species produces more individuals than the habitat can carry, excess
individuals are removed. If food supplies are limited, starvation and
disease operate to reduce numbers. If the population increases beyond the point where suitable cover is available, predators find easy
pickings. Predation, starvation, and disease thus normally do not
determine the average, long-term size of wildlife populations;
rather, they are simply instruments of destruction for surplus animals whose number and fate have already been decreed by habitat.

There are exceptions to all rules. Primitive man, as a hunter,
tended to kill only for food and other necessities, using relatively in-
efficient methods. In most cases he entered the natural community
simply as one more predator, and his own numbers fluctuated with
the abundance of prey. Modern man, however, hunting for sport
with highly efficient tools, has the potential of reducing a game species far below carrying capacity—even to extinction. Surprisingly,
hunting has been responsible for remarkably few such major reduc-
tions or eliminations of game species—the near-destruction of the
bison and the disappearance of the passenger pigeon being two no-
table exceptions. Most drastic changes in game (and nongame) species, which the uninformed decry as the fault of man as hunter, are

really due to man as destroyer of habitat. The changes we have wrought in the soil and vegetation of natural communities through farming, grazing, construction of roads, reservoirs, and cities, logging, and forest fires and overprotection from fire have affected far more animal species and populations than hunting.

But modern hunters still have the capability of decimating game populations below carrying capacity. How, then, can hunting be compatible with a continued supply of wildlife, not only for hunters but for all who enjoy nature? The answer lies in the principles of population dynamics we have just reviewed. The annual production of young game birds and mammals normally exceeds the carrying capacity of the habitat. Thus, we can substitute hunting as a mortality factor for some of the losses which starvation, disease, accidents, and predation otherwise would claim. Reduced to fundamentals, the annual surplus game population constitutes a crop which, under proper limitations, can be harvested for recreation by hunters without harm to the basic brood stock which a unit of habitat can support. Present-day federal and state hunting regulations aim at this goal. Where they are based on recommendations of competent game biologists, these regulations normally work well, although mistakes can occur since wildlife numbers and population trends are not often easy to predict. Where hunting regulations are based on political pressures—and this still happens—the results are not always so pleasant. But the principle—the substitution of hunting for other decimating factors—remains sound.

Returning to the question of what determines the number of animals that can exist in a given area, we have learned that this level normally is set by how well that area's habitat meets the requirements of that species. More often than not, this carrying capacity is determined by one of the several factors—feed, water, etc.—that are involved. Wood ducks nest in darkened cavities supplied by hollow trees, under natural circumstances. But most people are not keen on beat-up, hollow trees. To the suburbanite, they are something to be removed, or at least plugged with concrete. To the tree farmer, they are taking space that could produce a commercially valuable sawlog. Either way, wood ducks, bluebirds, and many other tree-cavity nesters lose. Consequently, lack of nesting cover frequently determines where and how many wood ducks can exist, although the same habitat may furnish other needs in abundance. Erection of suitable houses or nest-boxes—simulating natural tree cavities—frequently can work wonders in increasing the number of "woodies."

In the forested northern states, deer usually gang up in winter in those limited areas providing good food—often in cedar swamps.

Heavy winter snow accumulations limit deer movements, so they gather in these "yards" instinctively to be close to an available food supply. Forest habitat may supply an abundance of a whitetail's needs most of the year, but good winter yards are not so common, and predators and starvation chisel away at northern deer in winter.

As with the wood duck and the whitetail, so also with most wildlife species. One element of the habitat usually is most decisive in whether or not existence is possible and, if so, in what numbers. This vital element is called the *critical limiting factor*. It usually differs for different species in the same area, and often differs for the same species in different areas. But the lesson is always clear: if we can identify the limiting factor for the species we would like to add or increase on the land, and if we can aim a management plan at that factor, we stand an excellent chance of success. Much of this book is devoted to this point.

In leaving this discussion of populations and what makes them tick, remember that any plant and animal community is dynamic, always changing. The same is true for the carrying capacity of land for any single species in the community. Carrying capacity is a general level, an average around which the population fluctuates from year to year as food, cover, water, and other factors change. Nothing is simple in nature, so there are no simple recipes for increasing wildlife. Animals, and the communities in which they live, have evolved over thousands and millions of years to fit a specific niche in the world we share with them. If they don't always respond to our attempts to "help," it should be understandable.

TO MANAGE, OR TO PRESERVE?

Earlier we asked some questions which may now be easier to answer. Is hunting compatible with the current need and desire to maintain wildlife? Yes, if sound, scientifically based regulations limit the harvest of species and numbers to populations where annual surpluses are produced. Can we possibly equate management of a back yard for more wildlife to managing thousands of acres? Yes again; the principles are the same. Finally and most fundamental, do we—as representatives of the species that has changed and destroyed countless natural communities—have the right, the sheer gall, in fact, to try to "manage" nature? Should we not, instead, keep hands off and "preserve" what is left in its natural state? Many argue this point today, equating "preservation" with "conservation." I would ask these people first to check the meanings of the terms. "Conservation" means wise use; applied to wildlife, it means a sensible utilization of the resource without its depletion. "Preservation" means maintaining the status quo, freezing a given situation permanently. We have looked but briefly at the complexities of a wildlife community, yet even this quick inspection should make it clear that change is the rule. What shall be "preserved," when, and at what stage? The "balance of nature" is a dynamic, swinging, ever-changing balance at best. To attempt to freeze it, to stop the clock, is certainly tampering with nature. A few extant native prairies were saved some years ago by universities and other dedicated agencies. Protected jealously from disturbance of any sort, "preserved," they deteriorated, and their most characteristic grasses and flowers were stunted or vanished. Ecologists with a grasp of history pointed out that wildfires, created by lightning or Indians, periodically swept the old prairie communities. Sure enough, when controlled burns were made on the prairie relicts—with great trepidation at first—the results were nearly miraculous. Fire cleared away the accumulated, smothering duff of dead stems and leaves, and the prairie was reborn. Unnatural protection from fire has created similar stagnation in numerous forests, to the detriment of both wildlife and vegetation.

The only "preserved" species and communities in nature, in the literal sense, are fossilized remains. If we add to natural, constant change the alterations that man has made in every single area of this continent—directly through manipulation of the land where he lives and indirectly via air- and water-borne pollutants where he has not yet taken residence—then "preservation" is even more of an illusion.

I do not mean by this that we should "manage" every inch of the North American landscape. Even if this were physically and economically possible, in many situations we lack the knowledge of what to do and how to do it. Here, as elsewhere, basic understanding lags far behind technology, and the potential for harm is enormous. The potential for harm is just as real if we try mindlessly to "preserve"—to prevent with all our might the dynamic, changing forces which create and maintain the very thing we seek to save.

Where relatively natural communities and habitats remain, as in our wilderness areas and a few national parks and forests, we must limit "management" to those changes we are sure, through careful study, are sound; likewise we must limit "preservation" to be sure we are not suppressing those natural processes of change that are fundamental to the survival of these precious communities.

But in this book we are addressing ourselves primarily to areas that have long since ceased to be "natural"—a suburban yard, a farm, a hunt club on the Illinois River, Chesapeake Bay, or in the Sacramento Valley, a ranch in Montana, a lake in Wisconsin, an estate in Canada. In such areas, pre-man natural communities are gone. Nevertheless, though food chains may be simplified, soil and vegetation drastically altered, and the complexities of the community reduced, the English sparrow at your feeder and the starlings on your back forty march to the same old tune. If you want to substitute a cardinal for that sparrow and a pheasant for the starlings, you must pay the piper, too. Plan carefully and read long before you "manage" or "preserve."

You have two things going for you. Unless you are one of the fortunate few in charge of a hundred thousand acres of wilderness, you have more to gain than lose. Second, there is a lot more research, advice, and information on the handling of wildlife in altered habitats than there is for the management of wilderness areas. Availing you of this information is the purpose of this book.

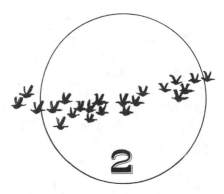

FIRST THINGS FIRST: PLANNING AND GETTING HELP

We live in an age of haste. It is all we can do to figure out how to make it through the day, or the week, or where to spend next year's vacation. Long-range planning is something the boss does, or that "someone in Washington" is handling.

However, if you really want results from wildlife planning, whether more birds at your feeder or more quail in front of your pointer, you are going to have to slow down. First, a long-range strategy, based on a lot of tedious-sounding items like soils and land use, is required for the best results, and often for any results at all. Second, it will take time for your plans to be fulfilled. Few of us can afford the money and manpower to create an ideal wildlife habitat overnight.

MAPPING

Before you can plan for the future you must know what exists in an area at present, and what features may either lend themselves to or prohibit certain types of improvements. The best way to discover and remember these features is by means of a map. If the land you want to improve for wildlife is a back yard or a few acres, make your own base map, using a tape measure (or you can pace off distances) and a compass. Make a working sketch with pencil as you go, and then transfer your measurements in ink to a large sheet of paper. Be sure to include the scale to which your map is drawn. The scale should be appropriate to the size of the area, and the completed map should contain as much detail as possible without being cumbersome to use. A scale of 1 inch on the map for every 10 feet on the ground is fine for a 100-foot lot, but awkward for a 1000-acre farm. You should also use a scale that fits convenient units of measurement—1 inch to 10 or 100 feet, or a mile, not 1 inch to 7½ feet or 9/11 mile.

For areas larger than a few acres, take advantage of the fact that most of the United States has already been mapped by experts, and obtain copies of their maps as a starting point for yours. The U.S. Soil Conservation Service maintains an office in most county seats. You will want to get acquainted with SCS in any event for the many assists they can provide, so use your quest for a good base map as a reason for your first visit.

Through SCS you should be able to order and purchase an aerial photograph covering your particular land. An "aerial" is probably the best of all base maps for large areas in that it shows vegetation, buildings, and other features already in place, saving the trouble of sketching them in. There may have been changes since the most recent photos, but these can be added. Again, if you are dealing with a large expanse, or with rough terrain on even moderate-sized areas, additional printed base maps are invaluable. Soil maps, showing fundamental soil types, have been prepared for much of the United States and are also available through local SCS offices, or from the state agricultural extension service at your state college. Topographic maps can be obtained through the Superintendent of Documents, Washington, D.C., or from various state offices.

Once you have purchased or drawn a good base map on which the property has been outlined, and distances or scale shown, start filling in the details. If you have drawn your own maps, you will need to sketch in these figures to scale; if you started with one of the several printed maps mentioned, many items already will be shown, and can simply be labeled.

First, draw in, or label, fixed, permanent features—permanent roads, buildings, and the like. Then add other items that have a pretty well established, predetermined use—fencelines that can't be removed, for example, or cropfields or pastures whose continued use cannot be changed.

Notes and detail on ponds, lakes, or waterways should be sketched in, along with as much information as possible on terrain. Identify such things as low, poorly drained sites (possible marsh or pond developments), steep slopes (where any plantings or changes must be aimed at holding, not disturbing, soil and preventing, not creating, erosion), springs, and so forth. Clearly, if the area is large and rugged, a professionally prepared topographic map is really a necessity.

Mapping present vegetation is vital. In a yard, or even a small estate, you can locate and label on the map individual trees and even shrubs. For large acreage more general information will suffice for a start—"oak-hickory woods, with some young walnuts," for example, or "second-growth popple," or "goldenrod and aster." In wooded sections it is important to note on your map not just the kinds of large trees (the *canopy*), but also what is beneath them. Have the woods been grazed or cleared, so that little or no brush or young trees (*understory*) exist, or is there a dense undergrowth, and if so, of what? If there is a pond, does it contain vegetation? What type—an algae bloom, rooted plants that may be good waterfowl food sources, or *emergents,* such as cattail, pickerelweed, or bulrush, offering good cover for marsh birds and young waterfowl?

Why so much emphasis on existing vegetation? You will recall that plants are a major key to animal distribution and abundance. Plant types are the foundation on which you will construct your management plan, the building blocks which you will retain, encourage, remove, or shift as you develop and follow through with that plan. But to know how plants should be manipulated, you need to know their relative values to wildlife, and to achieve this you must learn the names of the species—at least the common or dominant species.

Equally important, the more you learn about vegetation, the more you will know about the potential for management. Plants are prime indicators of soil, drainage, and other critical factors. The initial time spent identifying major kinds of vegetation on the land, and learning to interpret what they are telling you, can save countless hours and dollars that might otherwise be lost in futile planting or management efforts. Stands of red cedar, for example, usually indicate mineral soils—thin soil over bedrock or limestone outcroppings. Trying to establish moisture-loving plants on sites where red cedar predominates will normally be a waste of time. In the Appalachians, blueberries and huckleberries denote dry, relatively infertile soil. In the north, acid bogs are characterized by tamarack,

black spruce, and cranberry. Attempts to establish lime-loving
plants—such as most legumes—where existing vegetation shouts
"acid" can only meet with defeat.

Decidedly, a fundamental part of mapping and planning is
plant identification. If you are on your own—a one-man or one-
woman potential wildlife manager—you will have to undertake this
study by yourself. If it is a team effort—of sportsmen's club, garden
club, or just a group of friends and neighbors—do as a duck hunters'
group I worked with did. Pick one group member to specialize in
plant fact-finding. It needn't be a difficult or boring chore; there are
good, easy-to-use field guides to trees, shrubs, and wildflowers
available at bookstores. For your convenience, some publications
dealing with more specialized identification, and with the values of
various plants to wildlife, are listed at the end of this chapter.

SOIL ANALYSIS

In the process of mapping, itemizing, and acquainting yourself
with the characteristics of the area that you propose to manage,
don't overlook the most basic element of all—the soil. It is the stage
upon which your management drama will be played, the ultimate
food source for the plant and animal players, and a major determining factor in what you can do in the way of improvements for wildlife.

Soil is more than just dirt. It is composed of mineral material
(derived from weathering of the bedrock beneath it, or carried in by
wind, water, or ice), and organic material (the remains of plants and
animals). The study of soils is a science in itself, but a few elementary points will help in understanding its role in wildlife management.

First, soil—at least on relatively undisturbed sites—is more or
less arranged in layers or "horizons." On top, logically, is the topsoil, generally containing the most organic material, highest in fertility and often darkest in color. Next is subsoil, sometimes several
different layers with little or no organic material and often with
rock or mineral fragments. Finally, underlying all, is bedrock. These
layers vary in thickness from place to place. Bedrock outcroppings
may be at the surface, or rich topsoil may be several feet thick, or
merely a thin layer over mineral subsoils. Plainly, the soil profile, or
kinds and depths of soil layers, of your land will figure prominently
in what plants and, hence, what wildlife will thrive there.

Not as obvious but even more critical is the makeup of the soil layers themselves. Texture may be so coarse, as in gravel or sand, that rainwater filters through rapidly retaining so little moisture that only a few deep-rooted plants can live. Or the consistency may be so fine, as in clay, that the soil becomes rock-hard under certain moisture-temperature conditions. Soils may vary chemically from acid to alkaline, and range in mineral content from being deficient in certain essential elements to having such excesses of one element as to be lethal to some plants.

To understand the importance of soil, it is perhaps easiest to imagine a giant circulatory system. Physical and chemical reactions break down the parent bedrock, decomposing and releasing minerals which are absorbed by plant roots. Some of these mineral nutrients, incorporated into living plant tissues, build the bodies of animals eating the plants. As plants and animals die, the minute organisms responsible for the process of decay break down the complex, once-living tissues to their original form within the soil, where they are once again available to plants to recycle. This circulation of nitrogen, phosphorus, and other essentials of life is the basis of the food chains we have discussed.

In most natural communities, complex food chains and webs keep the resources of the nutrient "bank" tied up in living plant or animal tissues; they return to the soil rarely and usually only briefly. Territorial relocation of nutrients under undisturbed conditions is minimal; plants are stationary and most animals do not range far. But one slow, insidious natural force—the power of gravity, aided by moving water—works away steadily at removing nutrients, making withdrawals from the community fund. Mineral elements in soil dissolve in water, which, responding to gravity, flows downhill, draining nutrients away from land communities toward the sea. The water eventually evaporates from the ocean surfaces and returns to the land as rain, but generally the mineral elements remain at sea, never to return.

Man calls this process *erosion*. Natural communities resist erosion by their very complexity. While nutrients are locked up in living tissue they are not subject to loss through erosion, and the longer and more involved the food webs are, the greater their resistance to nutrient loss. As long as erosion losses are retarded so that they can be replaced by the slow process of decay and weathering of bedrock, the community is healthy and its soil base fertile. But processes which speed erosion, so that nutrients are lost faster than they can be replaced, will eventually deplete the soil and the com-

munity. Of all civilized man's detrimental effects on his world, few
equal in impact the hastening of erosion by agriculture, grazing, and
forestry. Annual crops—corn, cereal grains, and the like—now ab-
sorb the soil's nutrients, some of which are shipped away from the
land at harvest time while the remainder return to the soil once a
year, or even more often, for long periods of exposure to erosion.
Fast-growing, pulp-producing trees are substituted for long-lived
forests and are cut and shipped off the land, no longer dying in
place. Cattle replace native mammals, and they, too, are shipped
away, and the soil's nutrients with them. With food chains abbre-
viated, nutrients are exposed to erosion at rates of a score to hundreds of times greater, a loss hastened still further by transportation
of foodstuffs and raw materials.

I have lingered on the role of soil in order to emphasize why it
is a vital part of management planning. First, since soil fertility is essential to healthy wildlife populations, your plans must avoid any
measures which might accelerate erosion processes; instead, they
should be designed to retain and build soil nutrients. Second, since
variations in soils—chemistry, texture, depth, etc.—set limits on vegetation types and thus on animals, knowledge of the soil is prerequi-
site to management.

How do you find out about the soil on your land? Plant indicators will tell you much. What tree, shrubs, grasses, or flowers
dominate the area and seem to thrive best? Look them up in the
many books on plants in your public library; with a little searching
you will usually find what soils they prefer. If you are dealing with
more than a back yard or modest-sized lot, it is best to seek expert
help beyond this point. Your county agent, state agricultural agency,
state college, or U.S. Soil Conservation Service office can give you
information on soil maps, and on how to have your soils analyzed,
together with an interpretation of the analyses. Cost depends upon
the number of samples needed, which depends in turn on the size
and variability of the land. In most cases it is not expensive, and in
all cases it is money well spent in terms of the extravagant mistakes
it can save.

In undertaking small property management, there are some
facts you can gather on your own. Take a spade or posthole digger,
and dig holes, at least 2 feet deep if possible, at two or three different spots on your lot. What you are after is a sampling of each of the
soil types present. If the area is level and no larger than a half-acre,
chances are the soil is quite uniform, and a couple of holes at different points are sufficient. If the area is larger or uneven, holes should

be dug on high and low or other divergent sites. Check for notice-able differences as you go deeper—color changes, hardness of soil, presence of gravel or rock, etc. (If the area is in a subdivision where contractors generally remove and replace much of the top ground, you are apt to find a jumbled topsoil—probably including nails and bits of two-by-four—over a subsoil with little intergrading.) Make a note and sketch of the thickness and nature of the layering, if any.

From the earth you have removed, take the topsoil only (the up-permost, more or less uniform layer) and mix it thoroughly in a bu-cket. Remove about a cupful of the mixture, save it in a bag or bottle, and label the container "Topsoil, Hole #1," or whatever. Do the same for the next (subsoil) layer. Then fill your hole with water as a simple test of drainage. If the water disappears very rapidly, you have a coarse-textured "light" soil—largely sand and/or gravel (or else you have hit the storm-sewer tile). If the water, or most of it, is still there in an hour or so, your soil is probably "heavy," with much clay or minerals (something your spadework probably al-ready told you). Most soils are between these extremes. The water test gives you a clue as to whether the ground is light and easily drained, medium, or heavy and poorly drained—basic information for deciding what to plant.

Returning to the soil samples you laid aside, from each cup-size sample of topsoil put about ¼ cup in a quart jar (labeled by hole number), add a pint of water, shake it up thoroughly, and let the bottles stand until all sediment settles out and the water is clear. This may take three to four days or longer. When the water clears you can read off the components of your soil—coarse sand (if any) at the very bottom of the jar, fine sand (if any) next, silt above that, and clay, finest of all, on top. (The longer that water takes to clear, the more clay you have.) If half or more of the sediment is fine or coarse sand, the topsoil would be classified as light, sandy soil—easy to work up, but subject to drought and often needing fertilizer for best plant growth. If there is little recognizable sand and at least one-fourth clay, with much silt, your soil is heavy, it holds water well (too well, at times) but must be worked carefully or you will end up with a brickyard. Should the mixture be about 40 percent sand, 40 percent silt, and some clay, you are fortunate: you have good loam soil and will be able to grow most wildlife plants with a minimum of trouble.

For further examination of the soil left in your sample jars, visit your neighborhood garden center, hardware store, florist, or nursery and buy an inexpensive soil-testing kit. Use the kit and your re-

maining samples to check out "pH"—the scientific index of acidity-
alkalinity. The test will reveal whether your soil is acid or alkaline, and how much so. Repeat the pH test, according to the instructions furnished with the kit, at least twice on each sample to ensure accuracy. There will be a lot of other soil tests described on the kit labels and instructions, but don't take these seriously. The acidity-alkalinity test itself is reasonably reliable, worth the outlay, and, in conjunction with the other tests outlined in this chapter, will supply most of the information you need.

GOALS

At this point, between what you will have learned on your own and what you will have gained from others, you should have a valid picture of the material you have to work with—acreage, vegetation, soils, and the like, Now is the time to consider your objectives. Doubtless you've had these in mind all along, but it might be well to reflect on them again in the light of what you now know. Maybe you had in mind just a small pond for a bit of fishing, or to attract a few ducks and shore birds—but all you have is light, well-drained, seemingly bottomless soils. Perhaps you want a lot of pheasants as game to hunt with your friends, or to which you can lease hunting rights, but your land is so sandy that you can only grow pines. Or you might have figured to plant some good cone-bearing trees to pull in crossbills and finches in winter, but all you have is heavy clay. If such frustrations confront you, don't give up; some pointers for you are coming later. But do stop and consider the situation. If what you have does not lend itself easily to what you hope to have, there are two choices to pursue—resign yourself to spending a lot of work, money, and time in changing things, with no guaranteed success in achieving your goals, or rethink your situation, find substitute but nearly equivalent goals, and build on what is present rather than trying to start from scratch.

If your aim is better bird hunting, for example, and your soil won't support the fertile grain crops pheasants thrive on, think about quail, dove, grouse, or even chukar partridge. Be guided by what is there now. If you have spotted a few ruffed grouse, but no ringnecks within 100 miles, you can almost assuredly build a healthy grouse population quicker and cheaper than you can a pheasant population. If you planned to landscape your yard with fruit-bearing shrubs to attract more songbirds and discover your soil is too alkaline for the acid-loving dogwood, hollies, or bearberry you have in mind, try firethorns *(Pyracantha),* grape holly *(Mahonia),* and other fruit-bearers that thrive best in alkaline conditions.

In brief, fix your goals clearly in mind, and modify them or select appropriate alternatives where evaluation of existing conditions points squarely against what you first had envisioned. Look again at your map. What areas do you really have to work with? Be practical. If your back yard is the intended wildlife domain, you really are not going to move that big maple that shades half your lot, are you? If your sportsmen's club leases hunting rights from a farmer, where will he let you plant shrubs—on his best forty or that back corner between the woodlot and the road? Or, if you are inviting wildlife into a city park or subdivision, don't forget, whether you like it or not, that people's needs come first; only what's left after the sidewalks and parking lots is yours.

The purpose of this book is to help you carry out your plan. Each chapter is devoted to certain specifics, which may or may not be useful to you, depending on your goal. But all management for wildlife should keep certain fundamentals in mind:

1. The plan must be feasible biologically; it must depend on improvement from a natural base, from existing soils, plants, and communities.

2. The plan must aim to increase the basic productivity of the area, not simply pull wildlife into temporarily attractive deathtraps. In the same vein, it must not incorporate features that encourage erosion, deplete soils, or create situations that can be maintained only by constant artificial treatments—pesticides, herbicides, and the like.

3. The plan should make sense economically. It must be spaced out over a sensible period of time, and designed, in terms of equipment, within your ability to follow through.

4. Wherever possible, management should aim at maintaining and increasing plants and animals already native to the area, and should complement, not fight, existing terrain, watercourses, etc.

Remember, too, that the central theme of most plans to achieve greater wildlife numbers should be to improve interspersion, to attain wider diversity, and more edges where a variety of habitats meet.

A reading program of books on general wildlife topics, pamphlets, and articles on specific details, including but not limited to the publications listed at the end of each chapter of this book, will render invaluable assistance.

You can obtain help as well from a number of federal, state, county, and private agencies, all or in part devoted to wildlife management and conservation, or to related activities. Generally, these agencies provide one or more types of assistance—publications, financial aid, or consultation. Publications may be free, or you may have to pay for them. The best policy is to write the office involved, state your interests, and ask for a list of available reading matter. Order what you need and enclose payment, if any. Agencies through which financial assistance (or materials, such as seed, seedlings, etc.) may be available, under certain programs with specific requirements, should first be contacted by mail or phone. Briefly outline your situation and request information on rules and guidelines to aid programs for which you may qualify. (I'll have more to say about specific programs later.) Most public agencies offer some form of consulting field service—advice and assistance with planning. But keep one thing in mind: these agencies are usually woefully understaffed, with perhaps only one or two individuals assigned to handle inquiries throughout an entire state or region. Unless you are planning a major project for a sizable chunk of land, you may be pretty far back on the waiting line for a personal visit; if your project is an acre or two, the best you can hope for is to get a couple of key questions answered by mail.

The U.S. Department of Agriculture offers perhaps the most assistance. Its Agricultural Stabilization and Conservation Service (ASCS) provides cost-sharing for landowners who carry out a variety of wildlife and other conservation practices on their land, as well as payments—under various programs—for retirement of cropland. Farmers Home Administration (FHA) provides loans and technical assistance for landowners developing income-producing wildlife projects (fee-fishing, shooting preserves, etc.). The Extension Service of USDA offers a variety of useful publications and, through county agents, good advice and technical assistance. The Soil Conservation Service (SCS) also offers worthwhile publications, technical assistance, and cost-sharing programs for wildlife and other land use projects.

All four of these USDA agencies maintain offices (often shared) in most counties (usually in the county seat) of the United States.

34 One of the first steps anyone interested in carrying out wildlife management or conservation practices should make is to contact the nearest SCS and Extension Service Bureau. You don't have to be a farmer or interested in cost-sharing to find their literature, advice, and knowledge of other sources of help invaluable.

Two divisions of the U.S. Department of Interior can be of service in special areas. The Bureau of Outdoor Recreation offers advice and limited technical assistance on certain projects, including fish and wildlife developments, aimed at providing public recreation. The Bureau of Sport Fisheries and Wildlife is a source of publications and advice on projects involving certain wildlife species—primarily migratory birds. These bureaus are organized on a regional basis, but maintain an office in most state capitals.

The Community Resources Development Administration of the U.S. Department of Housing and Urban Development provides grants assisting towns in the purchase and development of land for parks, recreation, and conservation. If your interest is in helping your community by public projects along these lines, HUD may be of help.

At a more local level, every state has an agency responsible for administering, managing, and protecting wildlife. These state conservation departments or game commissions and their addresses are listed at the end of this book. Along with SCS and Extension Service offices, these primary state agencies are a must among your contacts. All provide useful publications, many offer technical assistance and advice (subject to the manpower limitations we have mentioned), and some furnish shrub and tree seedlings, or seed for wildlife plantings, free or at cost. Many states have other agencies—forestry and agricultural commissions or divisions, for example—offering specialized help. Since these vary in name and function from state to state, it is best to inquire about them through the conservation or fish and game department.

The National Audubon Society and National Wildlife Federation and other private agencies listed at the end of this book also have publications available on general and specific wildlife topics.

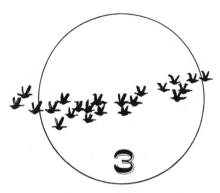

SMALL GAME: WHAT THEY ARE
AND WHAT THEY NEED

Currently there are nearly as many ways to classify game species as there were game biologists forty years ago. *Farm game,* for example, consists of those creatures, such as the ring-necked pheasant, cottontail rabbit, and bobwhite quail, primarily indigenous to agricultural land. *Big game* encompasses hoofed mammals—deer, elk, and moose. *Forest game* is primarily associated with big wooded areas and such inhabitants as the ruffed grouse and wild turkey. *Migratory game* are species crossing state and national boundaries in annual migration and subject to federal regulations, notably ducks and geese.

Some species, however, do not fit these man-made categories. Mourning doves, for example, migrate like ducks but are produced primarily on farmland. The woodcock doubles as both migratory and forest game, and squirrels are simultaneously farm and forest game. To classify this host of creatures, the multitude of categories goes on *ad infinitum.* There are *upland* and *wilderness game,* and even *webless migratory game.*

But for the purposes of this chapter, a simple, nontechnical definition of "small game" will be adequate: huntable birds and mammals of relatively small size that are commonly associated with farmlands and adjoining woodlands, including quail, pheasant, rabbits, squirrels, and the like. They occupy somewhat similar habitats and, in most cases, their management involves similar principles. Later we shall discuss waterfowl, forest game, and big game. Some of these groups also include species of small size, but they are members of different natural communities, with different management needs.

For the hunter, or the landowner who seeks additional income through lease or sale of hunting rights, small game and waterfowl usually offer the best return for management investments. Of course, you do not have to hunt to be interested in small game. The group includes common, desirable, and eye-catching species, well worth attracting and increasing whether for hunting or not.

RING-NECKED PHEASANT

Originally native to Asia, pheasants of several races were introduced into Great Britain and other European countries centuries ago. Descendants of those varieties that prospered were brought to North America over two hundred years ago by nostalgic English colonists who attempted—as they did wherever they settled—to establish birds and mammals familiar from home.

These early efforts were in vain. Success did not come until 1881, when twenty-one pheasants—probably Chinese ringnecks—were imported directly from China and stocked in Oregon's Willamette Valley. From this tiny beginning a booming population spread through the 180-by-40-mile valley; a hunting season opened just ten years later.

Appetites whetted by this success, other states inaugurated pheasant-stocking programs, as did private individuals. Game farms cranked out hundreds of thousands of birds from 1900 until the late 1930s. Some of these pheasants were descendants of Oregon's first twenty-one; others came from stock imported from Europe, and still others directly from Asia. By the early 1940s pheasants were solidly entrenched in nearly all states and regions where they exist today. Like the humans with whom they share the land, most pheasants in America are now a melting pot of races—part Chinese, part Mongolian, with a dash of English blackneck and a pinch of Japanese green, among others.

Whatever his "nationality," the pheasant filled a real gap. As the great North American grasslands vanished under the plow, the prairie chicken, sharptail grouse, and other native species of that community dwindled accordingly. Into this void strutted the pheasant, making himself at home over the vast farmlands of the Midwest, the cultivated land of the East, and the cropped and irrigated valleys of the West.

Despite repeated stocking, the ringneck has not become established in the southeast or south-central areas of the U.S., roughly below a line from northern Maryland through south-central Illinois and northern Missouri. Why? Very conceivably the lack of available calcium grit—a mandatory item for ringnecks—in much of this area is a deterrent. Also, possibly the high temperatures during the nesting season might curtail success since ringneck eggs are more sensitive to heat than are eggs of bobwhite and other southern natives. Whatever the cause, overcoming the barrier to pheasants in the South is a high-priority research project among game biologists.

In the meantime, the ringneck is having his problems in prime range where he has long been established. While never demanding a great deal in the way of cover, even the rugged pheasant must find shelter from storms and predators, and a safe place to nest. But the fertile agricultural soils, supporting the densest pheasant populations are under pressure these days. Modern clean farming practices and intensive use of every scrap of land have knocked out fencerows, roadsides, and odd areas of cover. Row crops, harvested and frequently plowed before winter, have replaced the hayfields which once gave some nesting space and winter protection. Neither has increasing agricultural use of pesticides and herbicides helped. In short, regions where cover was reduced to the point that prairie chickens and sharp-tails no longer could exist are rapidly becoming too barren even for the pheasant.

A short look at the life history and requirements of the ringneck will uncover the facts necessary to successful management for him. In early spring, the big, gaudy roosters announce the onset of the breeding season by crowing periodically from the boundaries of territories they select, patrol, and defend against other males. Polygamous by nature, the cock may have a harem of many hens, and the average is usually between four and eight. This polygamous custom, incidentally, plus the distinctive coloration of the male, makes the ringneck especially suitable as a game species. "Cocks only" hunting regulations enable the harvest of most of the easily distinguished roosters without hampering next year's production since each surviving male can breed with many hens.

The clutch of eggs, averaging ten to twelve in number, is laid in a shallow depression or scrape in the ground among dead grass or plant stalks, or in new growth 6 to 8 or more inches tall. Most nests are located in relatively open fields, along roadsides, or ditchbanks and the like; rarely are they in dense woods or heavy thickets. April and May are primary nesting months, and first hatches come in May over most of the range.

Hens will renest—perhaps several times—if earlier nests are destroyed before hatching, but they produce only one brood a year. Very young birds seen in late summer represent the payoff from the last nesting attempts by a persistent hen, not a second brood.

Young pheasants are able to get about actively within a few hours after hatching (an essential feat for ground-hatched birds), and forage for food on their own under the hen's alert eye. Insects make up the bulk of the chick's diet, as is the case with most young birds. At two weeks the youngsters can fly quite well, but brood and hen normally remain together for eight weeks or more. At sixteen to seventeen weeks the young are fully colored and full-grown—those that are still around, that is—since the average life span for pheasants is only eight months, hunted or not.

Dead stems of tall grasses make excellent cover for the first nesting attempts of hen pheasants in spring.

Ringnecked pheasants are tough customers, but even they cannot survive severe winter storms on the increasingly clean-farmed and denuded landscapes of the Midwest.

Brood bonds weaken in fall and the birds wander and disperse. Young and old still relish grasshoppers and other insects, but now feed primarily upon waste grain and weed seeds in harvested fields, and on wild fruits such as wild grapes and dogwood. As winter approaches, pheasants move to heavier cover and bunch up, the hens often in large groups of thirty to a hundred, while the cocks form smaller, separate bands.

Late winter is a critical season for pheasants over much of their range, and lack of food and adequate shelter are the chief threats. Ringnecks will range far and scratch deep for food—even through crusted snow—but when blizzards bring drifting snow, sleet, and ice across an increasingly clean-farmed and denuded landscape, even these rugged birds are put to the test. Despite the roughest winters, a few survivors usually emerge, feeding eagerly on early-sprouting greens where the sun has melted the snow. Before long the defiant crowing of the roosters rings in another spring.

What can you do if you want pheasants on your land? Unfortunately, if your region has no existing pheasants, and you're "outside" present pheasant range, the possibility is remote that you can establish a self-maintaining population, unless wildlife biologists come up with strains or races better adapted to your region. You can still have pheasants, of course, if you are willing to buy and release game-farm birds; but this can get expensive because they normally won't be with you long. You can also have good pheasant hunting in most instances—again, if you are willing to buy and stock birds regularly on a "put-and-take" basis.

If your land already supports some wild pheasant populations, there are management practices to try if you would like more ringnecks. Keep in mind that pheasants are basically farmland creatures. Relatively flat, treeless terrain, with grain crops and fertile soil, is pheasant country. If your land does not have these characteristics, even though pheasants exist in more favorable areas nearby, do not put much hope in raising big crops of ringnecks.

Because they like fertile, open farmland, pheasants are usually limited by factors that such lands lack—winter cover, adequate, unmowed cover for nesting, and a food source in late winter. We shall look at ways to fill these needs for pheasants and other small game in the next two chapters.

BOBWHITE QUAIL

Although he has some close rivals, to those who know him the bobwhite is the best loved of all our small game. In the South, a quest for "Mr. Bob" is the ultimate in hunting to the true sportsman, as I found when I moved to Maryland and was eventually invited to go "bird hunting." As a Yankee, I wondered what kind of "birds" we would hunt, but I was just barely smart enough to keep my thoughts to myself. Soon enough I learned there is only one "bird" for southern hunters, and that "bird hunting" is quail hunting.

On the other hand, on the northern fringe of his range, the bobwhite is classed as a songbird, closed to hunting in several states. Odd as it may seem, it is hard to say who loves him most, those who hunt him or those who shun the thought. But one thing is clear—the bobwhite is an asset anywhere.

He is a native of the eastern and central states, extending from central New England south to Florida, and west through southern Michigan and Wisconsin in the North, and through eastern Colorado and New Mexico in the South. Scattered populations have been introduced in several western states. On the northern and western fringes of his native range the bobwhite lives dangerously, in climates often too wintry or arid, and his numbers go up and down violently with weather cycles.

One of the many happy things about the bobwhite is the cheerful call of the male in spring—the "bob-bob-white" whistle which gives him his name. This call announces the start of the breeding season and proclaims his presence to nearby females. The male's territory—defended home ground in the breeding season—is not nearly as large or as carefully guarded as the ring-necked pheasant's, but the whistle-call still warns other males to keep their distance.

Calling, pairing (the bobwhite is monogamous, content with a single mate, unlike the ringneck), and mating starts in March and April in the South, and in April and May on the northern fringes of the range. The pair (his head markings and throat are white while hers are buff) build their nest together—a small depression scratched in the ground and filled with dead plant stems and grass. The nest is usually in an open site, not far from such clear ground as a roadway or tilled field, and in rather sparse vegetation, preferably amidst dead vegetation from the previous year.

The hen lays an average of thirteen to fifteen eggs, normally one each day. She begins to sit on and incubate the eggs around the clock when the clutch is complete, with brief absences to feed. The eggs hatch twenty-three days later.

How do all eggs in such large clutches hatch the same day when they are laid over a sequence of days? Because the embryo within the egg does not start development until the egg is warmed to nearly 100°F. During the laying period the hen visits the nest for only a few minutes, depositing an egg and leaving before her body can warm any eggs to the point where growth begins. When her clutch is complete, she remains in the nest constantly, warming all eggs to the temperature required for growth, and giving all an even start.

The young of most ground-nesters are precocious; they are up and about, able to walk, run, and feed on their own within twenty-four hours of hatching. If they hatched one per day for two weeks, the brood would be so handicapped that severe losses would occur. Young and hen are so vulnerable to predators during hatching that the sooner the new family is hatched, dry, and up and away, the better. Recent research shows that quail eggs which are actually touching one another hatch within a much shorter time span than do those that are separated. There appears to be a "clicking" type of communication between fully developed embryos that helps synchronize hatching time. This adaptation for survival is probably prevalent among many ground-nesting birds.

Within twenty-four hours of hatching, the young bobs, not much bigger than giant bumblebees, leave the nest with the adults, never to return. Both parents stay with the brood, unlike the ringneck where the cock could not care less, keeping them warm at night and leading them to adequate cover.

If, because of predation, severe weather, or other hazards, the hen is not successful in hatching her first clutch of eggs, she will try again—and again and again—until she is successful or until time, energy, or the season runs out. The same applies to most small game birds. However, such later nesting attempts usually show smaller numbers of eggs and poorer hatching success. Often, too, late hatches face more severe weather, scarcity of food, and more predation than do young from first nests. Consequently, management that helps increase the percentage of successful first nests often helps ensure better populations of bobwhite and other small game.

Through summer, quail families tend to remain together, frequently joining other families as the young mature, forming groups of twenty to thirty individuals. Their diet is still based on seeds and plant parts, but insects are now sought eagerly, especially by young quail who require the higher protein of animal foods for growth and development of their feathers.

With the shorter days and lower temperatures of fall, families break up and reassemble in different groupings. Individuals often travel a mile or more (a major expedition for most quail) from the range where they grew up, in a regrouping aptly termed the "fall shuffle."

By late fall, groups averaging a dozen to fifteen birds are formed, feeding, loafing, and ranging together as a covey through the winter. A covey's winter range seldom exceeds 20 to 25 acres, often much less in good habitat, and illustrates the principle of interspersion, or edge, in management. The closer together the covey's requirements (a variety of food and cover), the less the birds will need to travel, the smaller the home range, and, on the average, the more individuals per unit of land.

Since coveys commonly appear on the same few acres year after year, a close look at such ranges can help guide management plans. Briefly, the best winter ranges supply an abundance of seeds, the primary or sole winter food, at ground level. These seeds must be within reach on low stems, or, preferably, on bare ground in sparse vegetation. The choicest seeds in the world are worthless if they lie under thick ground cover. Unlike pheasants, bobwhite are not equipped to scratch for food through ice and deep snow, so severe winter weather is a real hazard. Ideal winter cover is that which permits quail to move easily on the ground, with some overhead vegetation. Sod-forming grasses and thick duff are generally unacceptable, but heavier cover—brush, a dense hedgerow, or woods—is characteristic of good ranges, furnishing escape from predators and hunters.

Oddly enough, the way a wintering covey spends the night may be a key to bobwhite survival. Quail are small as game birds go (less than half a pound), so conserving warmth is difficult. Bunching together at night to share body heat offers one solution, and also provides protection from predators for the ground-roosting bobwhite. A covey typically spends the night side by side in a tight ring, with wings somewhat overlapping and all birds facing outward. The roosting ring is disk-shaped rather than circular, so that no central, open hole permits body heat to escape.

Roosting sites depend on the region, and vary from brush and similar thick cover in the North to relatively open, herbaceous vegetation in the South, which, nevertheless, in combination with the topography, gives adequate protection from weather. Sites are always such that roosting coveys can explode upward and outward at the first sign of a nocturnal predator.

This roosting habit is critically important partly because of rather stringent cover needs—shelter from weather that is sufficiently open to permit escape—and partly because of mechanical limitations. It takes at least seven quail to form the heat-conserving roosting disk. Should there be fewer, holes in the formation permit body heat to escape. If small coveys, especially in the North, cannot find and join other coveys, their odds of survival in winter are slim.

In addition to suitable roosting cover, the bobwhite has other particular needs, including "dusting" sites. Many songbirds bathe in water; the bobwhite and many other ground-dwelling birds use dust to clean their feathers and rid themselves of external parasites. A necessary ingredient of the best quail range is at least one spot—the edge of a cultivated field or dirt road, for example—where the soil is bare, loose, and dry, and where bobwhite can scratch, squat, wallow, and thoroughly enjoy a dust bath.

We can learn much from the bobwhite, and our education might well begin with the distinctive requirements of his habitat. He demands cover sparse enough at ground level to allow easy movement, yet providing overhead protection and some patches of relatively dense growth in which he can escape his enemies. He needs an abundant supply of available seeds that he can find and reach on bare soil or low vegetation, and suitable roosting and dusting spots. Bobwhite is a coveying bird with no inclination for vast ranges. Manage your land to contain his needs within the most compact amount of acreage and, provided you are within good quail range, and have sufficient moisture and mild winters, your birds may multiply dramatically.

WESTERN QUAIL

The bobwhite may be best known and most widely distributed, but he is by no means the only U.S. quail. West of his native territory live five species of western quail.

All are more spectacular in plumage than the bobwhite, especially three species that sport a prominent head plume. One of these is the mountain quail, whose range stretches along the Pacific coastal states from southern Washington to southern California, and reaches as far east as western Nevada. Another is the California or valley quail, which makes his home in California and southern Oregon, and has also been introduced successfully along the coast as far north as British Columbia. The third is the Gambel quail—a desert-loving bird of the Southwest.

The remaining two species are devoid of head plumes but still strikingly marked. The Mearns quail, smallest of all, is limited to arid portions of Arizona and New Mexico. The big scaled or "blue" quail is found throughout New Mexico and ranges north into southern Colorado, west to central and southern Arizona, and east into Texas and the Oklahoma Panhandle.

These western quail nest in depressions scooped in the ground, as does the bobwhite. Most prefer nest sites under or beside brush or weeds, although mountain quail often nest under logs or at tree bases. Clutches average a dozen to eighteen eggs, somewhat fewer for the little Mearns quail.

On the whole, the habits of western quail resemble those of bobwhite, except that most western quail tend to roost in shrubs or trees, rather than on the ground. Dwelling in milder climates than the bobwhite, they have more to fear from predators than from severe cold. Some also are wider ranging, and have separate summer and winter grounds—especially mountain quail who "migrate" to lower elevations in winter.

The desert-dwelling species often run rather than fly when alarmed, and, as would be expected, are tied closely in numbers and distribution to rainfall and water supplies. In years when winter rains fail and little or no green, succulent vegetation exists, desert quail may simply fail to breed or nest. For this reason, the provision of dependable water supplies can be a primary management device for western quail in arid regions.

HUNGARIAN PARTRIDGE

Of the many exotic game birds introduced into North America, only three—the ring-necked pheasant, the Hungarian partridge, and the chukar partridge—have become successfully established to any degree. All three were stocked in almost all parts of the continent in considerable numbers at one time or another; all three eventually thrived in only a portion of the total area stocked, defining their own ranges in the New World.

The Hungarian or "gray" partridge came to us from southeastern Europe and western Asia. One of the first introductions was attempted before 1800, by a son-in-law of Benjamin Franklin. After more than a century and a half of stocking, the "Hun," as he is known to his friends, has made himself at home in northwestern North America along both sides of the U.S.-Canadian border, and extends from Alberta to Minnesota and northern Iowa on the southeast, and Washington and Oregon on the southwest. A second established range, with scattered populations, exists in the Great Lakes states, from southeastern Wisconsin and northern Illinois around the tip of Lake Michigan through northern Indiana and southern Michigan into Ohio. Scattered, isolated pockets survive farther east along the Canadian border.

Less pugnacious and conspicuous than the ring-necked pheasant, the Hun is always welcome in his adopted range, "a nice bird to have around." Choosing one mate and coveying much of the year, like the bobwhite, but larger (about three quarters of a pound when mature), the Hun does best in open small-grain country—the wheatfields of the Northwest. Wary and tough to hunt, he is a fine game bird.

Because the Hungarian's distribution is so limited, we shall not detail his habits and management. If you are fortunate to live within regions the Hun has adopted for home, and have some Huns on your land and want to hold onto them, take time to study their habits, learn the areas they frequent, and plan to maintain those areas in their present condition. Consult your state's conservation department—it will have at least one biologist who can help with advice on Hun management.

If your hope is to increase Hun numbers significantly, for hunting purposes, seek professional help. Compared to many upland game species we do not know much about Hun management, but it is pretty certain that, unlike the bobwhite, major changes in numbers result from major habitat changes on large acreages.

CHUKAR PARTRIDGE

Third on the list of successfully established imports among upland game, the chukar has found his home, after the usual nationwide stocking attempts, in semidesert country west of the Rockies. In arid portions of Nevada, Washington, Oregon, and adjoining states, this Asian native has become a prime game bird, elusive and challenging.

Out West the chukar tends to be a bird of public lands—broad stretches of beautiful but economically bleak country. Even states where he prospers have done little, beyond initial introductions, to manage for the chukar, and it is doubtful that you or I will buy up several square miles of semidesert to make the attempt. Intermediate in size between the bobwhite and the ringneck, the chukar is, however, easily produced on game farms. He performs well on release, if properly handled, and tastes like nectar. For these reasons, the chukar is a prime bird for shooting preserves and "put-and-take" hunting. If your interest lies along these lines, you will hear more about the chukar later.

MOURNING DOVE

The mourning dove is one of our finest, most beautifully colored, most welcome songbirds. He is also one of the most sporting of all game birds. Thus, to the nonhunting bird-lover, the idea of shooting a dove is incredible; to the hunting bird-lover, the idea of not being able to hunt doves is equally incredible. The mourning dove is simultaneously one of our most valuable wildlife viewing assets and our number-one game bird in terms of shots fired, hunters involved, and numbers harvested.

So far both hunters and nonhunters have been able to have their cake and eat it too. Northern states often closed to dove hunting, produce many of our doves; hunters in central and southern states account for most of the harvest, since northern doves migrate.

Despite intensive gunning, mourning doves have been on the increase in most areas over recent years—as much or more so in states
open for dove hunting as in those closed. In part this may be because of general habitat changes and the prolific reproductive potential of the species, in part to management efforts by state and federal agencies, and in part to the fact that some of the most
productive northern states allow no hunting.

Mourning doves do respond to certain land-management practices discussed in following chapters. Understanding why they respond depends, as with every species, on a knowledge of their life
history.

Unlike those small game birds discussed so far, mourning doves
are classed as migratory birds and thus are under federal protection
and hunting regulations. Their range embraces all of the United
States (with local exceptions because of unfavorable habitat), and
overlaps our borders north and south. Birds in the northern portion
of the range move south for the winter, usually to the Gulf Coast or
Mexico, but the mourner is a year-round resident in the southern
two thirds to three quarters of the nation. Some birds produced in
northern states also winter there, even though they may suffer
heavy mortality in severe weather. Bird banders often find that surviving northern "resident" doves have lost portions of their toes as
an apparent result of exposure to extreme cold.

Every animal has a reproductive potential designed to maintain
the species in the face of predation, starvation, and other mortality
factors. The small game birds discussed so far do this by hatching
one large brood of young each breeding season. Doves achieve the
same end with several small broods. The female lays two eggs per
clutch, may lay up to four clutches in one season, and often suc-
ceeds in rearing two clutches for an average total of four young on
the wing.

Mourning doves normally nest in trees. They build flimsy, flat
platforms of twigs, which are vulnerable to destruction by high
winds or heavy rain. Persistent renesting and the ability to produce
several broods a season help overcome these losses.

As the young depart on their own, and as adults wind up the
nesting period, doves build up in large flocks. Seed-eaters, they gang
up in fall to feed on waste grain in harvested cropfields. Flight patterns are established that encompass the daily needs—food, a source
of grit and water, and suitable trees for night-time roosting. Areas
that naturally, or through management, supply these basic requirements within fall migration or wintering range can normally attract
and hold large numbers of birds.

Mourning doves are among those species that have profited from the settlement of North America by man. Agriculture provides large open fields with attendant weeds and waste grain, making ideal feeding grounds. Man-made farm and stock ponds, and shelter belt plantings in the Plains states, have opened new opportunities, supplying water and nesting and roosting cover where little or none existed before. In the face of man the passenger pigeon became extinct; his close cousin, the mourning dove, has prospered and expanded in range and numbers.

RABBITS

Cottontail rabbits and mourning doves, oddly enough, have considerable in common. The cottontail is our most popular game mammal; the mourning dove our most popular game bird. Both are widely distributed and reasonably tolerant of civilization; both overcome mortality factors by producing several small batches of young a year.

With his close cousins (in most cases they are indistinguishable except to biologists) the marsh rabbit of the Southeast, the swamp rabbit, and the New England rabbit, the cottontail occupies most of the United States and parts of Canada. In forested areas of northern and western states he gives way to another relative, the snowshoe hare.

The typical cottontail begins life in a ground nest, a pit 4 or 5 inches deep scraped in the ground in open cover by the female, then lined with grasses, moss, or the like and finally padded on the inside with fur the female pulls from her own body. This nest is covered by the female with a lid of grass and leaves, flush with the ground and beautifully camouflaged. On the average, there will be four or five young in the nest, naked at first, but growing and developing rapidly and venturing forth for food and shelter, independent of their mother, between two and three weeks of age.

They need to be on their own fast since the female is capable of mating the same day a litter is born. Gestation takes only about twenty-eight days, so that—depending upon the limits set by climate—a single female may average two to three litters a year in the North and four to six in the South. Furthermore, some females born in early spring, in years of good food and weather, may even breed and produce a litter before fall. This mating talent is a primary reason why the cottontail survives. He outnumbers adversity.

Cottontails are vegetarians at all ages. In spring and summer they subsist on grass, sprouts, and nearly any fresh greenery. In

winter they turn to corn and other waste grain, if available, but their
mainstay in the North consists of the bark and twigs of shrubs and
trees, preferably from new growth. Sumac and apple are favored
sources. Because of his nearly universal taste for fresh greens and
young bark, the cottontail frequently finds himself in hot water with
gardeners, orchard owners, nurserymen, and foresters.

As an abundant, widely distributed, middle-sized, and fairly
defenseless species, the cottontail is a key part of many food chains
and pyramids of numbers. Over much of the country he is prey for a
vast array of predators, from the weasel, fox, and the coyote to
avian meat-eaters. In this capacity the cottontail serves as a buffer,
taking predator pressure away from rarer animals. As a food source
and as a buffer, he plays a seldom-appreciated but fundamental role
in determining wildlife abundance.

As if being dined upon were not enough, rabbits suffer from a
variety of "plagues." Virus-caused skin fibromas, warble-flies, tape-
worms, and, worst of all, tularemia run rampant through cottontail
populations, especially at peaks of abundance.

Yet the strong "spring" of the cottontail's reproductive potential
is equal to the depressing force of all these mortality factors, as long
as habitat meets his needs. Those needs are relatively simple since,
as might be expected in one so durable, the cottontail is most adaptable. Food is nearly any source of greens, although preferably
young grass and clover, in spring and summer, and adequate young
twigs and bark in winter. Cover from predators and weather normally is best supplied by brush patches and clumps, but piles of cut
brush, the burrows of woodchucks and other animals, and even cul-
verts, farm machinery, and outbuildings seem to be adequate substitutes. Obviously, food and cover must be low and within reach—a
heavily grazed woodlot with no ground-level cover is useless.

A "stay-at-home" like the bobwhite, the cottontail may live out
his life within the confines of a few acres if his requirements are
met. Thus, cottontail and quail reach highest per-acre populations
where food and cover are best interspersed, and both usually respond readily to management.

FOX AND GRAY SQUIRRELS

The squirrel family is a large one. For convenience, it can be di-
vided into two groups—"ground squirrels," primary western, and
"tree squirrels."

Tree squirrels include the little red squirrel or chickaree, the
handsome tassel-eared squirrels of the Southwest, and the flying

squirrels. Because of their distribution or habits, these species receive relatively little management attention.

Not so the gray and fox squirrels. Both are important game animals, widely distributed and well known by hunter and nonhunter alike. The fox squirrel ranges over most of the eastern half of the United States, tapering off with the last scattered trees on the edge of the Great Plains. The gray squirrel's range is similar, although he has a relative in the Pacific coastal states and another in Arizona.

While their general distribution is much alike, and both fox and gray squirrels have similar habits and life needs, the specific habitat each requires is different. These closely related tree squirrels illustrate the fact that no two species can make identical demands on the environment—occupy the same "niche"—in the same range.

The gray squirrel is basically a forest animal, thriving best in large stands of mature hardwoods or in heavily wooded bottomlands. In some eastern areas where fox squirrels are not found, grays may still occur along the narrow fringes of woods that are all that remain of unbroken forests, but by and large the gray is a "big woods" animal.

Most fox squirrels prefer more open country. While they do well in some dense woodlands in the Southeast, their ideal and predominant range is in small woodlots, open woods, and those fringes of trees extending along waterways, roadsides, and fence rows into open landscapes.

Because of those habitat preferences, man's impact has had a different effect on each species. Clearing forested land for agriculture, and thinning and pasturing much of the remaining woods of the eastern states, generally reduced or eliminated gray squirrels in many local areas. The same practices, provided the land was not completely stripped, plus shelterbelt plantings on the eastern Great Plains, in general boosted fox squirrel populations and extended their range both locally and to the West.

The fox squirrel is the larger of the two, with adults averaging close to two pounds, almost twice the weight of adult grays. Both can vary greatly in color. The fox squirrel is typically grizzled buff, or rusty above and orangish red to tawny brown below; the gray squirrel is silver-gray above, with a whitish belly. Yet local populations and races run the gamut from almost pure black to white.

Both species are tied closely to mast—fruits and nuts of trees and shrubs. Acorns, hickory nuts, walnuts, wild cherry and other fruits, and, in early spring, tree buds are diet mainstays. Corn is an important item where woods or fencerow trees border fields.

In fall, both gray and fox squirrels industriously "cut" nuts from trees and bury them, one at a time, an inch or two in the ground. These caches constitute the bulk of their winter food supply, essential in the North since squirrels do not migrate or hibernate. Apparently guided by scent rather than memory, squirrels dig up most of their buried treasure over the winter. Since the nuts they miss germinate as new seedlings, squirrels are assets to the future of the forest, especially in the case of hickories and walnuts, which bear nuts that must be buried to ensure germination.

Tree squirrels have two types of homes—leaf nests, and tree dens in hollow limbs or tree trunks. Leaf nests are the familiar bulky, leafy bundles that show up clearly in branches of hardwoods in squirrel range after leaf-fall in autumn. Most are built better than they look. Woven with twigs, and lined with shredded bark and leaves, they are remarkably snug and weathertight, although still subject to disaster in severe windstorms.

Dens in tree cavities are much more secure and permanent. Ideal dens are well above ground level, with an entrance about 3 inches in diameter which leads to a cavity 20 to 30 inches deep, although larger cavities often are used.

Leaf nests and dens may both be used at all times of the year for protection from weather, escape from danger, and rearing of young. In general, dens are used year round or in winter, while leaf nests, two or more of which are often built or rebuilt a year, seem to be mainly summer quarters.

Reproduction is a bit complicated. Full adults, in years of good food supplies, often produce two litters a year, one in spring resulting from mid-to-late-winter matings, and another in summer from late-spring breeding. Young females normally have only one litter. If born in spring, they produce young the following spring; if they are from summer litters, their first litter arrives the following summer. But mast crops vary. After a severe winter with limited food, reproduction can be cut drastically so that even mature females produce only one litter or none at all. Most litters average two to four young, and survival usually is excellent.

The main ingredients of good squirrel habitat are mature, mast-producing trees, especially white and black oaks, hickories, and walnuts, that furnish food and den-site shelter. A good variety of fruit-bearing trees and shrubs and an adjacent cornfield or two add luxury to the menu, but nut trees and squirrels are nearly inseparable. Given such, squirrels may live out their lives within a very few acres.

We have passed over some small game species in this chapter because their distribution is limited or because there is only local interest in their management. We have given the life-history highlights only of the most common. Sketchy as it has been, this coverage should provide clues to the key requirements of those species in which you are interested. Their successful management depends on practices, discussed in the following chapters, which can best improve habitat to meet these requirements.

More detailed infomation on small game in your area is usually available in printed form from state conservation or wildlife agencies. In most cases, one or more books have been written about each species and can be found at your local library. An excellent series of booklets on various game species, including such small game as the cottontail, pheasant, and squirrel, is available from the Conservation Department, Olin Corporation, East Alton, Illinois (write for titles and costs).

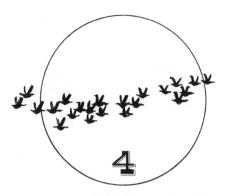

MAKING THE BEST OF WHAT YOU HAVE

Change is the rule in nature. Natural communities, as we have seen, are never exactly the same from minute to minute. One basic reason why they are not is a progressive shift—an "evolution" of sorts—that takes place, at varying extents and speeds, within the plants of the community.

Natural vegetation is far from permanent. Plant communities come into being, grow, reproduce, shift, spread, mature, and gradually die, to be replaced by other communities. Fields which were once under cultivation, and then abandoned, provide good sites to watch this process. In the first year after tillage ends, a crop of annual weeds and grasses springs up—usually the same weeds that plague your garden. By the second or third year, more permanent perennial grasses, wild flowers, and weeds become common, taking over from the annuals. As time goes by, these perennials spread out and dominate the scene. In many regions, brush may then appear, followed by tree seedlings. After many years, a young forest may cover the once bare field.

Natural ponds and small lakes, especially in regions of fertile soil, may provide a picture of all stages of this process occurring simultaneously. In the center we see open water with some floating and submerged plants. Closer to shore are emergent aquatic plants—

pickerelweed, cattails, and the like—and on the wet shoreline, sedges and reeds. Then, farther back from the water, are grasses, then brush and perhaps, depending on the region, trees. Return to the same pond twenty-five to fifty years later and, as a rule, each zone will have progressed inward. Eventually even what was once open water may be a forest.

A similar process occurs on barren, rocky areas, on burned-over soils, and on most denuded landscapes. Nature abhors a vacuum, and rugged, pioneering plants seek footholds on bare substrates, to be replaced by other vegetational stages over time, one succeeding the next.

This evolutionary replacement of plant communities is called *plant succession*. The speed at which it takes place and the species and general growth forms of plants that make up the various stages depend upon soil, climate, drainage, altitude, and other environmental factors. The abandoned-field and shallow-pond examples are typical of much of the eastern half of the United States, as well as humid areas of the West. In the Great Plains succession usually never proceeds past the perennial grasses; in desert country, scattered brush and cacti may be the "last word."

This "last word," an enduring community of perennials which, once established, tends to remain until disturbed by climate changes or natural or man-made catastrophe, is termed the *climax* plant community. The nature and composition of the climax vary with the same environmental factors that regulate the successional process. There are countless local exceptions, but in general, climax plant communities tend to be one of several types of deciduous forest in the eastern United States, perennial grasses in the Great Plains, various conifers or mixed coniferous-hardwood forests in the North and in the western mountains, and brush or scrub in the arid Southwest.

Plant succession is far more complicated than this superficial explanation suggests. It involves beautifully woven relationships between plants and their environment and one another.

Take just one example. A township in one of the Great Lakes states is cleared by fire or logging. But the soil, like a time-capsule treasure chest, holds the seeds of all the vegetation that once grew there, enabling it to grow again, all things being equal.

The sun beats on the exposed ground. Seeds of sun-loving species respond first—fireweed and other flowering plants, annual weeds and grasses, and aspen, white birch, and jackpine. The last three are tree species, which grow in spectacular numbers and with fantastic speed. Aspen, especially, may throw up tens of thousands of seedlings per acre, each growing several feet in the first year.

Two things happen during the initial two to three years. First, competition for light and nutrients results in success for only a fraction of the tree seedlings, the tallest and strongest. Second, down at ground level, the environment changes. Shaded by the sun-loving trees, many of the flowering plants and grasses die out. Others that can germinate and survive only in this shade take their place; among these are the first sprouts of slower-growing, shade-tolerant trees, pushing up quietly beneath the skyward-bound pioneers. Eventually, in the shade and protection of this second layer of the returning forest, appear seedlings of the slowest-growing trees which require the least sunlight—white pine, sugar maple, and yellow birch.

Fifty or sixty years pass. The quick-to-grow, sun-loving aspen, white birch, and jack pine are old and decrepit now, toppling to wind, rot, and disease, replaced by the next successional stage they have sheltered. In time this stage, too, matures and dies, and then the slowest-growing, most shade-tolerant and longest-lived trees in the sequence inherit the skyline—the persistent white pines, sugar-maples, and yellow birch. These comprise the climax, and will live and dominate until fire or tornado or blight or lumberman wipes them out and resets the stage.

So it goes in all vegetated parts of the world. Each group of plants strives and thrives under the environmental conditions best suited for it; each in turn modifies that environment, changing soil, ground-level temperatures and humidity, sun and shade, until conditions are better suited for other, slower-growing and longer-lived species. Each successional stage sows the seeds of its own destruction and in so doing paves the way for its successors.

Although perhaps nature's most dramatic "happening," plant succession is seldom appreciated because, except for the first few years, the drama unfolds so slowly. Modern, "place-hopping" Americans see no more than a scene or two of one act; to them, such a forest is at a standstill.

What does all this mean if we are simply interested in wildlife?

Hark back to the fact that plants are the basis of all animal life. As plant species change on a given site, so then must animal species. Animal succession parallels and is dependent upon vegetational changes. The whole is labeled *ecological succession*.

Look back at that *Lake states* forest for a minute. When it was cleared originally, and grassses, weeds, and seeding trees appeared, pheasant, quail, and cottontails prospered—especially if, after initial logging, farm crops were planted. Horned larks, ground-dwelling sparrows, and other songbirds moved in. As the small farms were abandoned and the young aspen and jack pine grew, snowshoe hare, deer, and ruffed grouse became more numerous, along with a different group of songbirds and small mammals. Much later, when white pine and maple took over, gray or red squirrels appeared, a few wild turkeys, various woodpeckers, and another sequence of animal species assumed dominance.

Some animals can exist in all stages of plant succession, but most can really prosper, or even survive, in only one. As a general and very important rule, most animals attain their greatest numbers in stages before the climax plant community. It is said that a climax plant community tends to have the greatest variety of animal species. This may be true, provided we take into account two important "ifs"—if we include all forms of animal life, especially insects, and if the climax community includes, as most do, when covering sizable acreage, a good deal of plant variety on local sites differing in soil, drainage, and slope.

The overriding principle of diversity still applies. There is little closer to a biological desert than a pure stand of climax trees, all of the same species, dominating and shading out all undergrowth. The cathedral-like silence of a mature redwood grove is a striking example. Before the lumber industry seizes upon this statement as one more excuse to cut down the last redwoods, it should be reminded that the carefully nurtured single-species, pure-stand sawlog plantings of today's tree farms are equally silent, but on a much larger scale. The greatest number and variety of wildlife always have been and always will be associated with the greatest diversity of plant species and growth forms.

Plant succession is important to wildlife. It is equally significant to anyone who would manage for wildlife because it is possible to manipulate successional stages, particularly the earlier ones. We can retard, speed up, or recycle the sequence, working toward that vegetational stage which is most favorable for the wildlife we seek to encourage. If, for example, you hope for a maximum variety of songbirds and mammals, game and nongame, with no particular emphasis on any one species, you should attempt to maintain a mixture of as many different successional stages as possible.

If small game is your goal, a mixture of successional stages is still desirable. However, the main thrust should be toward a high percentage of land in the early annual weed and grass stage, and in

midpoint brush, along with cropland, rather than later pole timber
or climax forest.

It is at this point that the careful background work we discussed earlier begins to pay off. Mapping and understanding physical characteristics—soils, topography, and drainage—and identifying existing vegetation are fundamental to managing ecological succession as it applies directly to your land. While there are broad, regional patterns in plant succession, some of which I have touched upon, there is great local variation, Disking three separate but superficially similar pieces of level ground within a square mile might produce desired annuals (providing excellent food and cover) in one instance, a preponderance of pesty sandburrs in the second, and a pure culture of stinging nettles in the third.

In every management measure you contemplate, you must follow some simple rules: (1) know what you have; (2) decide what you want, including whether your goals are feasible; (3) determine, through steps outlined here and in other references, and with professional advice if possible, how to achieve your goals; and (4) proceed with caution.

To "know what you have" means finding out all you can about the successional stages your land presently supports, and the sequences you can expect. Look carefully at abandoned fields, odd corners, and edges on your property and adjoining land. Find out when the soil on such sites was last disturbed so as to gain insights into yearly changes, which will be rapid in early stages of succession. Old fencerows often provide good clues to what later successional stages will bring in the way of brush and trees. If possible, ask for information from the biology or botany departments of your state university. Although plant succession is not his specialty, your county SCS representative usually has had ample experience with crop acreage "retired" under federal programs, and can provide some help. In the West, range and big-game management specialists at state universities and conservation agencies are a good information source—they struggle against or cooperate with succession constantly.

It bears repeating that if your wildlife goal is maximum variety, your plant goal should be the same. Through plantings and manipulation of succession, attempt to reach and maintain the greatest diversity of plant species and growth forms. If, on the other hand, your wildlife goal is a single species, like small game, your plant goal should be to supply the requirements of that species, again through plantings and by manipulating succession to maintain that stage or two associated with the maximum numbers of the game in question.

The practice of planting, or, alternatively, the practice of introducing or increasing desirable vegetation by retarding, setting back, or speeding up plant succession, are the two traditional approaches to managing land for game. In most quarters, planting has been the favorite approach. Manipulating native vegetation, while long having a few fervent advocates, has gained widespread recognition only rather recently.

In comparing these two techniques, planting in most instances is the quicker and more spectacular means of altering a landscape. In many situations it is also the only way to guarantee certain results. If a stand of pines, fir, or other conifers is desirable as shelter and as an attraction for wildlife requiring coniferous vegetation, these trees can often be established by planting, and survive and prosper in regions and on sites where nature normally could never produce them. Or, if space is very limited and a crop of seed important, planting annuals usually will yield far more pounds of seed per square yard than will annual weeds.

But native vegetation, encouraged or manipulated, has some definite advantages. It is a lot less expensive, for one thing. Disking, burning, and other techniques aimed at maintaining an early stage of succession, highly desirable for food and nesting cover for most small game, are a good deal cheaper in cash, man-hours, and equipment than is annual preparation of a seedbed, purchase and application of seed and fertilizer, cultivation, and all the other chores and expensive supplies that are involved in planting annual food and cover plots.

Important too is the very fact that native plants of the various stages of succession are native and natural. They are the food and cover sources to which native animals are adapted, and while each natural successional stage consists primarily of the same growth form—annual weeds, or grasses, brush, or trees—it usually contains a variety of plants differing subtly in cover and food values highly desirable for wildlife. Most native successional stages incorporate valuable diversity within themselves. Planted annuals, shrubs, or trees, on the other hand, usually are of the same species and age, each plot drably uniform throughout.

Native plants have another advantage. In years of drought or other exceptional weather, unfavorable to planted grains or exotic shrubs and trees, natives grow better and furnish more food and cover than do introduced material, simply because they are indigenous and adjusted to such extremes. Surely you have heard the old complaint that "this weather's tough on crops, but it sure hasn't hurt the weeds."

Which method to use must be dictated by the area and goals. If you can work with a couple of acres or more, and don't mind waiting a bit, a combination of encouraging and manipulating native plants, supplemented by plantings designed to furnish varieties of food and cover that nature is unlikely to provide, is the best bet and, hence, the most widely used approach. If you have a city or suburban lot of less than an acre, it is a bit silly to think of manipulating succession. Planting is for you, although you can still retain the native character by the choice of your plant materials. If you have the equipment and manpower, and are managing for monetary returns from wildlife via sale of hunting rights or operating a shooting preserve, the speed with which plantings can create game habitat may make it worthwhile to lean heavily in this direction.

Plant succession is like an old-time, hand-wound clock. It ticks along rapidly at first, the initial few stages following one another rapidly, then winds down gradually to a barely perceptible pace, and finally stops with the climax, until set back and simultaneously rewound when the climax vegetation is removed. Managing plant succession for wildlife is a matter of working forward with the clock to reach later stages, or of slowing or setting back the clock to earlier stages. The first is the simplest—all you need is patience.

If your land is primarily active cropland or a combination of cropland and woods, it is far easier and more desirable to establish vital early successional stages by sacrificing some cropland than by bulldozing the woods. Simply stop tilling the land. In most cases you do not even have to sacrifice much in the way of crop yields, either. Farm equipment has to turn around at the end of every field. With most farmers it is a matter of pride to make sure that these field-ends are planted and harvested. It may look neat but it is an economic fiasco; the extra time and trouble spent carefully planting and harvesting a few rows, at odds with the main alignment of the field, outweigh the yield of most heavily compacted field-end soils. It makes more sense to forget the turn-around and let succession establish wildlife habitat here.

Cropfield borders touching brush, woodlots or wooded fencerows and hedgerows offer even better opportunities. For several yards into such fields, effects of shade and root competition from the adjoining woody vegetation are such that costs of planting right up to the edge are seldom equaled by yields. "The juice ain't worth the squeezing," so you can turn these areas as well over to natural succession with no real economic loss.

This much can be done if wildlife is but a secondary management goal. If it is foremost, for income or pleasure, you can fallow even more acreage, let natural succession take hold and manipulate it to meet your wildlife goals.

MANAGEMENT TECHNIQUES

There are several tried-and-true methods for manipulating native vegetation, once established, each basically aimed at setting back succession to a more desirable stage, or maintaining a desirable stage beyond its normal lifetime. None is always perfect; each has advantages and disadvantages, as we shall see.

Burning

Lightning-induced wild fires have been nature's way of recycling succession wherever vegetation was abundant and dry enough to burn. In southern states, almost from first settlement, man used fire to clear off pine woods and keep them open as grazing grounds for cattle. Southern game managers found that quail, like cattle, did best in open woodlands, but dwindled rapidly when a dense brushy understory took over. Thus, carefully planned, controlled burning came to be a quail-management tool.

In the past decade or two fire has been used to set back succession to more desirable stages in managing a number of other target wildlife species. In the West, controlled burns have reclaimed large areas of chaparral brush for deer, setting back out-of-reach, slow-growing old plants, and stimulating succulent new growth from roots and crowns. In the East and Midwest, game managers employ controlled burning to eliminate or thin out old stands of planted or native grasses that have become too thick at ground level, provide little or no food, and are too short—because of density and competition—to serve as cover. Such single-species stands of sod-forming perennial grasses are nearly useless for wildlife, yet they occupy an amazingly high percentage of untilled land in the Midwest and elsewhere. Thinning by planned burning allows germination of a variety of seed-bearing annuals, creates diversity, and opens the stand so that ground-dwelling wildlife—like the bobwhite, cottontail, dove, and several songbird species—can move about, feed, and nest.

Fire also is cheap. Even with the precautions that are essential, most controlled burns for wildlife cost somewhere between ten and fifty cents an acre, compared with several dollars an acre to accomplish the same task with a tractor-drawn disk.

There are major disadvantages. Fire can be extremely dangerous in inexperienced hands. You can not just shut it off, as you
can a tractor or chain-saw. Never use fire as a tool until you have
cleared your proposal through your state conservation department;
in most states you are violating the law by setting such fires without
a permit. Further, in the process of obtaining permission you should
seek professional advice and guidelines. These will include specifications as to weather conditions, proper season of the year, and pre-
burn control measures—fire lanes plowed or disked, emergency
crews and equipment, etc.—and other absolutely necessary precautions. Obviously, fire is not for amateurs. If you control large
acreage, and suspect that a controlled burn might be useful, get professional advice and help first.

In an increasing number of states, strong laws designed to reduce air pollution are making it increasingly difficult even for professionals and public agencies to receive approval for using fire in
wildlife management. We have discussed it here, nonetheless, because if you explore other sources for advice, as you most certainly
should, you will read or hear about burning but perhaps not always
about the dangers, restrictions, and legal problems. Furthermore, on
suitable sites, under adequate, experienced supervision, and where
legally permitted, controlled burning is still a highly useful management technique.

Disking

More expensive, but safer and very often surer—at least for all
but the most experienced managers—are mechanical means of setting back succession. Foremost among these is the tractor-drawn
disk. In fact a sturdy disk, a good rotary-mower "brush-hog," and a
suitable tractor to pull them are essential equipment for managing
vegetation for wildlife on any sizable property.

Disking is best used to break up stands of sod-forming grass
that have reached the stage where they choke out other vegetation
and are too dense for use by ground-dwelling wildlife. This stage
usually is reached three to five years after seeding perennial grasses
such as brome or fescue, and in about the same time span after natural succession has been allowed to take hold on once cultivated
land. Thorough disking, which allows annual weeds to germinate
and restores the diversity of food and cover of early successional
stages, may be required at three- or four-year intervals.

Disking also is used as a second step, after mowing, to set back
brushlands or sapling stands to earlier successional stages. The rotary mower can chop woody cover within a few inches of ground

level. Annual disking thereafter will destroy and eventually eliminate root and crown sprouting by brush, and encourage growth of annual food plants and grasses, if such are desired.

Disks come in many widths, weights, and prices. The lightest, least expensive rigs will serve to break up grass stands of medium density on light soils. Tougher jobs—cutting thick sod on heavy or rocky ground, or following behind a brush-hog mower over stumps and roots—take progressively heavier disks which are a lot more expensive initially, but much cheaper in the long haul. If you have many rugged jobs, they will hold together longer and do the work in fewer passes over the land. However, heavy disks for hard jobs function well only when pulled by bigger, more expensive tractors. Economics thus begin to dominate the picture, underscoring the need for goal-setting and planning.

Mowing

Diversity and other benefits from existing vegetation, whether planted or the native results of plant succession, can often be improved by judicious cutting.

Extensive stands of tall grass furnish many small game species with cover for nesting and protection from predators and weather. A few tractor-width strips mowed in such stands provide openings where young animals can sun themselves and dry off after heavy dews or rains. The new growth, stimulated by mowing, furnishes accessible, palatable greens as a food source for cottontails and game birds. Similarly, strips mowed through brush create more edge by providing openings for sunning, dusting, and feeding.

Mowing, alone or in combination with other techniques, can be used to set back succession, particularly in woody vegetation. In those regions where brush and trees make up the latter stage of plant succession, various situations develop that are generally undesirable for wildlife.

First, the entire land area may be dominated by woody vegetation with little diversity. If this vegetation consists of brush or tree saplings, patches and strips can be opened by mowing to ground level. Vigorous disking after mowing helps prevent regrowth of woody vegetation and at the same time breaks up ground cover. Opened to sunlight and with the soil disturbed, such strips often develop good stands of annual food-producing plants typical of early stages of succession. They may also be seeded (by hand, if too rough for a seeder) to legumes and/or grasses. In either case, more edge is achieved, with increased variety of food and cover.

Mowing strips in large fields of grass and other herbaceous vegetation creates variety, produces openings in which young animals can dry off in the sun, and stimulates succulent new greens as a food source. Heavy-duty tractor-drawn rotary mowers, such as this one, are a valuable tool for creating edge in herbaceous or woody growth.

Second, where woody vegetation is not extensive, but consists of saplings all at the same age and of just one or two tree species of low value for wildlife, the tall growth shades out ground vegetation yet produces little or no food or cover. Here portions can be mowed and then disked to encourage earlier, more valuable successional stages.

Third, many brush stands, native or planted, may become "senile." Honeysuckle, sumac, and many other native and exotic shrubs furnish dense, low cover and an abundance of fruit, seed, or available browse when young and vigorous. But with age they become too tall, with too many dead branches, to supply good cover. Fruit production dwindles and the only parts in reach of browsing wildlife are old and tough or dead. Clipped off a few inches above the ground, many such shrubs sprout quickly, again yielding thick, low cover and succulent browse. With strong, mature root systems still intact, they will grow rapidly and fruit abundantly in a very few years.

Thus, mowing is an extremely useful tool for manipulating vegetation to increase habitat diversity and enhance food and cover values. It is a fast and relatively simple and inexpensive technique if you are properly equipped. For example, the old "sicklebar" mower, long used for hay-cutting, will serve well for mowing grass and herbaceous vegetation, and even very small brush and tree seedlings. But the newer rotary mowers will do the same jobs plus handle much tougher, older vegetation. These rotary mowers range from "stalk choppers," widely employed in farming to chop corn stubble after harvest, to heavy "brush hogs," specifically aimed at clearing brush and young trees.

Rotary mowers come in two to four blade designs and in many patterns, weights, and sizes; the heavier the model, the more it costs. The biggest can cut off and chop up any tree the tractor pulling it can run over. The style for you depends on the work you require and what you can afford. Seek advice from several farm-equipment dealers, and remember two general rules. First, if you can justify and afford it, get the mower able to handle your toughest job; heavy-duty mowers can handle easy mowing, but lightweights will fall apart if you ask too much of them. Purchasing a heavier, more expensive mower can be cheaper in the long run than constantly repairing an initially inexpensive "economy" model. Second, as with a disk, a mower must be matched with the tractor that pulls it. It is foolish to try to pull a brush hog that can chop up trees 3 inches in diameter with a tractor that can't crawl over a seedling.

Other tools

There are other means of managing existing cover to enhance wildlife values. In any stand of trees and brush, whether forest, woodlot, or old fenceline, competition is at work: competition for sunlight, for growing room, and, down at root level, for soil nutrients. As a result, trees and shrubs with high value for wildlife may be crowded out or retarded in growth and fruit production by species with relatively low values. An ax or chain-saw can be employed to "release" particularly valuable trees by cutting out competing neighbors. But be *careful*. Here, as always, remember that there are few, if any, "bad" trees. A tree that is useless to a quail may be essential to a fox squirrel. This is particularly true of old, over-mature trees—the kind that most foresters quickly eliminate because they "take up valu-

able space" and furnish little usable lumber with their partly hol-
low limbs and trunks. If your ambition is to have a variety of interesting wildlife, such veteran trees are among your most valuable assets. They provide den and nest sites for numerous mammals and birds, and a direct or indirect food source for many more.

The ax and saw are best employed to "release" valuable oaks, walnuts, or other trees in situations where they are relatively rare and dominated by competition from an overstory of very common trees. Like all management tools, these implements should be used to increase, not reduce, habitat diversity.

What about herbicides? A score or more of highly effective and relatively inexpensive weed and brush killers have been used by farmers, land managers, and wildlife managers for a number of years to set back succession, reduce competition, and promote habitat diversity. In general, properly applied, they do the job quickly and efficiently, and often more cheaply than other methods. But we are learning that, depending on the herbicide, they can be very dangerous to people, wildlife, or desirable vegetation.

Because we still know so little about long-range effects of herbicides, and because even the little we do know is frightening, my advice is to avoid them. There are few dry-land vegetation problems for wildlife that cannot be handled by other methods; we shall discuss marsh and pond problems later. If you feel you must use an herbicide, despite this warning, at least do three things: (1) consult your state conservation department first about your legal situation (most states now require that a permit be issued before herbicides can be used), and for professional advice; (2) when applying the herbicide, follow the manufacturers' instructions to the letter (if anything, reduce the recommended concentration slightly; never exceed it—much of our herbicide problem comes from the lethal idea that if a little works, a lot will be even better); and (3) treat the smallest possible area.

Grazing domestic cattle, sheep, or goats is sometimes employed to set back succession on areas dominated by old stands of heavy grass and brush. Grazing has the advantage of producing some income from wildlife land either through pasture rental or as alternate pasture for your own livestock. It has the disadvantage of being tricky; it is quite easy to overdo the job and end up with a wasteland.

By nature, grazing is primarily a tool for larger acreage, such as public lands, but it can be effective if your property is fenced to hold livestock, and dominated by heavy grass or dense brush. In this case the key to success is frequent—almost daily—inspection,

66 and immediate removal of the animals when the job of opening up thick vegetation is accomplished. If the livestock is your own, this should be no problem. But if you are renting grazing rights, be sure the contract spells out that you call the shots as to when the livestock comes and goes, with suitably stiff penalties for any departures.

The essence of this discussion is that native vegetation that exists, or can exist—through fallowing formerly cropped land and initiating plant succession—on your land should be the base on which to construct a wildlife management program. Native vegetation has major advantages. It is free; and it is indigenous, and hence best adjusted to local and regional environments and stresses. By the same token, native wildlife species are already adapted to the food and cover native plants afford. Finally, native vegetation can be managed by combining an understanding of plant succession with the tools we have mentioned to speed up or set back succession's "clock."

The extent to which you can use native as opposed to planted vegetation varies with your land, goals, and time-table. In a small suburban lot, use plantings; you don't have space and you probably don't have time to depend upon succession. On larger acreage, lean hard upon native plants and succession if your goal is a variety of wildlife and you can set aside ample land.

PLANTING FOR SMALL GAME

$\mathbf{A}$s a rule, most individuals and agencies attempting to improve wildlife habitat overwork plantings and underrate natural succession. As was pointed out in the previous chapter, succession is usually cheaper and often provides better diversity, and the resulting vegetation frequently is used more quickly by native wildlife. However, succession is usually slower than planting, especially for later growth stages, and somewhat less dependable—you don't always get what you hoped for. So if you have a lot of land and time, lean hard on succession—the bigger the area, the more the economy of succession will be apparent—with plantings in key sites where nature can't provide the habitat you need. But if land is limited and you are in a hurry (and don't mind added costs), planting is for you. Most improvement programs lie somewhere between the extremes and require both techniques.

Successful upland habitat management demands a familiarity with sources and care of seed and planting stock, planting methods, and specific plant materials and techniques. Even if you are not especially interested in small game, the basic ideas and methods used in creating this particular habitat apply as well to plantings designed primarily for songbirds, forest wildlife, and other upland species to be discussed later.

There was a time when most of the plants recommended for wildlife habitat improvement were foreign or "exotic" species, but today's increasing understanding of ecology and natural communities has brought about wider use of native vegetation. This is a healthy trend; native plants are adjusted to our soils and climates and are less apt to spread as pests because "controls"—usually in the form of insects and other animals—have evolved along with the plants. Equally important, wildlife normally will use familiar food and cover more readily than they will new "unknowns." Work with bobwhite quail and other species has demonstrated clearly that plantings bearing highly palatable but unfamiliar fruits and seeds may not be used for a year or more, until the local fauna has had an opportunity to get acquainted with the new food source.

Native materials must be emphasized, but not to the exclusion of some of the most valuable, proven foreigners which, for certain food, cover, and decorative uses, are hard to beat.

PLANTING DESIGNS

We are well acquainted with the objectives—*interspersion, diversity,* and *edge.* To achieve these with plantings, you must observe two overlapping principles. First, keep food and cover close together, and create as many small areas as possible in which a species can find all its needs. Second, the greater the variety of plant species and growth forms you provide, the greater the variety of wildlife you will attract, and the better the chance that the particular species in which you are interested will find suitable food and cover at all seasons.

Design your plantings to have maximum contact—edge—with other cover types. As an example, imagine a cropfield bordered by good, natural fencerow cover on one side, and suppose that you can afford to devote a quarter of an acre of this field to provide food for wildlife. First, situate the food patch next to the fencerow cover, not in the middle of the field where—when the cash crop is harvested—it will be an island small game cannot reach without exposure to weather and predators. Second, make the food and cover contact zone as long as possible. In this field, a food strip 20 feet wide and 500 feet long, bordering the fencerow, will be much more effective than the same quarter-acre placed as a 100×100-foot square in one corner.

This small patch of field corn will serve small game well in winter because it adjoins good permanent cover.

Always maximize edge in planting designs; use rectangles, strips, and irregular shapes rather than squares or circles. Furthermore, many small plantings are more advantageous than a few large tracts. To grasp this idea, visualize a small farm with 80 acres in corn, 20 in a woodlot, 20 in pasture, and 40 in oats and hay, all in neat, orderly blocks. Such a farm might support one covey of quail or two or three pheasants in the one spot where cropfields, woods, and pasture join to provide essential cover and food. If you could tumble this farm in a giant blender and thoroughly mix the ingredients, the resulting interspersion and contact between cover types would produce far greater wildlife on the same acreage.

You can achieve the same effect as this hypothetical blender by carefully selecting where and what you plant. Where good permanent cover exists, consider a border of food, and grass for nesting; where natural food is abundant, add permanent cover. Where two or more areas of good cover are isolated from one another by open ground—as fencerows on either side of a field, or a woodlot and a small brush patch, for example—connect them by planting a hedge of permanent cover. This "bridge" serves as a protected travel lane for wildlife and multiplies the value of each of the former islands of cover.

The use of interspersion and edge is an effective erosion-control practice as well as being beneficial to wildlife. Grass water-diversion terraces and contour strip-farming break up the deadly monotony of big, single-crop fields, and soil and wildlife both benefit.

WHAT AND WHERE TO PLANT

Plants for wildlife in general, and small game in particular, fall into three groups: annuals; perennial grasses and forbs (nonwoody, broadleaved plants, such as the clovers); and woody perennials—vines, shrubs, and trees. Although all groups can furnish both food and cover, annuals are used primarily for food production; perennial grasses and forbs for nesting, summer cover, and food in the form of greens; and most woody plants as winter and escape cover. In each group there are some species that double as both food and cover; where space is limited, these plants are especially valuable.

Unless you have unlimited land and funds and are planning an arboretum, you cannot plant everything, so you will need to make choices. In selecting, refer back to your goals. Do you want maximum numbers of a particular species for hunting or other use? Or are you aiming for a variety of game, or simply maximum diversity of wildlife of all types—game and nongame? Does your target species or group reside all year and reproduce in your area, spend only the winter or breeding season there, or just pass by as migrants?

From this book and other sources, learn all you can about the basic habitat requirements of the wildlife you favor at the seasons they are present. Try to spot those factors that are most likely to be limiting population size on your land—lack of winter food, nesting or escape cover, and so on.

With this background you can narrow the range of plant materials to certain groups and growth forms—even a list of species. At
this point, the information discussed in Chapter 2 comes into use.
How much of the land in question can be devoted to plantings for
wildlife? What are soil, slope, shade, and drainage conditions?
These *site factors,* along with the climate in your area, determine
which plants will thrive and which have no chance at all. Match
these site and climate factors against the requirements of those
plants you have listed as most desirable. You can discover specific
requirements from this book and other source material, from local
nurserymen and seed dealers, and from the advice of state conservation departments, agricultural colleges, or other agencies listed
in Chapter 2.

In the rush to get started, do not overlook the eventuality of
problems with plantings. Some plants useful for wildlife tend to
spread. If your land and equipment cannot control this, avoid these
species. For best results, many plantings, both annual and perennial,
require cultivation, mowing, and fertilization, and this must continue for several years after planting for some perennials. If time or
equipment won't permit such maintenance, look for carefree species or reconsider your plans. Looking to the future is especially important for shrub and tree plantings that may take years to reach
maximum usefulness. Can you tie up a site for that long, or will it be
needed for grazing, a roadway, or a building? Visualize shrub or
tree plantings as if they had reached full growth. Are they far
enough from that fenceline so that it can still be maintained? Are
they growing up into power lines, encroaching on a driveway, or
causing snow to settle and drift over a road?

As you plan, weigh all elements carefully. Select a list of plants
that are adapted to available sites and furnish the wildlife requirements desired, and start investigating seed and plant sources. Check
first with your state conservation and forestry departments. In many
states, these agencies produce and supply shrubs and trees for wildlife plantings free or at cost. Normally, these will be small seedlings
with certain necessary restrictions on their use, but such agencies
are still the best source for acquiring in quantity locally adapted
species of known usefulness. A few states also supply seed of annual or perennial wildlife food plants.

If your state agencies do not supply plant materials, or if you
want varieties they do not stock or larger, older specimens, turn to
commercial dealers. There are excellent private seed companies
and nurseries in most areas of the United States that carry plant ma-

72   terials useful in wildlife work. Most are aware of the growing interest in such plantings; some even specialize in plants for wildlife.
State conservation, forestry, or park departments or your county
SCS office can usually provide a list of these dealers. Also consult
your local nurseryman or seedsman; what he doesn't carry in stock
he can often order for you.

Regardless of the source, insist on getting just what you want
and order, particularly if only a specific variety meets your needs.
For example, there are dozens of hybrid grain sorghums, but only a
few will mature seedheads in short northern growing seasons. If
you live in a northern state, make sure you order one of these, and
that you get what you order. Similarly, there are numerous shrub
honeysuckle varieties, most furnishing good cover. Some bear
hardly any fruit, but one variety—amur honeysuckle—is an outstanding fruit producer. Don't just ask for or be satisfied with any
unnamed honeysuckle.

PLANTING, BEFORE AND AFTER

Success with plantings requires more than careful selection of
plant species; planting sites need to be prepared in advance. Preparation can range from working up a well-fertilized, finely pulverized, firm seedbed—for seeding certain annuals and perennial
grasses—to "scalping" small squares in heavy sod before planting
shrubs. What is required depends upon what is being planted, so
heed instructions from seed dealers, nurseymen, and other sources
of information.

More than a few plantings fail because the plants are dead before they ever get in the ground. Seedling shrubs and trees usually
are packed and shipped bare-rooted—a virtual necessity—since digging, handling and shipping costs would be prohibitive otherwise.
With expert, modern packing methods the plants arrive in fine
shape (at least from reputable sources); problems come after arrival.
Since the roots are surrounded by moist packing material, and the
package is wrapped so as to be nearly airtight, conditions are ripe
for a deadly heat build-up. To prevent this, open the crates or bundles on arrival, moisten the packing material, and place the loos-
ened bundles in a cool, shaded spot with adequate ventilation. Remember that the roots must be covered and kept moist.

Bare-rooted materials that cannot be planted within twenty-
four hours should be *healed in,* as described later. While bare-
rooted plants are most susceptible to loss between arrival and plan-

ting, even seed can deteriorate if not stored properly. Keep seeds cool, well ventilated, protected from rodents, and well away from any chemical herbicide containers. Though many seeds retain good germination rates for a year or more if properly stored, it is wise to buy only what you can plant in one season.

Once you are ready for planting, be sure that you have adequate instructions, and follow them. Some seeds and seedlings take hold and grow under almost any treatment; you have to work at failure. In other cases—as with some of the best perennial grasses—directions as to planting season and seeding depth must be carried out to the letter to prevent failure. Avoid jeopardizing any planting by taking the little extra time to carry out what seem like overly fussy instructions.

Obviously, planting for wildlife habitat—done right—takes time and care, from initial planning to maintenance once plants are established. But don't let all the precautions deter you. Many of the best annuals, perennials, shrubs, and trees are easily established if you bother to find out what they require and meet these requirements.

ANNUALS

Annuals are plants that live only one growing season, germinating from seed and dying with the frosts of fall. "Wild" annuals can survive only by producing enough seed in one year to guarantee future generations, unlike perennials that will have another chance to set seed or can reproduce from wintering roots. Consequently, annuals are nature's traditional seed producers. Man took advantage of this characteristic to develop today's highly bred grain—corn, wheat, oats, rice, and the rest.

Plant succession can be manipulated to maintain early stages of seed-bearing annual "weeds" as a wildlife food source. Compared with these "weeds" that spring up via natural succession, planted annuals cost more and have less variety, but are often more dependable, and normally produce far greater yields per acre. Certain planted annuals furnish cover, but they serve primarily as a concentrated food source for seed-eating small game and nongame.

For this reason, small game species often thrive on land farmed for grain, provided that the farm is not so "clean" that no cover remains. Waste grain left after harvesting, along with the seeds of annual weeds that survive spraying and cultivation in cropfields, are a staple food source for pheasants, bobwhites, and doves, as well as many waterfowl. Consequently, farming is compatible with management for small game and other wildlife on the condition that adequate year-round cover is left or planted. In fact, a landscape well diversified with small cropfields and permanent cover normally is more productive than the same area all in heavy cover.

Not long ago the annual "food patch" was the most popular single habitat management technique for small game. The routine recommendation was that if you wanted more quail or pheasants or rabbits, plant a food patch. With accumulating experience, wildlife managers are now less naive. We have learned that lack of food is not always, everywhere, a limiting factor. Instead, as a general rule, it appears that food shortages—and, thus, the need for planted food crops to supplement natural sources—are critical mainly in the North where winters are long and severe. In brief, and with the reservation that there are many exceptions to every rule in wildlife management, the farther north you live, the more you should be

Tracks of deer, squirrel, pheasant, and cottontail, and the battered condition of the stalks, show how well wildlife will use a few unharvested rows of corn in the North—if those rows are near cover.

concerned with providing food. Moreover, a planting that furnishes concentrated supplies of highly palatable food can entice wildlife to specific locations, even though the general area has adequate, albeit less tasty, food sources. Thus, food plantings, even in the midst of plenty, can be used by both hunter and bird-watcher to pull wildlife into gun, binocular, or camera range.

There are two primary ways to create annual food sources. If the land is farmed for grain crops, it is cheaper to leave an unharvested portion than it is to make special plantings. Corn is ideal for this purpose, but small grains are useful as well. Remember, unharvested crops left for wildlife should adjoin good cover; a strip in the middle of a large, harvested, bare field is next to useless. How much should you leave? Bordering good cover, a strip 10 feet wide is good and one 30 feet wide is better, but more than this is probably wasted. If you can leave only a square corner patch, a tenth-to a quarter-acre is good; more than a half-acre is probably wasted. Also, when you know in advance that you will be leaving part of a cornfield or other row crop, cultivate this portion only once. That is enough, in most cases, to ensure a seed yield sufficient for wildlife while giving annual weeds and grasses a chance to furnish some cover and additional food between the rows.

Similar rules should guide you in planting annuals specifically for wildlife. Place food plots tight against good cover, and keep them small. For odd corners or patches in natural cover, plots of a quarter-acre to a half-acre are good. Adjoining roadside or fence-rows in good cover, a food strip 30 to 40 feet wide is adequate, with one exception. To create habitat on bare and exposed northern sites while waiting for conifers or other permanent cover to grow, strips of sorghum, corn, or other annual foods may need to be 50 to 100 feet wide. With this expanse, if the windward half is covered by drifting snow, at least some food and cover will remain in the lee.

In choosing annuals to plant where moderate to heavy snowfall prevails, stay away from weak-stemmed annuals. Soft-stemmed plants, tall or short, bend or break under the impact of severe weather after frost. This bending and collapse of stems is called *lodging*. Wherever snow or heavy winter rains and wind occur, plants susceptible to lodging furnish little or no cover; in the North, their seedheads are often buried under snow and ice. Buckwheat, a highly palatable small-game food, is a case in point. The first heavy rain after frost knocks buckwheat flat; the first snow locks it away for the winter. Some other foodbearing annuals, such as soybeans, get limited winter use by wildlife in the North because, while they don't lodge, they lose their leaves after frost. The food is there, but borne on bare stems, and small game must risk exposure to weather and predation to use it.

Where blackbirds congregate in late summer, fall, and winter—and this includes an increasing number of northern as well as southeastern states—certain seedbearing annuals planted as a winter-long source for local birds can be wiped out in days by these flocking migrants. Sorghums with light-colored seeds (including most grain-sorghum varieties), buckwheat, and most millets are especially vulnerable; annual lespedezas are least so.

Therefore, in considering plants suitable for the North, don't waste time and space on varieties that end up buried under snow or furnish too little cover to be inviting. In the South beware of plants that serve only as blackbird bait.

These reasons, and others, underlie the use of mixtures of several annuals. One or more varieties may succumb to lodging or blackbirds, or may fail to set seed because the growing season is too wet, dry, hot, or cool, but some usually make the grade. Many state conservation agencies have developed food patch mixtures for small game designed to be totally successful in good growing years, and to provide some success under the worst conditions. The Virginia mixture, for example, is useful in many middle Atlantic and southeastern states. It consists of Korean lespedeza, German and browntop millet, buckwheat, milo, rape, cowpeas, and two varieties of soybeans, broadcast in roughly equal parts at 30 pounds per acre. Missouri's food-patch mixture works well in the lower Midwest—2 pounds each of dwarf or grain sorghums and soybeans, and 1 pound of millet.

In the northern states, where snow is a problem, I like a mix of 15 pounds of grain sorghums, 10 pounds of black amber cane, and 5 pounds of either buckwheat or millet, broadcast at 30 pounds per acre. The buckwheat and millet mature early and attract small game in fall, even though much other food may be available, because of their palatability. In severe winter weather, the tall cane with tasty seedheads tends to lodge but is held above snow by the stiff-stemmed sorghums. As winter ends and the cane seeds have been gobbled up, the grain sorghum—fully as nutritious but less sought after—is available, still above snow, to pull birds through the last critical weeks.

If you are serious about feeding or attracting good numbers of small game or other wildlife by providing a concentrated food supply, treat food-patch plantings as you would cash crops. This means

soil tests to determine the need for lime or fertilizer applications.
Annuals are expensive, not only because they require time and
money to replant every year, but because in nearly all cases fertilizer must be applied each year as well. This gets costly but it is
foolish to stint; plantings repeated on the same ground without fertilizers soon become stunted and yield little food or cover, particularly in the case of such prolific seed producers as the sorghums.
Yearly fertilizer applications can be reduced by practicing crop rotation on food strips or plots; plant annuals for two years, then seed
down the area to a legume grass mixture to be plowed under as
"green manure" after one or two growing seasons.

While some natural weed growth may be desirable in an annual planting for ground cover and variety, weeds compete with
your crop, and this competition must be kept within reason. For
food plots planted in rows, a single cultivation usually is ideal, giving the planted annuals an adequate head start without eliminating
later weed growth. Where annuals are broadcast or drilled so that
cultivation is impossible, careful use of a suitable herbicide will
control weeds. If you object to herbicides, as I do, because of both
known and unknown dangers, you can often beat weed problems
by plowing and disking the planting site as early as possible, allowing it to lie fallow until weeds sprout, disking thoroughly, and then
planting. Where perennial weeds, such as quack grass, are especially troublesome, it pays to plow in spring, disk several times
through summer and fall, and then plant your annual crop the following year.

In planting any annuals, be certain to obtain and follow instructions as to planting season, depth, rate, and equipment. There are
three basic planting methods—broadcasting the seed, planting with
a grain drill, or using a corn planter. Broadcasting is simply scattering the seed at random by hand or by "cyclone" seeders which
range from small, portable, hand-operated devices resembling a
flour-sifter to tractor-mounted power-take-off rigs. For broadcasting, sites are plowed and thoroughly disked, and the seed spread
and then covered by light disking, dragging, or rolling. Broadcast
planting is simple since no expensive planter is required, and furnishes random growth that gives good cover. But it takes more seed
per acre than other techniques, and annuals that need space and
cultivation, such as corn, do not turn out well if broadcast.

Corn planters, obviously, are used for corn and also sorghums
and other large-seeded annuals. Highest food yields per acre result
where annuals are well spaced (as with the corn planter) and culti-

vated. However, wider rows and intensive cultivation mean less cover. If you have good permanent cover and need food, border the cover with a few well-spaced and cultivated rows of annuals. If both food and cover are necessary, broadcast or drill your food plot, and avoid wide rows and cultivation. You will get less food per acre, but the denser growth of weeds and planted crop will furnish the cover that makes the food usable to small game.

The grain drill is perhaps the most flexible planting tool. It handles a variety of seed sizes, and row width can be varied by leaving all seed "gates" open or by plugging them in various patterns to adjust both to the space requirements of different annuals and a desirable balance between food and cover.

Let's look at some annuals recommended for wildlife plantings.

Field corn, grown in most states, is a palatable and nutritious wildlife food that ranks high on the list for pheasants, quail, squirrels, turkeys, and cottontails. In the North field corn's stiff, tough stalks hold the ears above all but the deepest snow. Even as a harvested cash crop corn is a valuable wildlife asset, for after it has been cut for silage, the leftovers make a prime attraction for doves; or, if it has been picked as grain, missed ears and kernels are gleaned by waterfowl and upland game.

The major drawback to field corn is its need for space—meaning wide rows and a minimum of weed competition—and consequent low cover value. For this reason, plant corn tight against good cover, never alone in the middle of a bare field.

There is some evidence that game birds find sweet corn and popcorn even more palatable than field corn. These varieties are shorter, have weaker stalks, and thus often provide more accessible ears and better cover than field corn in the South. But in the North heavy snow can crush and bury sweet corn and popcorn so that they furnish neither food nor cover.

Sorghums have in recent years become increasingly popular for both commercial grain production and wildlife plantings. There are two basic groups—"forage" varieties and "combine" or grain sorghums. Forage sorghums are used commercially for cattle silage. They are tall (usually 5 to 10 feet in good soil), leafy, and slender-stemmed, with open seedheads. Black amber cane, orange Waconia cane, and sudan grass are best known, along with Sudax, a newer hybrid. They tend to be more adaptable to poorer soils then grain sorghums, and the dark-seeded types, like black amber and sudan, are often more palatable to game birds and less susceptible to blackbird damage. But because of their weak stems, forage sorghums lodge and flatten in severe weather.

The grain sorghums are shorter—1½ to 3 feet—with stouter stems and tight seedheads. They come in a vast assortment, from older varieties, such as milo maize and redbine, to numerous hybrids developed for combine harvesting. Make sure you select a variety that will produce mature seed within the growing season of your region.

Grain sorghums are less tolerant of weed competition and poor soils than are forage varieties, but under good conditions have few equals for seed production. They are best used as a primary food source—like corn—planted in wide, cultivated rows, tight against good cover, or mixed with forage sorghums and broadcast or drilled to furnish both food and cover. In this combination the stiff-

Grain sorghums are a versatile wildlife crop: flooded, they feed waterfowl; on upland sites their stiff stems hold seedheads above snow.

stemmed grain sorghums support the forage sorghums as they lodge, and the resultant tangle gives good cover and food through the winter.

All sorghums are warm-weather plants and should be seeded in late spring or early summer, about the time corn is 6 to 8 inches high. Planted too early, the seed lies dormant and may rot. You can take advantage of the difference in seeding time to create a good food plot by drilling forage sorghums right over wide corn rows when the corn is a few inches tall. The stout cornstalks support the lodging sorghum in winter.

Sorghums can be broadcast (using 20 to 30 pounds per acre), planted with a grain drill, plugging two of each three gates (10 to 15 pounds per acre) or in a corn planter set for 20-inch rows (6 to 10 pounds per acre).

Millets are another group of annual grasses with good wildlife food potential. Like sorghums, millets are warm-weather plants and in the North should not be seeded until June. Drill the seed shallowly, 10 to 15 pounds per acre for best seed yields, plugging every other hole in the grain drill and using the "2 pecks of wheat per acre" setting. For thicker cover but reduced seed yield, broadcast or drill at 30 pounds per acre.

Several millet varieties are useful in wildlife work. Pearl or cattail millet is the tallest (2 to 3 feet on good soil) and stiffest-stemmed, with a tight head of large seeds resembling grain sorghum. It is the only millet that stands up well in snow, but the stalks tend to lose their leaves and furnish little cover in severe winters. Both pearl and Japanese millet are used frequently for waterfowl plantings.

Proso and browntop millets are shorter (averaging 12 to 18 inches) and have more open seedheads, with medium-sized and highly palatable seeds. They are usually the number one choice for planting dove-hunting fields in southern and central states, and do well into the Great Lakes region. Since doves feed on seeds dropped on bare soil, plant millets for dove fields in 42 inch rows, and cultivate to keep between-row ground clean. Several fields of 1 and 2 acres often attract and hold doves better than do big plantings. In managing dove fields, keep in mind that federal regulations permit shooting over standing crops of fields harvested by normal farming practices, but prohibit knocking down or manipulating millets or other crops to lure or bait doves for hunting.

German or foxtail millet has small and less palatable seeds and lodges easily. It is used to some extent for dove fields and for seeding between corn rows after one cultivation to provide ground cover.

The lespedezas offer a variety of small-game benefits. Korean lespedeza (low cover in foreground) is a prime annual food source; sericea (background) is taller, perennial, and makes good cover.

Soybeans, cowpeas, and other large-seeded legume crops furnish good yields of nutritious seed, usually sought after by quail, pheasants, and the large game birds. Nearly all are next to useless for food patches where deer are plentiful; deer usually snip off the plants soon after sprouting. Most furnish little shelter and hence are usually mixed with other annuals that are better cover producers.

Annual lespedezas are small-seeded legumes that come close to topping the list for food plantings for quail in particular. There are three varieties. "Common" is one type, the least desirable since it is expensive, not readily located at dealers, and the lowest-yielding.

Kobe is excellent for the deep South below a line across northern Arkansas, Tennessee, and North Carolina. Korean is best from Kobe's northern limit up into northern Missouri, Kentucky, and Virginia.

The advantages of annual lespedezas include low susceptibility to deer and blackbird damage, ready growth in most soils, erosion control value, and the fact that as legumes they add nitrogen to soils in which they are grown. They have good forage value and are frequently planted for pasture. Plant seed in early spring—March to April in their northern range, earlier in the South.

While Kobe and Korean are annuals, they reseed readily and on good sites will maintain themselves year after year, especially with some assistance in the form of a light disking and fertilizer application on established plantings in late winter.

There are other useful examples among the various plant families. Sunflowers are added to some food-patch mixtures for small game, but are probably most useful for attracting songbirds. Rape, a leafy member of the cabbage family, furnishes an excellent source of greens, sought by most small game, well into fall. Flax and buckwheat are also ingredients in many mixtures, the seeds of the latter being exceptionally attractive to pheasants and quail. Both flax and buckwheat are useless as cover in northern winters.

PERENNIAL GRASSES AND FORBS

These plants usually have their greatest small-game value as cover, especially nesting cover, although most provide some food in the form of seed or succulent green parts relished by rabbits and most game birds (particularly in late winter and spring). Their usefulness extends well beyond small game; perennial grasses and legumes are widely employed for erosion control and as soil builders. They can, for example, be seeded between the rows of crops such as corn, after the last cultivation, to tie down the soil and supply at least some wildlife cover in winter after crops are harvested. They are then plowed under as "green manure" the following year.

Many perennial grasses and forbs are quite easily established; some are difficult. In any event, careful site selection and preparation and adequate knowledge of requirements and characteristics are, if anything, even more important with these species than with annuals. The very fact that these are perennials means you will expect good performance from them for several years and will be tying up a planting site for the same time. Planting season, rates, and depths are especially critical.

Where space is at a premium, as on a working farm, these plants can be used along roadsides, field borders, equipment turn-arounds at field-ends, or at woods borders where tree competition minimizes crop production. They make ideal cover for the banks of ditches and dikes since they hold down the soil but don't clog the waterway with roots. In woodlands, perennial grasses and legumes are the standard plantings recommended for fire lanes or for strips cleared to create diversity, and wildlife sunning and feeding sites.

Instructions may call for use of a *nurse crop* when planting many of these perennials. The nurse crop is a fast-growing annual that partially shades and protects slow growing perennials, and helps reduce weed competition during the critical first year until the young perennials can make it on their own. Oats are an excellent "nurse," as are most small grains, and provide some nesting cover if planted early. Small grain nurse crops usually are seeded at about 1½ to 2 pounds per acre, mixed with the perennial seed. If the "nurse" should get too thick and threaten to crowd out the perennial crop, mow the area (set the mower high—at 6 to 10 inches) after mid-July when most nesting is over.

As is true of all plantings, some care after the first year helps ensure a longer useful life for perennials. The various techniques discussed in Chapter 4—mowing, grazing, spraying, and burning—can be applied as needed, just as for native vegetation. Where recommended, periodic fertilizer applications can greatly increase growth and life spans.

Legumes dominate the list of perennial forbs with top wildlife and conservation values. As a group they tend to furnish more food, at least as seed, than do the grasses and have the asset of fixing nitrogen in the soil. Most benefit from liming, both in preparing the site and as a maintenance practice. The "hay" legumes, commonly used in hay, forage, and pasture plantings, include alfalfa and the clovers—red, ladino, sweet clover, etc.—and are usually seeded at 8 to 10 pounds per acre, alone or mixed with perennial grasses. Alfalfa is particularly useful as pheasant nesting cover, especially mixed with brome grass. Sweet clover makes good pheasant cover and yields a useful seed crop for birds, but tends to become too tall and rank for smaller game birds and often plays out after two years. Ladino and red clover are shorter, serve well for nesting for small game birds and cottontails, and are at the top of the list for supplying greens for all forms of wildlife.

Annual mowing of these legumes often helps prolong the life of the stand. If you mow, however, remember to delay cutting until late summer when dangers of destroying nests, nesting wildlife, and young are minimal. If you plant legumes as a source of greens for small and large game, on farm or forest land, and plan to mow periodically to maintain fresh, succulent growth, make sure these areas are cut short early in the year, before ground nests are underway. This reduces the danger that nests will be initiated, only to be destroyed by your regular mowing routine.

Sericea lespedeza is a top choice as a perennial soil-binding cover, with wildlife values, for erodable sites on poor soil.

Sericea lespedeza is an exotic legume introduced into the United States and widely used by conservationists. Although related to the annual lespedezas, sericea is a true perennial, dying back to the crown in fall and sprouting again the following spring. With neither green parts or seeds especially useful as food sources (annual lespedezas are much better quail food plants), sericea's great value is as cover. On erodable slopes and poor soils (except waterlogged sites) where few other plants can survive, sericea will usually produce excellent, soil-binding cover. This trait, together with relative ease of planting and maintenance, makes sericea invaluable. Its one drawback is that after frost the small leaves and stems are so brittle and dry that a dense stand is sheer misery for a hunting dog. For this reason, avoid sericea or limit it on areas to be used intensively for bird hunting, such as shooting preserves.

Sericea will grow from northern Florida to northern Illinois, and from the Atlantic Coast west to eastern Oklahoma and Texas. In the northernmost portion of this range the growing season is usually too short for seed to mature, but good cover can still result.

Plant sericea in early spring, using 30 to 40 pounds of hulled, scarified seed per acre. Plowing isn't necessary; only the top 2 or 3 inches of soil need be pulverized, and the seed requires only shallow covering (less than ½ inch), or none at all. These traits mean satisfactory stands can often result from broadcasting seed by hand on newly worked roadsides, slopes, or ditchbanks, with no additional treatment. The best, quickest results, naturally, take more work—a light harrowing or disking, followed by cultipacking, and sowing seed. On level sites no covering is needed, but slopes should be rolled or cultipacked after sowing so rains won't wash the seed away. Regardless of how you plant it, sericea demands patience. There is usually little growth the first year. But first-year sprouts will grow well the second season, dormant seeds will germinate for several years, and the stand will thicken each season. Never give up and plow under a sericea planting that has had less than two full growing seasons to make a showing.

Crown vetch is a prominent feature along many interstate highways. The U.S. Soil Conservation Service has promoted this plant as an erosion-controlling groundcover for steep cutbanks and overpass slopes along new highways—and for good reason. Crown vetch thrives as well as sericea on poor soil and does as good a job of holding soil. In addition its bunchy growth and attractive, sweet-pea-like flowers make crown vetch more visually appealing. It is a bit too soon to comment on wildlife use since few tests have been completed. Chances are that crown vetch will prove to be of low food and moderate cover value but, like sericea, will provide one of the very few dependable perennial cover plantings for steep, nearly sterile soils.

Crown vetch will grow in just about any region that receives 20 or more inches of rainfall annually. To date there are three main named varieties—Penngift and Chemung for the eastern states, and Emerald for the Midwest.

Bird's-foot trefoil is another legume sometimes touted for wildlife. It makes a fairly good ground cover and cattle pasture on poor soil, but does not seem to offer much small-game food or cover value. To my knowledge it accomplishes nothing for wildlife and erosion control that sericea or crown vetch can't do better.

Perennial grasses offer fine nesting cover for cottontails and nearly all small game birds; depending on the species, they may also be useful as a food source or furnish fall and winter wildlife cover. As with legumes, seeding times, rates, and methods vary, so get adequate advice and instructions.

Reed canary grass is a tall, persistent, and easily established perennial. Residual foliage from the previous year makes excellent early nesting sites for pheasants, and this is one of a limited number of grasses capable of furnishing cover in the teeth of northern winter weather. The planting site, however, is important. On fertile, low, moist soils, canary grass soon becomes too dense to be usable by small game, and rank growth leads to lodging under snow. Best results come on dryer, upland sites.

Brome grass, if unmowed, likewise offers prime pheasant nesting sites in the form of residual cover in stands a year or more old. More susceptible than canary grass to lodging and weather, brome still makes good cover in fall and in mild winters. Sow brome about ½ inch deep in early spring (April or May in the North), mixed with oats as a nurse crop, and mow or harvest the oats for best results.

Timothy, perennial ryegrass, blugrass, orchard grass, and fescue are all used in wildlife plantings, depending on local site and regional climate conditions. Your state conservation department can usually advise as to which of the many perennial grasses you should select.

Prairie grasses are less well-known, but possess all the advantages we have mentioned for native plants. (Most of the above varieties are exotics introduced from other continents.) North American prairie grasses available commercially at present include big bluestem (up to 8 feet in height on ideal sites, and very leafy), little bluestem (2 to 5 feet, a handsome grass for "wild" landscaping, and better on poor soils than its larger cousin), Indian grass (4 to 8 feet), and the various switch grasses, of which Blackwell switch grass is perhaps best known and, to date, most widely used and tested in wildlife work.

The species named are all warm-season grasses which make their best growth in summer, and are deeper-rooted and more heat- and drought-resistant than most exotics. For wildlife, especially small game, they have additional advantages. Primarily clump-forming bunchgrasses, these natives furnish the tall, overhead canopy with open travel space at ground level that small game prefer; they also furnish better cover in northern winters than do brome or other imports. For nesting and winter cover, they are tough to beat.

Why, then, haven't these native grasses been more publicized? Partly because interest, know-how, and equipment have only recently evolved to the point where seed supplies are available commercially. And partly because success with most natives is not as fast or simple as with many exotics.

Tall, native perennial grasses are coming into their own in plantings for small-game nesting cover and shelter.

Consequently, obtaining and following expert planting instructions is a must. Seed depth, site preparation, and planting times are especially critical. If you plan to use these grasses extensively, a suitable, special purpose grass seeder is essential. In general, native grasses are planted early in spring as soon as heavy frosts are past, and seeded shallowly in a firm seedbed. They are slow starters—often so inconspicuous in the first year as to be unrecognizable. As with sericea lespedeza, be patient. Allow at least two full growing seasons for a good start, and three for useful cover in many sites. But these species are worth the wait.

If seed of native grasses is not available from local sources (and it probably won't be), contact your county SCS representative or state college of agriculture. Ask for planting instructions from these same contacts as well as from the dealers they recommend.

A last word on perennial grasses and forbs—they often provide peak effectiveness as small game cover and food when planted in mixtures. Midwest pheasant experts, for example, currently agree that a blend such as 4 pounds of alfalfa and 4 to 6 pounds of brome grass per acre give perhaps the best of all planted pheasant-nesting cover. Similar mixtures also are highly rated for cottontail management. Missouri's conservation department suggests a "rabbitat" planting (to occupy a 20 × 200-foot 1/10-acre plot, next to permanent cover) of 1 pound each of ladino clover and brome, timothy, and orchard grass or bluegrass. Pennsylvania cottontail biologists push a blend of 2 pounds each of orchard grass, redtop, and red clover, 4 pounds of timothy, and 1 pound of alsike clover.

These legume-grass mixtures make a variety of palatable food available over a long season, and the legumes retard the tendency of non-native grasses to form overly dense, undesirable sod.

WOODY PERENNIALS

Woody plants are used in small-game management primarily to supply winter and escape cover, with food a secondary although sometimes important consideration. Nesting use by small game is limited to doves and, of course, squirrels. Shrubs and trees are essential habitat ingredients for a host of birds and mammals, so well-designed plantings offer a real bonus by attracting a variety of other wildlife in addition to small game.

Use woody plantings for thicket cover in odd corners, protected travel lanes linking woodlots or other large permanent cover areas, and along woods borders (using shade-tolerant shrubs), field edges, and roadsides. In choosing sites, remember the need for diversity, and for keeping food, nesting cover, and protective cover close to one another.

Don't overlook opportunities for shrubs and trees to do double duty as windbreaks, shelterbelts, or screens near buildings, or in erosion control. In the Plains states, or wherever wind or snow is a problem, a windbreak of conifers and deciduous trees, at least ten rows wide and placed at a right angle to prevailing winds, provides blessed relief from howling gales for both people and wildlife. There should be at least four rows of such low-branching conifers as spruce or red cedar on the inner lee side. Where heavy snow is likely, leave a snow "dropout" zone of some 75 to 100 feet between the windbreak and buildings, roads, or whatever you are shielding.

To control potential or existing erosion and gullying on poor soils and simultaneously benefit small game, try thicket plantings of autumn olive, indigo bush, rose acacia (also called bristly locust), or speckled alder. Besides tying down erodable soil and furnishing wildlife food and cover, many of those shrubs are nitrogen-fixing soil builders. Where streambank erosion is a problem, plantings of red osier, silky dogwood, or purple osier willow along the outside stream curves (where the current hits) offer effective control and have strong wildlife fringe benefits.

We discussed sources of planting stock and precautions in buying earlier in this chapter. I must stress again the need to learn site and climate requirements of the various species before selecting shrubs and trees, and the need to think ahead. Woody plantings are a long-term proposition; don't waste them on sites whose future use is in doubt. To size up what your plantings will look like when mature, try to visit a good nursery, a state game-management area, an arboretum, or an SCS plant materials center. If you have time and a green thumb, you can save money by growing your own planting stock from cuttings or even seed (most libraries have good "how-to" books in their garden sections), or by transplanting stands already existing on your land.

If you purchase seedlings, review procedures covered earlier in this chapter for care on arrival. If planting must be delayed beyond one or two days and the materials are bare-rooted, they must be healed in. Dig a V-shaped trench about a foot deep in a shady, protected spot. (If no shade is available, make a wind and sun screen of burlap or scrap lumber.) Untie and loosen the plant bundles and spread the seedlings along one side of the V, with their roots below the surface. Cover the roots completely with soil, water thoroughly, and then tamp the soil. If watered to prevent drying out, seedlings handled in this fashion will stay healthy for a week or more.

The critical point throughout is to prevent the roots from drying. Seedlings with exposed roots can be lost in a matter of minutes on a dry, windy day. Remember this while planting, and carry your seedlings in a bucket of water or well wrapped in moist peat moss or burlap.

Proper site preparation is important. If the planting is to be fairly extensive, and the shape and location lend themselves to the equipment, it is best to plow and disk the site thoroughly to set back weed competition for the critical first year. If there is a heavy stand of grass, plow and disk in fall and disk again in spring prior to planting. Where only a few seedlings are involved, or where areas are inaccessible to tractor or rototiller, competition can be reduced by scalping—removing with a spade the top 1 to 4 inches of soil, along with weed and grass roots, in a patch at least a foot in diameter. Seedlings are planted in the centers of the bare spots.

Most trees and shrubs can be planted successfully in spring before they leaf out, or in fall after leaves are gone. Avoid planting or moving during the active growing season and when moisture-losing leaves are fully out. There are several planting techniques. Which to use depends upon the location and size of the planting, and the time, money, and equipment available. For extensive plantings on suitable terrain, a tree planter is by far the best. This tractor-drawn rig, seating one or more riders who place the seedlings, cuts a planting furrow and covers it and the seedlings in continuous operation. So equipped, an experienced crew can plant as many as 1,000 seedlings an hour. Most state conservation departments and SCS offices can provide a list of tree planters available for rent in your area.

Hedges, travel lanes, and other elongated row plantings can also be handled with a tractor and two-bottom plow. First, cut a backfurrow by making two rounds with the plow. Then harrow or disk, plow a new furrow on the ridge of the back-furrow, set the seedlings in this furrow (anchoring them with a little soil), and cover the roots by cutting another furrow. As a final step, firm the soil along the new planting with the tractor wheels.

Where seedlings must be planted by hand and only a few plants are involved, dig a hole—after scraping the site as described—deep enough to accommodate the roots without crowding or doubling them over. Place the seedling in the center, cover the roots, and stamp the soil down firmly with your foot all around the seedling. If much planting is to be done by hand, use a narrow, sharp spade, or

a planting bar or "spud." Plunge the spade or bar into the center of
the scalped spot at about a 20° or 30° angle and then push it upright,
to create a V-shaped hole. Place the seedling in the hole against the
flat side. Then plunge the bar or spade straight down into the
ground, 3 or 4 inches from the sloping side of your first cut. Pull the
handle toward you, pressing the soil against the bottom roots, and
then push forward, packing the upper soil. Tramp hard around the
seedling to pack it firmly and to close the last hole. Once you get the
hang of this method, you can plant with surprising speed.

Regardless of how you plant, be sure to set seedlings at the
same depth from which they grew previously, or slightly deeper,
and—most vital—*be sure the soil is packed firmly around the roots.*
A seedling with its roots in air pockets in loose soil is as sure to die
as one dropped on bare ground.

Spacing is important in shrub and tree plantings. The tendency
is to plant seedlings too close because it is hard to imagine how they
will look when mature. But crowding results later in shaded-out,
dead lower branches, eliminating valuable ground-level cover.

As a rule, spacing between plants within a row should average
at least 2 to 3 feet for shrubs such as dogwoods and honeysuckle, 5
to 6 feet for shrubby trees like Russian olive and the taller Viburnums, and 8 to 10 feet for medium-sized conifers and deciduous
trees. Between rows, spacing depends on maintenance plans. If the
planting is to be cultivated, leave adequate room for tractor and cul-
tivator. If cultivation is not planned, placing can be similar to that
within rows. For best results, stagger your planting so that the seedlings in the first row are opposite the spaces between seedlings in
the second row, and so forth.

Where feasible, new plantings should be cultivated once or
twice annually for the first year or two to reduce weed competition.
If this is impossible, mulching with shavings, ground corncobs, and
the like helps retain moisture and keeps weeds down. Occasional
fertilizer applications for certain species on some soils may be necessary for optimum growth and vigor. If you have had your soil
tested and learned the requirements of the species planted, as you
should, you will know when and where such assists are worthwhile.

Some woody plants lose their effectiveness for small game long
before the end of their life span. Shrubs planted for low, dense escape cover often grow tall and spindly after eight to ten years.
Lower branches and some main stems die, and fruit production declines. Full usefulness often can be restored by severe pruning—
back to a few inches above the ground—by hand or rotary mower in

92 late winter or early spring. This may seem like wanton butchery, but results can be amazing. A multitude of new sprouts and stems push up so rapidly that cover and fruit are better than ever within two seasons or even one. Dogwoods, honeysuckles, autumn olive, sumac, shrub lespedezas, and many other multistemmed shrubs can be managed in this fashion.

The strip of bark on these "half-cut" young pines will keep the top alive for many years. Net result: a living brushpile.

"Half-cutting" lower branches of large old conifers (and some other trees) simultaneously creates a living brushpile and admits more growth-stimulating light at ground level.

Some conifers planted specifically as dense winter and escape cover for ground-dwelling small game, and not designed primarily for windbreaks, dove nesting, or other purposes requiring taller growth, also lose their effectiveness with time. Shade from upper branches kills out understory vegetation and lower limbs, creating a ground-level desert. Conifers that have reached this point can be topped—cut off 4 to 5 feet above the ground so that sunlight can reach the lower branches and ground. But it is better to act before they are too tall, by using a technique called *half-cutting* or *cut-and-bend*. This treatment works well on many conifers (and some deciduous trees) when they are 6 to 8 feet tall. In spring after the sap has risen, make a cut in the trunk with a hand- or chain-saw 3 to 4 feet above the ground, opposite the direction you want the top to fall. Cut just deep enough so you can push the top over, leaving a connecting strip of bark and wood. The lower branches, no longer shaded, grow vigorously while the connected top should remain alive indefinitely, its tip again growing upwards. (Five to six years later you may need to repeat the process with this tip.) The result is a low, dense, living brushpile forming ideal winter cover. On conifers too large and old for this treatment, and on some deciduous trees, lower limbs can be half-cut and bent down to form a living umbrella of cover that is equally effective.

The list of woody plants with wildlife values is almost endless. At this point we will describe some species especially desirable for small game; in later chapters we will discuss varieties employed in managing forest game and songbirds. Nature makes no such distinctions. A shrub that bears palatable fruit or furnishes good escape cover is used by most wildlife in the area, game or nongame. So the distinctions I make are only a matter of degree.

We have encountered lespedezas previously among the annuals and perennial forbs. A third group, the *shrub lespedezas,* are also popular in small game plantings. There are two main varieties—bicolor and Japonica. Both have their greatest value as highly palatable quail food, either supplementing native foods or—where supplies already are adequate, as is often the case in prime quail range—used to attract coveys into hunting areas.

Bicolor lespedeza does well east of the Great Plains and south of U.S. 40 in the Midwest, and U.S. 30 in the East. Of the several strains, "natob" is the hardiest in the North. Since it thrives in partial shade, bicolor is ideal for the shade- and root-competition zone along woods borders. Planted as seed or seedlings, bicolor prospers in most soils unless too waterlogged. A healthy ⅛-acre plot produces enough seed to feed a quail covey all winter, and the leafy canopy shades out ground cover so that the seeds fall on bare soil, providing ideal feeding conditions for bobwhite. Fallen seeds resist deterioration and are avoided by rodents and most songbirds.

Bicolor stands tend to lose vigor with age and should be cut back early every third or fourth spring to a few inches above ground.

Japonica lespedeza is closely related to bicolor and bears seed even more prolifically in its prime range, from Massachusetts and Tennessee north and west to mid-Illinois, Indiana, and Ohio. Japonica dies back in fall and hence does not require periodic clipping.

Not long ago no wildlife planting was considered complete without at least one *multiflora rose* hedge. An import from Asia, multiflora seemed to be the all-purpose wildlife shrub. It grows rapidly on nearly all sites, except where wet or shaded, and in most regions except the northernmost states. Its dropping branches form thorny tangles, impregnable to predators on the outside but open beneath for ground-dwelling game. The heavy crops of fruit, clinging to the stems for months, are not highly palatable, but do furnish a nutritious emergency food source available above snow. Covered with small, perfumed white rose blossoms, multiflora hedges are most handsome and, at first, were considered cattle-proof and publicized as "living fences."

Time and experience brought disillusionment—not with multi-flora's values, which remain great, but with the fact that wide hedges were virtually unhuntable. Dogs might venture once into the thorns to pin down a covey, flush a pheasant, or retrieve a cripple, but could rarely be forced a second time. Game was as invulnerable to the hunter as to the predator. On the other hand, thick-coated beef cattle were seldom daunted by the "living fence" (some even seem to enjoy a good tickling), and filtered through thin spots like water through a sieve.

The worst blow was multiflora's ability to spread, not by suckers or runners, but from seeds consumed with the fruit by birds and deposited in droppings far from the initial source. Impenetrable bramble jungles grew up in abandoned fields, old pastures, woods borders, ditches, and any open area not used for crops or active pasture.

Why discuss a shrub now in disrepute? Because you might come across the older literature, published before all the facts were in, which sings its praises, and some state agencies and private nurseries still promote its use. And because, while multiflora's faults outweigh its values in most situations, there are some sites where local conditions, management, and climate control its spread and on which multiflora can still be a great escape-cover planting. But never plant multiflora without inspection and approval of the site by a competent biologist.

Other shrubs once recommended for small-game plantings have not passed the test of time—not because they are dangerous, as in the case of multiflora, but because they fail to accomplish their purpose or are not as good as newer varieties. Coralberry, ninebark, and most privets are examples; their heavy crops of fruit that looked like such fine wildlife food proved to be so unpalatable as to be used rarely. Tatarian honeysuckle and Russian olive are other old-timers, which, while still useful as food and cover, rate a poor second to more recently discovered relatives.

Tatarian has been supplanted by *Amur honeysuckle* in the affections of most game managers. Both species bear quantities of palatable fruit sought after by game and nongame wildlife alike, and both furnish good cover, especially if cut back periodically. But Amur's fruit ripens later and remains on the shrub longer into fall and winter, while Tatarian's fruits drop and are lost before they are needed most.

Russian olive's new competitor is *autumn olive*, in my opinion one of the finest of all wildlife shrubs. On good sites, autumn olive bears fruit and furnishes cover in its third season. The abundant red berries (twenty-four plants at Beltsville, Maryland, produced 900 pounds in one year) are retained well into winter, although most are soon consumed. From black bears and raccoons to wild turkeys and warblers, wildlife finds these fruits irresistible. Clipped at three-to-five-year intervals, autumn olive makes good, dense escape cover, although this practice reduces fruit production. For best fruit yields, plant in blocks with 8-foot spacings between plants, or at 6-to-8-foot intervals in rows spaced 10 to 20 feet apart. Use closer spacing if your goal is cover and you plan to clip.

Among native woody plants of particular value for small game are the *sumacs,* whose bark and new shoots provide a staple winter food for cottontails, while the persistent fruits, held well above snow, offer valuable emergency nourishment for a variety of birds. Bayberry, elderberry, blueberry, blackberries, and the shrub and flowering dogwoods are other extremely useful native woody plants. Wild plum is a top thicket-type escape cover and food source both north and south. By all means, place such native vines as the wild grapes and woodbine (Virginia creeper) high on your list. Planted in the sun along woods borders, fence corners, or other sites offering climbing opportunities, wild grapes in particular are difficult to beat as small-game food and cover.

There are hundreds of shrubs useful for small game, including most of those we will mention later in connection with forest-game and songbird management. Those cited here are chosen because they are available and useful in most regions, don't require kid-glove treatment, and have time-tested small-game values. More good native species are not included because, unfortunately, many as yet are not commercially available in quantity at reasonable prices.

The evergreen *conifers,* aside from furnishing dove nesting sites, serve small game primarily as winter cover. Some species, including red cedar, are a food source as well. In selecting conifers, lean toward heavily branched species offering dense cover—spruces, firs, and cedars, for example, in preference to most pines. Many conifers are choosy as to soil type and drainage, so know your site and the requirements of the species. You will find that the wide range of conifers includes some suitable for nearly every purpose. White spruce and white pine, for instance, do well in open shade and can be planted among aspen or birch stands to add cover diversity. Pfitzer junipers and other low, spreading conifers make top-notch holding cover for newly released, hand-reared game birds, besides sheltering native game. Don't forget half-cutting as a means of preserving ground-level cover in stands of upright conifers.

Conifers are hard to beat for cover in northern winters. Deciduous shrubs (foreground) lose much of their cover value with their leaves.

For winter cover, a mixed planting of shrubs and coniferous trees is hard to beat. The best sites are slopes that face south out of the wind but catch the sun; the worst are windswept tops of knolls and ridges. Plantings may be in a circle, square, rectangle, or curved with contours, but should be at least 150 feet wide for adequate shelter from winter weather. Plant conifers in the center, using red cedar, Black Hills or white spruce and similar thick-branching species. Place fruiting, thicket-forming shrubs (wild plum, honeysuckle, bayberry, and the like) around the evergreens to furnish sunning and loafing cover and a food supply, and to catch blowing snow.

COST-SHARING

Planting, even on a moderate scale, can be expensive. You may be able to cut costs by participating in one of several federal and, in some areas, state programs designed to stimulate interest in wildlife and soil conservation projects. Depending upon county, state, and region, a variety of plantings may qualify for reimbursement of part or most of the planting costs, Acceptable practices include plantings designed primarily for wildlife as well as such projects as windbreaks, seeding diversion terraces or retired fields, and reforestation, all having important fringe benefits for wildlife. To find out how you can qualify, contact your county Soil Conservation Service or Agricultural Stablization and Conservation Service offices and state conservation department.

Don't overlook the direct financial returns some plantings offer while benefiting wildlife. Conifers planted for sale as Christmas trees are a prime example. While growing to salable size they furnish shelter; if cut above the lowest one or two whorls of branches they will continue to supply ground-level cover. The growing demand for natural materials in decorative dried-flower arrangements has created a market for fruit- and seedpod-bearing branches as well as the traditional Christmas greens. Selective pruning can benefit your shrubs and trees as well as your pocketbook.

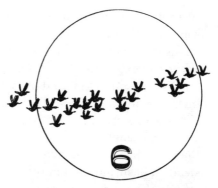

GILDING THE LILY: ARTIFICIAL ASSISTS

There are times and places when artificial "assists" can supply wildlife requirements—food, water, escape and nesting cover, and certain special needs—that cannot be met by natural means.

Two schools of thought exist on these assists, philosophically and at a practical level. As long as men are interested in wildlife, there will be those who fight any attempt to manage or manipulate nature; obviously, they have a particular horror of artificial measures. I sympathize with the "hands off" view when it is applied to wilderness and other natural areas. But on land already drastically altered by man and his activities, it seems shortsighted not to employ all means—within reason—to restore wildlife.

On the practical side there are also grounds for opposition to certain "artificial" management techniques. Large-scale attempts at feeding game in harsh winters, for example, have a well-documented history of failure. Usually initiated in northern areas by well-intentioned citizens after severe winter snows or ice storms, such feeding projects normally take the form of massive scattering of corn for pheasants, or hay for deer. Major emergency feeding programs for ringnecks seldom are much help; on good range, enough birds usually survive without help, and their high reproductive rate puts the population back in business in one breeding season. Where winter cover is inadequate, feed alone—without shelter—is not enough. Since people rarely go back into areas where cover still exists, most corn ends up spread along roadsides or in the open where birds that find it are subject to heavy loss from automobiles and predators.

For this reason, most professional wildlifers take a long-range view and would prefer to see the money, manpower, and energy that are spent on massive emergency winter feeding, focused instead on basic habitat improvements.

Rubber-tire nestboxes, concrete waterholes, and even brushpiles are not the most aesthetic of objects, and "gilding the lily" may not appeal to you. If you wish, nevertheless, to give any of these techniques a try, avoid the dangers that are inherent in some. First of all, artificial devices are a temporary means of filling in missing gaps in habitat, not an end in themselves. Used properly, they can be of help while plantings grow and management of natural vegetation proceeds. Second, always bear in mind that feeders, nestboxes, and other such aids have the potential of doing more harm than good; they can become deathtraps if not properly placed, guarded, and maintained.

This chapter is aimed at small game, although some methods are useful for other species as well. Artificial assists primarily for waterfowl, songbirds, and other wildlife groups are covered in appropriate chapters later.

FEEDERS AND FEEDING

While supplemental feeding may not be successful on a large scale, its use on limited areas can be worthwhile. Applied locally and with common sense, it may aid small-game populations through periods when natural foods are so scarce as to be a limiting factor—particularly at winter's end or in severe cold and snow. Feeding can also attract game within camera or gun range. Thus, quail feeders are sometimes used in the South—much as plantings of bicolor lespedeza—to attract quail coveys from heavy brush to huntable areas.

Supplemental food can be scattered on the ground, or provided in various types of feeders. Each method has advantages and problems. You will see warnings about food rotting if in contact with the ground; some songbird books advise spreading food on plastic, or removing it daily if not consumed. With grain—and you should use only grain, never commercial pelleted poultry food, for ground feeding—such precautions are absurd. Most seed and grain available to wildlife in nature comes from lodged seedheads and waste grain lost or missed in harvesting. It is exposed to weather and usually in contact with the ground all winter. If this food were dangerous, grain-eating wildlife would have been extinct years ago. The major disadvantage of ground-fed grain is that it is easily covered by ice and snow. Squirrels and some other species will still locate and reach it, but snow-covered grain is lost to quail and many other species until the next thaw.

There are some definite advantages to feeding on the ground. It is cheaper, since no feeders have to be purchased or constructed. Even more important for the recipients is that feeding sites can be switched frequently, thus minimizing the opportunity for predators to concentrate on a few feeding stations in constant use.

Corn is the best grain for ground feeding because it is more easily visible and less prone to deterioration than small grains. In most cases, corn can be fed on the cob. Cobs are cheaper and less likely to be buried in light snow. Most game species can pull the kernels off the cob and, in so doing, usually drop and miss enough to feed smaller wildlife.

Man-made feeders require money and time. Since they are often too much trouble to move, they may become death-traps where predators are a problem; it doesn't take long for predators to wise up and keep a watch on regularly visited feeding areas.

For this reason, feeding stations established by feeders or by ground-fed grain must be located in or at the edge of good escape cover. They should be checked regularly for signs of predation, and moved as soon as any such evidence is spotted.

There are dozens of feeder designs, some styled for one species, others for more general use. Many state conservation departments will furnish construction plans on request, as will local and state Audubon clubs and the National Audubon Society. Good, ready-made feeders, especially for quail, are advertised in most outdoor and nature magazines.

Whether you build or buy them, good feeders should incorporate certain features. They should be so constructed or fastened that cattle, deer, and weather won't knock them down. Where commercial pelleted foods are used, or where small grain is confined without ventilation, as in metal feeders, the food must be kept dry. The better metal feeders available commercially feature small feeding slots and serrated metal edges, minimizing chances for squirrels, raccoons, and opposums to consume the full contents at one sitting. Finally, feeders should be easy to refill; the weather in which they are needed most is when you will be least willing to fiddle with intricate lids and latches.

There are several easily built devices for feeding ears of corn above the snow. For squirrels, ears can be impaled on large nails or spikes driven through a strip of wood, and the strip wired or nailed to a tree. For pheasants, and turkeys, as well as squirrels, and for many smaller species that will feed on kernels knocked off and dropped, a chicken wire sleeve holding several ears and open at the top for refilling is simple and effective. Attach the sleeve by nails or staples to a board and wire the board to a tree, within reach of game birds on the ground.

Baskets made of fur-farm wire or chicken wire, like old-style open incinerators, can be bought or built and filled with ears of corn. If you place them on the ground, brace them with stakes or posts so they won't be knocked over. Better still, especially where deep snow is likely, hang them 6 to 12 inches above the ground from a limb or crossbar. Wooden, V-shaped hoppers for ear corn, constructed with lathes or rough-cut branches and suspended between trees or posts, are often recommended. These and other large devices are usually cumbersome or impossible to move if predators concentrate. For this reason small, easily handled feeders are best for small game.

One last reminder—never begin supplemental feeding unless you will have the time, interest, and money to continue through until critical weather or food shortages are over.

BRUSHPILES

As we have seen, "living brushpiles" can be created by half-cutting trees of the right size and species, and are superior for many reasons to piles of dead material. But trees suitable for half-cutting are often not present at the right time and place, especially where habitat management for wildlife is just getting under way. Freshly cut material frequently is easier to come by. It is a natural by-product of such commercial practices as pruning orchards or managing woodlots for timber production, and of such wildlife work as removing weed trees to release valuable mast producers, clearing lanes and openings in large stands of pole timber, and cutting back overage shrubs to promote new growth.

Properly located and constructed, brushpiles make excellent escape and winter cover for ground-dwelling small game, not only

Brushpiles offer excellent interim cover while new shrub and tree plantings grow. These piles are part of a line forming a wildlife travel lane between two wooded areas.

cottontails but quail and pheasants as well. Follow the same rules for placement as for cover plantings—in fence corners and gullies, adjoining feeding areas or nesting cover, along road and field edges, bordering woodlands or clearings, or in a series close together to provide and secure travel lanes between permanent food and cover. Brushpiles are well used in areas newly planted to tree and shrub cover; about the time the piles deteriorate and become useless, the growing plants should be big enough to take over the job.

Don't just throw brush in a haphazard heap. For maximum longevity and wildlife value, follow time-tested methods. Make a pile at least 5 feet high and 10 to 15 feet in length (or in diameter, if circular). Several piles of this size are better than one giant stack. For the base, use the largest limbs or logs (6 inches or more in diameter are best) and lay them parallel and about 4 to 6 inches apart. This spacing allows use by rabbits and other small game, but is too tight a squeeze for most predators. Then add a second layer, also of larger limbs or logs, at right angles to the base layer. Finally, having ensured access at ground level, add finer material, again with alternating layers.

So constructed, with only a few large pieces touching the ground where rot works fastest, a brushpile can have a useful life of ten years or more. Oak, locust, or other rot-resisting materials make the longest-lasting base; if sumac, apple, basswood, maple, or other clippings palatable to cottontails are available, place them near the base or so draped at the sides as to be in reach.

No brush or clipped-off woody material is useless, even if not sturdy enough or sufficient to create a model brushpile. Scattered in grass plantings, especially among tall grasses prone to lodging, such as reed canary grass grown on wet sites, branches and small tops support grass stems that grow up through them. The combination supplies cover that neither ingredient could furnish alone. Even discarded Christmas trees help beef up natural cover for a season or two where winter shelter is scarce.

If you are ultra-cottontail-conscious, you may wish to carry the brushpile idea a step further, as do some state agencies and sportsmen's groups—especially beagle clubs—in the rabbit-hungry northeastern states. Where a source of flat rocks is handy—as in most of New England—you can build a permanent den. Pile the rocks as if building a small igloo, leaving a 4-to-6-inch-wide tunnel system at ground level, with at least two or three exits, and top with brush. Or build a brush pile over sections of old 6-inch pipe or tile. At least one state publication actually recommends throwing rolls of old wire, discarded farm equipment, car bodies, etc., into gullies to furnish rabbit cover. Junk probably works fine, but the idea is ghastly—an extreme example of how singleminded obsession with one goal can lead to disaster. There is enough junk abandoned over the American landscape without deliberately adding more.

ARTIFICIAL NEST STRUCTURES

We will discuss man-made nest devices for waterfowl in Chapter 7; with small game they are used mostly for squirrels. The traditional squirrel nestbox is made of durable lumber. Rough-sawn cedar or cypress heartwood are best; more expensive initially, their long life span makes them much cheaper in the end. Where squirrel hunting is popular, state conservation departments usually have printed material on box construction and placement available on request. Try to obtain such instructions; they are based on local conditions and experience and thus preferable to the general directions given here.

A typical box, built from 1-inch lumber, measures 7 x 9 x 18 inches in height. To shed rain, the top should be cut large enough so that it overhangs ½ to 1 inch on all sides, and should slant forward at a 30° angle. Plan and cut the box sides, front and back, accordingly. Use screws to fasten the top so that inspection and cleaning are easier. Cut or bore a circular entrance hole (2½ inches in diameter for gray squirrels, 3 inches for fox squirrels) in one side, where it

will be nearer the tree and more accessible, near the top. Entrance
dimensions are important—these sizes admit squirrels readily but
keep out such predators as raccoons.

For maximum drainage and air circulation, use ½-inch-mesh
hardware cloth (heavy-gauge and galvanized after weaving to reduce predator problems) as the box "floor." You don't need to add
nest material; the squirrels will soon take care of this.

Maryland's Department of Game and Fish pioneered a long-
lasting nest structure for squirrels, made of rubber tires. An ordinary auto tire is cut in two, each half making one nest. Slits are cut
on each side, about a third of the distance from one end, and the
smaller end is folded up and inside the larger and fastened with
bent roofing nails or heavy wire. The result is a snug, kidney-shaped
structure with a roofed-over entrance. One problem, however, is
that the steel beading must be removed from the inner rim to permit
cutting and folding. This is a tough job, requiring special equipment
or much hard handwork.

*Snug housing for squirrels from half a used tire. Note nature and positions
of cuts, folds, and fasteners.*

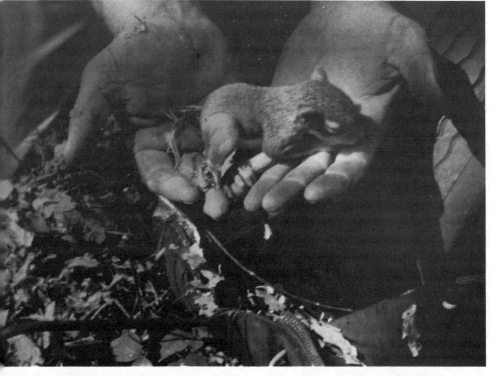

One of a litter of gray squirrels produced in a rubber-tire nestbox.

Place squirrel nests about 20 feet above the ground in trees sturdy enough for support. This is high enough to minimize vandalism; placing them higher won't be any advantage for the squirrels but will make necessary inspections more difficult. Tire nests can be hung from branches with an S-shaped steel hanger. Wire wood boxes securely in place, circling box and tree trunk at two points to prevent tipping. Plastic-covered wire is best since it resists weathering and the ends, twisted together in fastening, will untwist slightly to permit tree growth. Boxes can also be nailed to trees, but avoid nails on valuable timber species. Bolt or screw a wood or strap-metal strip securely to the back of the box, letting the strip project above and below; then nail the projecting ends to the tree trunk. Use large galvanized nails, and leave a gap of 2 inches or so between tree and hanging strip to allow for trunk growth.

Check boxes periodically—once a year, if possible—for necessary repairs or problems. But watch out for bees; they like boxes, too.

Several recent studies indicate that they are, when used where natural hollow den trees are few or absent, and where food is abundant. Such situations frequently occur in farm country; cornfields and other crops provide a food supply, but available timber often is too young to be cavity-prone, or is managed for timber production whereby overmature, hollow trees are removed.

Although never widely employed as yet, artificial nests for doves have been tested in several states. They are simple and inexpensive to construct. One good design starts with a 12-inch square of ½- or ⅜-inch-mesh hardware cloth. Trim the square to make a circle, then cut a pie-slice wedge out of it, overlap the cut ends about 3 inches, and fasten them together to form a shallow cone. Wire or nail the cone about 6 to 16 feet above the ground in the fork of two limbs, or at the angle where a limb leaves the trunk. Bend the edges down slightly so no rough ends protrude.

If doves find your cones attractive, they will bring the nest material. The cone's advantage is that it provides a reasonably secure base for the flimsy little twig nests—so prone to wind and storm loss—that doves construct. So far there have been few instances of much use by doves, unlike the immediate response squirrels often make to nestboxes.

MAN-MADE WATERING DEVICES

Artificial "waterholes" for wildlife are employed primarily in arid portions of the West where lack of free water can be a critical limiting factor for many species. Invented for desert-dwelling quail, they were initially called "gallinaceous guzzlers." Now known simply as "guzzlers," they are in use in dry country for a variety of wildlife, including big game.

The basic design includes a hard-surfaced (concrete or asphalt) collecting apron, covering an area of about 300 square feet and so situated as to catch a maximum of rain and run-off. The water runs into a storage tank of steel, concrete, or fiberglass, covered and below ground level to minimize evaporation. Openings at the back or sides, and one or more ramps, give easy access for wildlife. Guzzlers must be located where silt and water-borne debris won't fill them up, and on rangeland they should be fenced to keep out cattle.

These are not devices to be thrown together by amateurs. To be effective, guzzlers must be large enough in size and properly designed, built, and located. So constructed, they can cost $1,000 or more in labor and material. If you have this kind of money to invest, and are located in arid country where you suspect water may limit numbers of wildlife species in which you are interested, contact your state conservation department for advice.

Small, shallow depressions or dugouts are sometimes lined with plastic, concrete, or asphalt in more humid regions, to catch and hold rain and run-off as a temporary wildlife water source. In these regions water is unlikely to be critical for wildlife, since water is usually available in the form of dew or succulent plant parts. However, such catchment basins, like birdbaths, can attract wildlife for viewing. They should be located out of the wind, and well shaded to reduce evaporation and growth of algae.

ODDS AND ENDS

Grit is sometimes scattered or supplied in feeders for gallinaceous birds, although it is doubtful that a shortage of grit is ever a serious limiting factor. In those few areas where soils supply little or no natural gravel or rock fragments, graveled roads or lanes become grit sources.

Some western quail, including the valley or California quail, roost off the ground. Where densely foliated roost trees, such as live oaks and junipers, are scarce or too recently planted to be of use, artifical roosts have been employed with fair success. A wire-covered frame, about 8 by 16 feet, is supported about 6 feet above the ground by posts. Wood or metal may be used for the posts and frame; 2-inch pipe works well. Brush is piled on the frame, using fair-sized crooked or forked branches to minimize packing, and the roost is ready for occupancy.

As the years go by, it is likely that modern man will tend to use these and new, artificial assists for wildlife more widely. Not intrinsically "bad," and quite helpful as temporary stopgaps while plantings and vegetation managed through succession come of useful age, the danger of artifical devices is the possiblility that they may someday be accepted as full and complete substitutes for natural food and cover. Should this come to pass, wildlife management will have become zoo-keeping.

WATERFOWL: WEBFOOT REQUIREMENTS
AND HOW TO MEET THEM

Rare indeed is the person who loves wildlife and the outdoors but has not succumbed to the lure of water and waterfowl. Increasing numbers of landowners holding title to a couple of acres or more rate a pond of some sort high on their "want list"—as the construction of hundreds of thousands of farm ponds bears witness. Sometimes the goal is attracting waterfowl for viewing or hunting. Sometimes fishing or swimming takes priority. Yet, even here, most folks end up thinking it would be nice to have a few ducks around.

Farmers in prime waterfowl-hunting regions find that they can glean excellent income from leasing annual hunting rights, or charging daily blind-fees—on occasion earning more per acre than from farming. It is hard to find a sportsmen's group that is not interested in improving waterfowl production and hunting on local waters. Modern city and suburban planners look to water—and waterfowl—as an attractive and unusual "natural touch" in new developments.

Unfortunately, wild waterfowl are not always cooperative. You can develop upland sites with food and cover plantings and be reasonably certain of attracting and increasing at least some terrestrial game and nongame wildlife. Not so with waterfowl. For one thing, most are migratory. With the exception of the wood duck and such localized species as the Florida and Mexican ducks, most of the

United States sees wild ducks and geese only during spring and fall migration or in winter. Further, it takes more than just water to support, produce, or attract waterfowl. There are far more water areas in North America—natural and man-made—than there are ducks to use them. Ponds, lakes, streams, and marshes must contain adequate food and cover plants of the right kind, and the best plants won't tolerate just any old water. The location and setting of wetlands, and the surrounding shorelines and uplands, must be suitable as well to attract waterfowl.

So, perhaps even more than in the case of upland wildlife, extensive developments for waterfowl can be a costly waste of time without adequate advance information and planning. While what we cover here may help avoid some problems, it is imperative to seek advice from state and federal sources. Fortunately, most states have competent waterfowl biologists, who have developed effective management techniques. State and federal biologists are few and overworked, so don't expect on-the-spot field assistance, but you can obtain highly useful literature from state conservation departments, the U.S. Soil Conservation Service, and the U.S. Bureau of Sport Fisheries and Wildlife (regional offices are listed in the Appendix).

WATERFOWL GROUPS: THEIR CHARACTERISTICS AND MANAGEMENT POTENTIAL

An understanding of waterfowl and their requirements is basic to any management effort. A duck is not "just a duck"; waterfowl are an extremely diverse group, both in habits and in the habitat they find suitable during breeding season, in migration, and on wintering grounds.

North American waterfowl vary in size from giant trumpeter swans to tiny teal; in color from white snow geese and sooty black ducks to colorful wood ducks; in range from the mallard, common across the continent, to the Mexican duck, limited in the United States to part of the Rio Grande valley. Some nest in tree cavities, some in reed clumps over water, others in grassy uplands. Some feed mainly on fish, some primarily on submerged aquatic plants, and others graze like sheep.

Passing by the swans, mergansers, and sea ducks, there are three major groups of waterfowl that are of primary interest, and about which enough management information is available for practical application. Let's look first at the geese. Generally larger than the ducks, with longer necks and less-flattened bodies, geese also

are characterized by having excellent balance on land, since their 111
legs are set farther forward under their bodies than is the case with
most ducks. Thus, while they eat aquatic plants and invertebrates,
they also forage frequently on land, grazing mn greens and feeding
on grain. This is important for management; it means that suitably
planted uplands in migration and wintering areas can attract geese
even if adjacent waters support little or no food, or if the nearest
water areas are a considerable distance away.

The fact that many Canada geese and, more recently, an increasing number of blue and snow geese winter farther north now
than they did a few years ago is adequate testimony to the attractiveness of waste-grain food supplies left by modern corn-harvest-
ing equipment. Such "short-stopping" of southbound geese in fall,
as a result of agricultural waste grain and deliberate management
efforts by northern state and federal refuges, has become an extremely touchy issue with southern hunters and game agencies.
"Their" wintering geese often no longer show up.

Most geese nest in the far north, for the most part well beyond
the reach of public or private management and—at least until very
recently—beyond disruption by human activities. As one consequence, as long as hunting is carefully regulated, population
changes are caused mainly by year-to-year weather fluctuations on
the breeding grounds. Another consequence is that "management"
for most geese means attempts to attract them for viewing or hunting during migration or in winter. There are some interesting exceptions. The northern Great Plains and Great Basin states and the Pacific Northwest are the heart of the breeding grounds for the big
western race of the Canada goose. And the largest of all North
American geese—the recently rediscovered giant Canada—which
traditionally nested from the eastern Prairie states across much of
the northern Midwest, has been re-established by state, federal, and
private efforts over much of this region.

These races, along with Canadas that have been induced to
breed in the Northeast, offer an opportunity for management for
production, rather than simply for harvest or a migration-viewing
"spectacular."

North American ducks contain two waterfowl groups of prime
interest for management—"divers" and "dabblers." Divers include
the canvasback and redhead, greater and lesser scaup—or "blue-
bills"—the ringneck, goldeneyes, and others. As their name implies,
divers feed under water as a rule. Short legs placed well to the rear
of the body help them dive and swim; they also make agile movements on land very difficult.

As a result, management to attract diving ducks can be difficult for private landowners. Upland grain and grass plantings hold no appeal, and the aquatic food plants most divers prefer grow well only in certain inland and coastal waters—most of them large and under public ownership.

Since breeding grounds for nearly all divers in the United states are limited to the northern states, only a relatively few state agencies and private individuals have an opportunity to work with production habitat for this group.

Among the ducks, more management attention is focused on the second great group—the dabblers or "puddle ducks." These include such favorites of hunter and bird-watcher as the pintail or "sprig," the mallard, the teal species, black duck, wood duck, gadwall, and baldpate or widgeon. They are a diverse group, but all are able foragers. In water, they normally feed by "tipping up"—pivoting forward and downward with head, neck, and forebody under water, gleaning food from the bottom in the shallows. With legs placed farther forward than the divers, dabbling ducks can walk well and feed comfortably on land. These traits make them the most versatile feeders of North American waterfowl—with a diet ranging from aquatic insects, plants, and seeds to acorns and waste grain—and also more susceptible to management. It is considerably simpler to plant upland grains, flood natural or planted lowland feeding areas, or manipulate shallow water to establish food sources attractive to dabblers than it is to work with the rather finicky deeper-water aquatic plants divers prefer; it is also feasible over a much broader range of soils and waters.

From the production standpoint as well, most dabbling ducks offer greater management possibilities to more landowners and state agencies than do divers. For one thing, most dabblers select nesting sites in upland habitat—easier to establish and manage than the over-water nest habitat of the canvasback and redhead. For another, as a group, dabblers' breeding range covers more of the United States. The mallard, for example, now breeds in most states; the wood duck's primary breeding range is the eastern half of the United States but it is a year-round resident in the Southeast. If most of the management ideas that follow are slanted toward the dabbling ducks, these are the reasons. Divers could well benefit from habitat improvements, but their habits and range render the development and implementation of management techniques more difficult.

Because most waterfowl are migrants, generally breeding to the north, wintering to the south, and pausing en route in between, and

because many species are prime game birds, webfoot management
has two aspects: management of breeding and brood-rearing habitat, aimed at increased production; and habitat manipulation designed to attract birds during migration and winter, for increased hunting or viewing opportunities. In certain regions, and for some species, efforts aimed at one goal may achieve both.

In either case, financial assistance frequently is available to the landowner from federal and state sources, along with considerable literature and technical aid. Again, check with state conservation departments, county SCS and ASCS offices, and the U.S. Bureau of Sport Fisheries and Wildlife for possible cost-sharing programs covering preservation and development of waterfowl habitat.

IMPROVING NATURAL WETLANDS
FOR WATERFOWL PRODUCTION

Obviously you cannot beat wetlands within prime, natural waterfowl breeding range in the northern United States and Canada as sites to manage for increased waterfowl production. The wood duck, mallard, and giant Canada goose are exceptions to some extent, since their breeding range is more extensive in the States, and we will cover some production management techniques for these species later.

Geese and cornfields go together. Crop residues left after mechanical harvest of corn have altered wintering patterns for geese across much of North America.

But, if you are fortunate enough to own or have a voice in the control of natural wetlands in the northern Great Lakes States, New England, the Pacific Northwest, or the northern Great Plains—especially in the old pothole country of the Dakotas, western Minnesota, and the Sandhills of north-central Nebraska—you have a head start. Here the first rule is simple: Don't make any drastic changes without professional advice, If you have a good, natural wetland area that harbors breeding waterfowl, you hold an increasingly rare piece of America's wild heritage. Be careful not to destroy what you seek to improve. Because such areas are becoming more scarce and important, advice from state and federal agencies will be easy to come by. Further, for prime production areas, financial assistance in the form of leases and easements—to guarantee preservation—and cost-sharing for improvements (up to 80 percent in some counties) are often available. Again, state conservation departments and local or regional offices of the U. S. Fish and Wildlife Service are the best sources of information on management advice and cost-sharing information.

In implementing advice for improving natural production areas, there are some basic principles to keep in mind. For example, consider social factors among breeding and nesting birds. Most wild waterfowl will not tolerate crowding. Breeding males defend territories, keeping out other males of the same species, even when hens don't object to close neighbors. For this reason, a maximum shoreline, along or near which many species choose nest sites, is important. Construction of islands and open channels, both discussed later in more detail, can help in this regard.

Because waterfowl respond to the same factors of habitat variety—edge—that hold for all wildlife, best natural marshes for production are about 30 to 40 percent open water and 60 to 70 percent beds of emergent aquatic plants, exposed hummocks, and the like, well interspersed. Best marshes are at least an acre in size and hold water year-round. Water need not be deep; emergent cover plants require shallows, and the submerged aquatic vegetation that furnishes food directly, or in the form of the insects it harbors, cannot grow beyond depths penetrated by sunlight. To maintain nesting cover, the surrounding uplands should not be burned or mowed, and grazing should be halted or curtailed.

In addition, hunting on natural production areas must be carefully controlled. Since most female waterfowl return to nest where they grew up and learned to fly, heavy, early-season gunning can "burn out" locally produced ducks, leaving few or none to return the following spring.

Marshes choked with vegetation no longer furnish the balanced open water-plant cover mixture waterfowl find most desirable.

Areas of open water created in marshes overgrown with vegetation usually bring an upsurge in waterfowl use and production.

Natural wetlands may become too crowded with emergent plants—especially cattails—to provide the amount and interspersion of open water and cover needed for good brood-rearing and production habitat. When this occurs on small areas, removal by hand is most effective and safest. Simply pull out a portion of the offending plants.

On large areas with water-control structures, water levels may be lowered and openings created in the exposed vegetation by burning, mowing, or even plowing. If mowing is possible, cut at ground level in early summer, before seeds are set, and again when new growth is 1 to 2 feet high. Reflooding with 1 to 2 feet of water usually kills out any emergents surviving such treatment. If control structures don't exist, the same procedures can be followed in dry seasons that expose and dry out emergent plant beds sufficiently. As a last resort, weed-killing chemicals often work well, but remember to obtain expert advice and official permission before considering herbicides, many of which are prohibited or strictly regulated by state laws. Control techniques are best applied when undesirable vegetation is flowering, or just before, since the plants have not yet seeded and their food reserves for regrowth are low.

Openings in areas too packed with vegetation, or which dry in summer so that no open water remains, can be created by ditching with a dragline, or blasting. Both methods remove emergents, result in open water too deep to permit regrowth, and, in drier sites, can create open water by cutting below summer water tables. Dragline or bulldozer ditching and dredging have advantages over blasting. Blasted openings leave no exposed soil banks useful for loafing and nesting birds, and usually fill in more rapidly. Ditches to create permanent, open water in lowlands may qualify for federal cost-sharing. Ditches 4 to 5 feet deep and with 2,000 to 10,000 square feet of surface are best. Recommended spacing is one opening of such size for each 2 to 4 acres of marsh.

Blasting to create potholes or open water in lowlands has been employed for years. It became something of a fad in the 1960s, with the discovery that inexpensive ammonium nitrate, mixed with fuel oil, formed a blasting agent often cheaper, more readily available, and simpler to use than dynamite.

Thousands of potholes were blasted in private and public wetlands. And, sure enough, these small, open-water areas were used by ducks. But, as time permitted closer studies, it became apparent that the sighting of a duck or two on blasted potholes might not be all that important. For example, research at the Delta Waterfowl Research Station, in Manitoba, showed that blastouts (55 feet long, 26

feet wide, and 5 feet deep in this instance) were used by males and
pairs of several duck species for loafing and—if suitable food plants
volunteered—for some fall feeding. But there was little or no use for
nesting or brood-rearing, and no apparent effect on production.

So small blastouts are probably just frosting on the cake in
many cases. They are still useful in wetlands too thick with vegetation or too dry in summer to maintain waterfowl, where no other
means exists for creating water-holding openings. This is often true
for small areas where the work is too limited to be worthwhile for
dragline and heavy-equipment contractors. On large projects, drag-
lining actually is cheaper than blasting—even with ammonium nitrate—but where all else fails, explosives will do the job. Remember,
however, that their use is closely regulated by state and federal
laws. Consult your state conservation department for advice and
procedures, and hire a licensed blaster.

Management to increase waterfowl production on natural wetland areas is not always a matter of creating more openings. The ratio between water and cover may be askew in the opposite direction—too much open water. Where this is the case, manipulation of
water levels can help, if feasible. Construction of islands, and even
rafts, may be recommended, although islands are much more easily
built during creation of new, man-made wetlands. Water-level
changes, islands, and rafts are all discussed elsewhere in this chapter.

Predator control on waterfowl production areas is con-
troversial, although the controversy no longer need be over whether
or not control "works." Thorough, recent studies leave little doubt
that drastic removal of predators that take eggs, nesting hens, and
ducklings will increase waterfowl production. The problems that
arise are those of economics (effective predator control is very expensive) and aesthetics. Can we justify killing one group of animals
to increase another? The best course seems to be to concentrate on
providing adequate nesting and brood-rearing cover, including
man-made nest structures and islands, plus spot control of certain
predators where they exist in large numbers. The snapping turtle,
for example, is one of the most serious predators on ducklings
where its range overlaps waterfowl breeding grounds. There are
several ways to hold down snapper numbers. One of the best involves rigging 4-foot lengths of chalkline (or similar heavy cord)
with large fishhooks, baited with old chunks of meat or fish. Tie the
free end of the line to a sturdy stake or steel post driven into the
bottom in water 2 to 4 feet deep. A series of these staked lines, tended daily for a week or two each spring before waterfowl broods
hatch can do much to minimize losses. Don't overlook selling the

turtles, or using them yourself. Snapper meat is delicious and makes up more than a little bit of the turtle soup you eat in restaurants or buy in cans. In the southeastern states, check around for commercial turtle trappers who, in return for keeping their harvest, will remove more snappers in twenty-four hours than you probably dreamed existed.

Large bass, pickerel, and northern pike are rough on ducklings, too. Resist the temptation to stock these fish in new or established waters slated primarily for duck production.

CREATING NEW WETLANDS FOR WATERFOWL PRODUCTION

As with all wildlife improvements, advance planning can save many dollars, man-hours, and frustrations for anyone contemplating development of new breeding areas for ducks and geese. Obvious but sometimes ignored first steps are to be certain that the land in question lies within the breeding range of waterfowl, to determine which species are most likely to occur, and to learn all you can of their breeding, nesting, and brood-rearing habitat requirements.

Next, check out the potential site. Your county SCS workers are an excellent source of advice and detailed literature, and may often survey and lay out a plan for your land. They will point out certain site requirements. The soil must hold water, for example, so sites dominated by gravel, sand, or rock outcrops seldom are feasible. Commercial soil "sealants" are available, but they are costly. Clay soils make the best water retainers, and applying a clay lining that is a foot or more deep and well packed usually will seal a pond bottom, even over gravel. Peat and muck are poor choices since they furnish an unstable substrate for plant growth, and create a water chemistry that is unfavorable for most good waterfowl food and cover plants.

The potential water source should be sufficient to maintain suitable levels at all seasons (there should be no danger of drying up in summer while broods are still flightless), with a minimum risk of heavy flooding in wet spells. Water quality is especially important for production areas; prime vegetation for food and cover requires clear, nonacid water. Consequently, to minimize turbidity, as well as siltation, the site must be such that surrounding uplands are or can be protected from erosion. For the same reason, carp must be excluded and livestock use kept to a minimum.

Shoreline and upland areas around the site, in addition to being free from erosion problems, should be suitable for preserving or establishing, and managing, adequate nesting cover. Shorelines should slope gently to allow for growth of emergent aquatic plants, valuable as brood cover. Remember, too, that breeding wild birds do not tolerate crowding, so plan a maximum of shoreline that is as irregular as possible.

Studies in prime breeding range in the Prairie states tell us that an ideal design includes one or more good, large lakes, ponds, or marshes for use by adult birds and broods, with a series of smaller "satellite" potholes, level ditches, or impoundments close at hand for nesting pairs. In Maine, small marsh impoundments 5 to 10 acres in size were better duckling producers than either larger or smaller units. It boils down to variety and edge, plus specific needs of the birds involved; provided all requirements are met, a cluster of several small-to-medium-sized wetlands will usually beat one large unit.

As a general rule, the best new wetlands are created by damming natural lowlands with adequate, protected watersheds. Dredging or blasting can be employed, but are often more costly and the results less satisfactory. Dams on impounded sites must be constructed of impervious material, adequately shaped and packed. Keep trees and brush off the dam, and incorporate an emergency spillway to handle unusual water volumes. Here, again, SCS guideline literature is excellent.

The primary advantage of impoundments over dugouts is that impoundments can easily be equipped with water-control devices, which in turn permit water levels to be lowered or raised at will, and the impoundment drained completely, if need be. This is important for several reasons. New impoundments tend to be quite fertile in their early years; fish grow rapidly, vegetation thrives, and waterfowl use is heavy. But, as time goes by, productivity declines. This process is apparent to laymen pond owners and professional waterfowl managers alike, though often only through hindsight since it happens slowly.

Although there is much still to be learned, research tells us that the decline in fertility stems from chemical changes in flooded soils and, to a lesser extent, in the water itself. Some essential nutrients become "locked up," either in dead organic material—primarily plant parts, that decays slowly under water, especially in cooler, northern climes—or as a result of being altered to less available compounds. Certain minerals—particularly soluble iron—that retard plant growth tend to increase in submerged soils. Exposure of the bottom soil to sunlight and air can produce rapid decomposition of organic material, again freeing locked-up nutrients, and alter other chemical compounds to reduce toxic or growth-retarding levels. Disking can speed up these processes by helping break up and aerate drained soils, and expose them to sunlight. In most instances, the result is a renewal of fertility—often spectacular—leading to vigorous plant and animal growth on reflooding. In addition, the breakdown of organic bottom deposits drastically slows the rate at which these materials fill in shallow wetlands, eventually creating dry land. Thus drainage can set back succession as well as renew fertility.

Hence, this is one major value of control structures. In nature, drought periods accomplish the same end. The dry cycles that shrink prairie potholes periodically, to create duck shortages, actually serve to renew the fertility and prolong the life span of these highly productive natural wetlands.

Control of water levels also makes possible manipulation of food and cover plants for waterfowl. As we shall see later, drawdowns can encourage growth or permit seeding of annual food plants that attract birds in fall and winter. Partial drawdowns can be used to encourage growth of bulrush and cattail, where more brood cover and nesting cover for redheads and canvasback is desired. Repeated drawdowns during growing seasons often lead to establishment of willows and other brushy species. These, like cattails, can be desirable where brood cover is scarce and open water too predominant.

Where the relationship between open water and emergent cover is disproportionate in the opposite direction—with too few openings—control stuctures again can come to the rescue. Raising water levels sufficiently can kill out cattails, willows, and other emergents.

Waters that are too turbid or muddy for good plant growth because bottom soils contain much fine (colloidal) clay often can be cleared, at least partially, by a drawdown which speeds up decay, releasing carbonic acid which, in turn, helps precipitate out the clay particles.

Manipulating water levels won't cure all wetland problems, but it is effective in so many instances that new wetland construction projects should incorporate control structures wherever possible. Detailed advice as to the best structure (and there are several, from "dropboard" devices to "flap gates" and valves), as well as timing and likely effects of manipulation for your area and project, should be sought from SCS and conservation department specialists in your county and state. In general, if you seek rapid establishment of brush and other emergent cover, or are simply after good stands of fall-seeding annuals every year, a partial drawdown annually is most effective. If you seek to renew productivity of submerged aquatic food plants and fertility in general, more complete drainage at lower intervals (every four to five or more years, for example) is best.

If the area to be flooded in a new permanent impoundment contains brush and trees, and the primary goal is waterfowl, these woody plants should be cut and removed if possible. True, they make rather good emergent cover temporarily. But as they die and fall, their decay creates large amounts of tannic acid, resulting in dark tea- or coffee-stained water, which many of the most valuable aquatic food plants will not tolerate. Where tree and brush removal is not feasible and tannic acid staining occurs, application of agricultural lime can help.

Water-control structures are important in managing manmade wetlands for waterfowl. Dropboards placed in this slotted concrete structure will impound water to flood the marsh in the background to the desired level.

Uneven terrain in a newly flooded impoundment will furnish many desirable loafing and nesting sites for waterfowl.

To increase edge, and offer nesting and loafing sites secure from such nonswimming predators as skunks, it is often desirable to plan for island areas in new impoundments. In uneven terrain, flooding may leave exposed dry hummocks. These are desirable, so don't bulldoze out such high spots. In building islands, usually the first question is how big they should be. The answer is not easy because there are many variables. In general, small circular islands—10 feet or less in diameter—seem best for nesting geese. Geese are big and tough enough to fight off most predators, and a small island is easier to defend. For ground-nesting ducks, bigger islands, 50 feet or more in diameter, are often recommended, and an X-shape may increase nesting density. For both ducks and geese, the exposed land area seems best when about 2 to 4 feet above high-water level.

Erosion is the island's worst enemy. More than one owner's or manager's smile has faded as the carefully spaced islands on his new impoundment dissolved or washed away. Three things help ensure permanency. First, locate islands in the lee of headlands or beds of emergent vegetation that reduce wave action. Second, pro-

tect island shores by *riprapping*—placing rocks, concrete chunks, or
logs at the waterline. Third, tie down the soil with perennial vegetation, especially grasses, which provides nesting cover as well. The
easiest method is mulching the bare soil heavily with perennial
grass, such as orchard-grass, cut when seedheads are ripe. The
stems provide temporary protection, and seeding occurs naturally.
To establish switchgrass or other good but slow-growing perennial
nesting cover, plant rooted pieces or "clones"; don't wait for a seeding to take hold.

This sounds like a lot of trouble but, if built and protected
properly, good island nesting areas are well worth the effort—and it
is far easier to create them before flooding. Too many times, islands
are ignored in new wetland construction, often because thoughts
are directed toward plantings. As we will see later, aquatic plantings receive more attention than they deserve.

Muskrats pose a threat to earthen dikes and dams, both new
and old. Muskrats don't always build houses of vegetation in shallow waters. Many—the so-called "bank rats"—set up housekeeping

*Holding water through all seasons for several years killed the trees in this
impoundment. Fallen trunks furnish loafing sites and some cover, but tannic acid from decaying wood will reduce chances for many desirable
aquatic plants to take hold. It would have been better to remove all or
most trees before flooding.*

in burrows with entrances tunneled below waterline along shores. Such burrows can undermine and weaken or eventually extend all the way through a dam or dike, causing leakage or complete loss of impounded water. Control of muskrat populations thus is essential. Precautions can be taken when impoundments are constructed, or, in some cases, these safeguards can be used to fortify threatened older dikes and dams. These measures include laying heavy-gauge, galvanized, mesh fur-farm wire or chicken wire along the face of the dam, from the base, or well below water level, to a foot or more above high-water mark—or riprapping with stone or concrete blocks placed along the same expanse, which has the added advantage of minimizing or eliminating erosion. Where extreme problems occur or can be anticipated, a deep, narrow trench, excavated by a ditching or trenching machine (which can be rented), can be cut along the midline of the dam and filled with concrete as a permanent barrier. It must extend well below the waterline to be effective.

Federal and state financial aid often is available for new impoundments for waterfowl production, especially in prime natural breeding range. Federal guidelines to be met in order to qualify for cost-sharing usually require a minimum of 1 surface-acre of water in a new impoundment with more then half the shoreline fenced to exclude livestock.

MANAGEMENT FOR WOOD-DUCK PRODUCTION

For many who would like to lend a helping hand to produce more wild waterfowl, but who don't live in the major breeding-ground areas of the North, the wood duck provides a fine opportunity. Unlike most ducks, woodies breed predominantly in the United States, throughout nearly all states east of the Great Plains, and along the Pacific Coast south to central California. The drake is perhaps the most beautiful of North American waterfowl. Once considered nearly extinct, but now a common species, the wood duck's range and ability to adjust to civilization and to man-made waters and nestboxes make him an ideal management target. Tolerating people, he remains wild and cautious without becoming a free-loading nuisance as mallards will.

Most management efforts, public as well as private, have centered on providing artificial nesting sites. Wood ducks nest in tree cavities, like woodpeckers. The destruction of lowland forests, combined with modern forestry practices which urge removal of old, hollow trees to make room for more commercial timber, greatly reduced natural nest sites for the woody. Years ago, biologists with the Illinois Natural History Survey explored the use of man-made structures, simulating hollow trees, to increase wood-duck production. The technique worked; other states, led by Massachusetts, picked up the idea, and today nestboxes are a standard management device in woody range.

Early nestboxes were made of wood, carefully covered with bark and placed in sheltered spots in deep woods. They looked great but had a major drawback; they were so well camouflaged that wood ducks seldom found them. In addition, wooden boxes had a relatively short life span and, especially when located in trees, were easily entered by predators. So metal structures, durable and a thwart to climbing predators, were tested—often placed in the open on posts over water, with no attempt to make them look "natural." They worked well.

From these experiments came the present array of wood-duck nestbox styles. Before we discuss some of them in detail, remember the instructions that apply whenever building and erecting artificial nest structures for wildlife. Boxes should be simple to build, erect, and maintain, and durable and light enough to handle easily. If located over water, they must be placed above the high-water mark. Construction amd mounting should be such that wind or waves don't easily shake or move the structure. Adequate nest material must be added and boxes checked and maintained annually. Finally, and most important, every effort must be made to make structures predator-proof, lest they be deathtraps.

Through time and numerous experiments, three basic wood-duck nestbox styles have gained greatest popularity: the wooden box with minimum interior measurement of 9 x 10 x 20 inches deep; a vertical galvanized metal structure, 24 inches tall and 12 inches in diameter with a 3 x 4-inch elliptical entrance; and a similar metal box mounted horizontally, with the entrance at one end. Construction details and plans for making one or more of these styles can be obtained from most state conservation departments, or by writing the Government Printing Office, Washington, D.C., and requesting U.S. Dept. of Interior, Bureau of Sport Fisheries and Wildlife, Wildlife Leaflet #458, "Improved Nest Structures for Wood Ducks." Acceptable boxes are available from some private commercial sources, and are usually advertised in outdoor publications.

In my opinion, the horizontal metal box is most effective for over-water locations. It is easier to build than the vertical counterpart and less prone to starling competition. Starlings also nest in

Vertical metal nestbox for wood ducks. Note projecting ends of hardware-cloth ladder, placed inside entrance to facilitate escape of ducklings. Cone-shaped top helps guard against predators climbing down from above, but this box is wired close to the tree trunk and is vulnerable to raccoons.

darkened cavities, and often pre-empt wood duck boxes. The larger opening in the horizontal box discourages them because of its size or the greater light it admits. Use a 2-foot length of 12-inch diameter furnace pipe, and close one end completely with wood (durable cedar or cypress is best). Close the other end partially, leaving an opening 4 inches high and 11 inches wide at the top as an entrance.

As you should do with all structures, attach a strip of hardware
cloth about 4 inches wide on the inside of the box, from the entrance edge to the floor, as an escape "ladder" for the ducklings.
Add about 3 inches of sawdust and wood shavings as nest material.
Horizontal boxes of the same dimensions can be constructed of
roofing paper, fastened around a 24 x 12-inch tube of fur-farm wire.

When erecting woody boxes of any style, locate them conspicuously, so they can be found. If on posts over water, boxes
should be 4 to 5 feet above expected high-water lines; in trees, 30 to
45 feet above ground seems best. Where a considerable amount of
suitable water is available, place boxes in groups of 5 to 10, spaced
within each group 50 to 100 feet apart. Steel or wooden posts or
metal pipe may be used for mounting.

Placing boxes over water excludes nonswimming predators,
but doesn't bother such nest-robbers as raccoons and blacksnakes.
Several types of predator guards have been tested, and designs usually are included with literature on box construction available from
the sources cited. Aluminum sheets have been fastened sandwichlike on both sides of the mounting post, 1-inch waterpipe has
been used as a post, and 3-to-4-foot lengths of aluminum downspouting have been placed around posts, but—in some areas—eventually all these obstacles have been circumvented by persistent raccoons. Where nestboxes are new to an area, and raccoons not yet
knowledgeable of their contents, these devices may be effective for
years—even unprotected boxes may not be raided. But, sooner or
later, one enterprising 'coon will learn what's up, and from then on
it's trouble.

To date, the only foolproof (or raccoonproof) guard for overwater boxes is the old "rat guard"—so named for its long use on
mooring lines to keep rats from entering ships at dock. As used for
nestboxes, this guard is an inverted metal cone, 36 inches in diameter at the bottom and fitted snugly to the mounting post at the top.
Raccoons climbing the post can't reach over or around the cone;
snakes can't slither through if no gaps are left at the top.

Boxes mounted in trees are harder to protect. They should be
vertical in style, with a cone-shaped top to prevent squirrels and
'coons from entering from above, and mounted away from the trunk
on a metal bracket. The government publication mentioned details
these features.

Other wildlife—besides the undesirable starling—may nest in
woody boxes. In the North, these can include such ducks as the
goldeneye and hooded merganser. Screech owls, great-crested fly-

catchers, and tree swallows have all been recorded; their use should be welcomed—all are good additions to any wildlife area.

Nestboxes alone won't guarantee healthy wood-duck populations. Food and cover, especially for broods of youngsters, must be adequate. Woodies need a lot of fairly heavy cover emerging above water, especially for brood production. Wetlands with about 25 percent quiet, open water, and 75 percent emergent plants or flooded shrubs—well interspersed—are ideal. Desirable plants include bulrush, spatterdock, cattail, buttonbrush, smartweeds, arrowhead, and flooded tall grasses, sedge, and rushes. Where such cover is unavailable, successful production has been obtained on small, quiet ponds with shorelines overhung by dogwood and shrub willows. Emergent vegetation provides food—in the form of insects falling to the water from leaves—as well as shelter. Deep, open water exposed to strong wave action is seldom used by woodies.

Brood loafing sites—muskrat houses, logs, small islands—are important. We have discussed island construction, and will cover other loafing assists later. Beaver ponds, small, shallow lakes and ponds, wooded streams and rivers and backwaters are all good wood-duck habitat, if adequate emergent or shore cover exists or can be established.

SOME ARTIFICIAL AIDS TO WATERFOWL PRODUCTION

Goldeneyes and hooded mergansers will use wood-duck boxes for nesting, as mentioned. Some other waterfowl species will use man-made nesting structures as well. (Remember, however, that while protected nest sites can enhance nesting success, successful hatches are but the first step. Proper habitat for adults as well as broods must also be available.)

Mallards have utilized man-made nests in a number of areas. (No one is yet certain why some flocks take readily to such devices while others do not. Acceptance probably relates to an imprinting or learning process.) There are two basic types of mallard structures—open baskets and enclosed boxes or cylinders. The open basket, elevated over water, seems to attract use more quickly, but is subject to predation where crows are common. This nest consists of a cone of ¼- or ½-inch-mesh galvanized hardware cloth, 8 to 10 inches deep and 24 to 26 inches in diameter, wired into a frame of ¼-inch steel rods welded to a 1-inch pipe. The pipe is slipped into a larger support pipe driven into the marsh or pond bottom, so that the base of the cone is 4 to 5 feet above highest water levels. Nests of this general type have been tested successfully in Iowa, the Dakotas, and other Prairie and Plains states, again where crows are uncommon in nesting seasons. (A descriptive folder entitled "New Homes for Prairie Ducks," among other references at the end of this chapter, will give additional information.)

Both baskets and enclosed boxes should be guarded from climbing predators, like wood-duck boxes. Nest material—grasses, hay, or soft straw, preferably with a base of wood shavings—must be added and, in the open basket, wired in place. All styles receive best use if mounted over open water, 1 to 3 feet in depth, or among scattered emergent vegetation. Boxes over thick weedbeds or dry land get less use. Make sure the mounting post is solid and driven deep into bottom soils, and avoid sites where windblown masses of ice are prevalent.

Four-unit "mallard motel." Two wire and roofing-paper nestboxes are wired atop the 2x4 crossarms; two crates below are equipped with wire and paper entrance funnels (to help protect nests from crow predation) and landing platforms. Tight-fitting metal "rat guard" cone protects nests from climbing predators.

Nesting mallard hen keeps a wary eye on photographer from a wire and roofing-paper nestbox. Wooden insert helps contain nesting material.

Enclosed structures often receive less immediate use than baskets, but they do hide eggs from crows and other avian egg-eaters. Crows learn fast and may even begin to raid darkened boxes, in which case extended or mazelike entrance tunnels may be necessary. Rectangular structures with internal measurements of 18 to 30 inches long and 10 to 14 inches wide and high, either open at both ends or with one opening 6 to 8 inches wide by 10 to 12 inches high, can be made of nearly any material. Wood, galvanized metal, or wire wrapped with reeds, roofing paper, or the like will all suffice.

One good, durable, and fairly simple box is based on a 2-foot length of 12-inch diameter furnace pipe, the same as that used for metal wood-duck boxes, mounted horizontally. For mallards, close one end a third of the way to all the way with wood, and leave the other end open. Fasten a wooden partition, 4 inches high, inside the box, midway across the bottom, and place nest material between the partition and the rear of the structure. Punch three or four drain holes in the bottom.

Another useful style is formed by bending a 30x48-inch piece of heavy-gauge fur-farm wire into a rectangular framework, 12x12x36 inches long. Staple a 4-inch wooden nest partition midway to the inside bottom. Wrap the wire frame with roofing paper, sisalcraft, or heavier, pebbled material, to cover sides, top, bottom, and one end, and fasten with wire. The open end forms the nest entrance. Lightweight paper will wear out in time, but the box is easily rewrapped.

Use of enclosed boxes by mallards often can be hastened or increased by fastening an 8x10-inch wooden "landing platform" or perch to protrude from the base of the entrance.

Mallards, at least those of game-farm origin, tolerate closely spaced nest sites. Consequently, where large numbers of stocked birds occur, two to four boxes are sometimes placed on a single mounting post. A simple "motel" mount uses two 30-inch 2x4s, nailed opposite one another about 24 inches from the top of a wooden post. Boxes are then nailed or wired on top of this double crossarm, one on each side of the post. Two more boxes may be added, wired one atop each of the first pair.

Wire and roofing-paper basket is one of several workable styles of nest structures for Canada geese. Marsh hay nest material is being wired in at basket corners to prevent loss in high winds.

Canada geese frequently use man-made nest structures and sites. Geese like somewhat elevated nest locations in open areas, which they can defend more easily—especially when over water— and from which they can keep a close eye on their surroundings. Small islands constructed for geese have been described. Beyond this, the imagination of waterfowl managers has run wild, producing dozens of devices—of wood, straw bales, rubber tires, washtubs, wire, etc. Almost every state conservation department has its own favorite design, specifications for which usually are available on request. The book *Homegrown Honkers* (see references at the end of this chapter) also contains ideas for nest structures.

Some of the more effective and relatively simple designs include a galvanized metal washtub, filled with hay or grass and firmly fastened between four posts—or a platform made from 1x8s (spaced to allow drainage and ventilation) nailed to two 2x4s, in turn nailed to four guyed posts. A durable but harder-to-construct structure is a wire basket, with the rim made from a 10-foot length of steel reinforcing rod bent to form a 30-inch square. One-inch-mesh wire is fastened to the rim with hog-rings or wire, to form a basket 9 inches deep, and the whole is mounted 18 inches over water between four steel posts.

Certain general rules apply to all styles of nest structures for geese. Predator guards are not as vital as for ducks, but are a big help. Nests should be over water, deep enough so predators can't walk to them. Avoid areas where wind, wave, and ice action are severe; these big structures are vulnerable to damage. Geese are territorial. The gander defends the nest site and a surrounding area from other geese, so structures must be well spaced for maximum use. Spacing of at least 100 yards usually is necessary, although this distance sometimes can be reduced after a flock has used structures for several years. A small island, raft, rockpile, or anchored log, within 20 to 30 yards of the nest, helps reduce the need for spacing. Such "gander stands" serve as loafing sites for the belligerent males; located near the nest, they apparently serve to minimize territorial aspirations.

Anchored logs are valuable as loafing sites, where such are scarce naturally, on any waterfowl production area. They afford protection from many predators and are used heavily for resting and sleeping by adults and broods.

Small piles of rocks, islands, or exposed natural elevated spots deliberately left during impoundment construction, all pay their way as loafing areas. Wooden rafts, made of scrap lumber, or with a

frame of 4x4s or 2x4s to which 1-inch boards are nailed, can increase use of open-water ponds or lakes lacking natural resting
sites. Anchor rafts securely with chain or heavy wire, and avoid
wind- and wave-swept areas. Blocks of styrofoam may be added to
increase buoyancy. Specialists with time to putter have created effective "floating islands" for nesting and loafing waterfowl by con-
structing boxlike rafts that hold soil and can be planted with
grasses, rushes, and other suitable growth.

INTRODUCING AQUATIC PLANTS

Almost inevitably, the first thought of most individuals or
groups who have constructed a new waterfowl impoundment or
taken an interest in an established wetland area is: "What can we
plant to produce or attract more birds?" Their thought is that planting wild rice, duck potato, sago pondweed, and other "famous"
food plants, acclaimed in outdoor magazine stories and otherwise
associated with vast hordes of waterfowl, will solve all problems.

Unfortunately, this most popular management scheme is seldom productive. (I'm referring to planting aquatic perennials, not to
seeding annuals—a practice, discussed later, that can be quite successful.)

The basic problem is that in nearly all regions water plants appear *(volunteer)* and become established very quickly where conditions are suitable, even in new impoundments, miles from the nearest wetlands. Also, as we shall see, most of the best plants for
waterfowl are quite fussy about the habitat in which they grow and
prosper. These two elements—rapid volunteering and specific requirements—dictate that the most that planting aquatics can achieve
is a speeding up of the natural process of growth in suitable new
waters. In old, established wetlands, planting perennial aquatics
usually is hopeless; species that don't occur are absent because the
area does not meet their needs. Every planting attempt possible
won't make them grow as long as those needs are not fulfilled.

Nevertheless, because perennial plantings can hasten vegetation establishment in new waters and—on rare occasions—improve
older or natural areas, and because many people will insist on trying anyway, we shall discuss this subject briefly. An essential first
step is to learn to identify at least the common aquatics, using reference books available at most libraries, or sources suggested by state
agricultural colleges or conservation departments. Identification is
important for three reasons: (1) you can avoid introducing pest

plants, such as water hyacinth, alligator-weed, water lettuce and others that can plague you ever after; (2) you can recognize the most useful species for waterfowl; and (3) you can learn the site or habitat factors desirable plants require.

Once you've learned to tell "good" from "bad," you have two alternatives. To buy, transplant, or seed all desirable species, hit or miss—or to take time to analyze basic factors in the target wetlands that will determine which plants have the best chance, and where and how they should be planted. With either approach, start small. Try a few test plantings before expending lots of time and money on what may be wasted effort.

Clearly, the careful-analysis approach is best if you are really serious. Among the site factors important to aquatics are water turbidity and color. Is the water clear or muddy—or stained brown, indicating acid conditions? What is its chemistry—acid or alkaline, hard or soft, brackish or fresh? Establish its stability—whether levels fluctuate greatly. Also research the bottom conditions. Is the bottom hard or soft, with sand, gravel, silt, or clay? Some features can be determined simply by observation. Others require chemical tests, which you can attempt yourself with a testing kit or—at relatively little cost—have done by local or state water-quality testing agencies.

In general, waters that are turbid, acid, organic-stained, low in calcium, or subject to major fluctuations in level are least productive of desirable perennial plants. Unfortunately, many of these conditions prevail in man-made impoundments. It may be possible to alter some of these factors by liming or, where control is possible, by temporarily drawing down water levels. Where improvements are not feasible, some plants—not of the greatest value, but still useful—may prove tolerant. In acid-stained waters, for example, watershield and naiads serve as good food plants and are fairly easily established. In like fashion, spatterdock, cattails, needlerush, and certain other emergents—often considered undesirable in prime, productive wetlands where "better" plants will thrive—can be a blessing on lower-quality areas, where they may create the only emergent cover.

On the whole, stable impoundments are best managed for submerged aquatics and true emergent plants, such as the bulrushes, whereas fluctuating waters should be managed for annual food plants (millets and the like) and woody emergent cover (buttonbush and willows). Where water levels can be controlled or changed, an impoundment that has proved unproductive under one of these two conditions may be productive if managed in the alternative fashion.

Let's take a quick look at some key groups of aquatics, notably those which enrich waterfowl production areas. Submerged plants, characterized by having vegetative parts entirely underwater, serve as primary food sources for diving ducks and as an important diet item for many dabblers. The pondweeds (*Potamogeton* species) are among the best, and sago pondweed is a favorite. Where waters meet their rather demanding requirements, submergents can be transplanted by pulling or digging in spring, balling the roots in mud to keep them moist, and embedding or simply dropping them into the new site, with small clusters of plants weighted with fence staples or similar sinkers. Choose a site with a soft, muddy bottom, the same depth as that from which the plants were removed.

Duckweed or "duckmeat"—tiny, floating plants often covering water surfaces in favorable areas—are useful food, especially for ducklings. They need calm, sheltered water and are easy to move— simply scoop up a quantity in a bucket of water.

Emergent plants are those which are rooted under water but have vegetative parts protruding well above the surface, and they are highly important as brood cover for all species and as nest sites for some ducks. Some provide food; all tend to attract insects, which are important in the diet of ducklings. The bulrushes are among the best emergents, since most supply seed as well as cover. Alkali bulrush is important in salt wetlands of the Southwest, but special management is required to establish a seedling bed, so get local advice. Wild rice, another widely acclaimed food and cover emergent, requires fresh, not stagnant, shallow water in a sunny location and with a soft mud bottom. Since fertile seeds sink and work their way into the bottom, they can be broadcast on the water surface, and require no covering. Wild rice is difficult to establish. It suffers from various insect pests and diseases, and a bed successfully grown one year may disappear the next.

Less desirable emergents, such as cattails, may survive conditions where nothing else will grow, and are far better than no cover at all.

Vegetation at shoreline also is valuable for food and cover. Wild millet, rice cutgrass, sedges, smartweed, and some panic grasses are among the best. As with emergents, they are established by transplanting clumps, for small projects, or seeding with seed gathered from established stands.

If no source of local wild material for transplanting is available, a number of aquatics can be purchased from commercial nursery specialists in Wisconsin and other states. Advertisements appear in most outdoor magazines. Remember to start modestly; don't spend a lot of money unless and until pilot tests show encouraging signs. Small new plantings may have to be fenced or screened for protection from muskrats and wood ducks until a good stand is established.

Techniques for planting to attract migrant and wintering waterfowl and for managing uplands are discussed later.

ATTRACTING WATERFOWL IN FALL AND WINTER

Geographic location, water quality, and other factors limit opportunities for most of us to create breeding areas for large numbers of waterfowl. But there is always the likelihood of attracting at least some species during fall migration and on wintering grounds. In fall and winter, nesting cover, loafing sites, small potholes for breeding pairs, and emergent brood cover, among other factors, are unnecessary or much less important. Food, in quantity and readily accessible, and open water for safe resting become critical. And wetlands that can never meet breeding-habitat requirements may serve beautifully, under management, to draw and hold birds for viewing and hunting.

When considering specific techniques, keep in mind that waterfowl—as migratory wildlife—are under jurisdiction of the federal government. The Bureau of Sport Fisheries and Wildlife (BSFW) of the U.S. Department of Interior sets the regulations under which waterfowl may be hunted, propagated, or held in captivity. Rules having special application in management include the so-called "baiting" regulations. These prohibit "artificial" feeding to attract ducks and geese for hunting—deliberately scattering grain or other food, or knocking down standing grain crops (as distinguished from normal agricultural harvest procedures), for example. Other regulations prohibit use of captive birds as live decoys to attract wild birds. Where there is use of either baiting or live decoys, hunting is forbidden not just on the specific site, but on surrounding areas over which birds may pass on their way to and from bait or live decoys. Take care that your plans won't run afoul of these regulations. If any doubt exists, contact the nearest local, state, or regional BSFW office for clarification.

Many privately owned, man-made waters in the U.S. are designed primarily as fish ponds, stock-watering sites, or all-purpose farm ponds. In most cases their design and use is such that they offer little to attract waterfowl. Good fishing ponds, for example, are steep-sided and deep. Margins are kept clean of overhanging growth to permit easy access, and aquatic plants are discouraged. Improvements for waterfowl use can be made, although often with some detriment to fishing. Grading one shoreline to a 5:1 or 6:1 slope will encourage emergent plants at shoreline and permit seeding attractive grasses. Where control is possible, water levels can be lowered in summer to expose shallow areas. As explained later, annual plants, such as smartweed and millet, often volunteer (or can be seeded) on exposed bottom soils. Raising water back after these plants set seed, in fall, provides a prime feeding site. Such partial drawdowns, timed properly, can be helpful to fishing as well where stunted panfish are a problem. They force small fry out of protected shallows into deep water where bass can thin them out.

Management of adjacent uplands to provide food—especially for grazing geese—and provision of loafing rafts and logs help make fish and stock ponds more attractive to waterfowl. Fencing to exclude cattle from all but one end of a stock pond makes possible better shore and upland management for ducks and geese.

Natural wetlands along migration routes or in wintering areas often can be improved. Brackish-water coastal marshes are an example. Their physical and chemical make-up render them more productive and more easily managed than many freshwater areas for such highly ranked perennial food plants as widgeongrass, sago pondweed, and saltmarsh bulrush. In addition, tidal marshes and brackish coastal flats are home for numerous wet-soil grasses—saltgrass, cordgrasses, and the like—whose seeds, stems, sprouts, or roots are prime duck and goose foods. Management of brackish tidal areas may entail controlled burning or grazing, or installation of flap-gate structures to manipulate water levels by utilizing tidal influx and outgo. For details on brackish-water management, consult state or federal conservation agencies or SCS offices, or visit one of the numerous state or federal waterfowl refuges in coastal areas.

Established natural or man-made freshwater areas are often managed to attract waterfowl by encouraging stands of such plants as millet and smartweed, whose seeds are prime foods. These annuals germinate and begin growth on exposed bottom soils. They will tolerate "wet feet" and some flooding, though not prolonged submergence, after they have begun to grow, and are most attractive to migrating and wintering ducks if flooded shallowly after their seeds mature.

The cycle of summer drought and low waters followed by fall rains and flooding, normal to many river backwaters, shallow lakes, and marshes, creates ideal conditions for natural growth of wild millet ("barnyardgrass") and smartweeds. Many famous gathering spots for migrant and wintering waterfowl, such as the Mississippi River bottoms in Illinois, owe their attractiveness primarily to these conditions.

Where water-control structures exist or can be installed, these natural "drawdowns" can be duplicated without depending on nature's whims. When effecting drawdowns, remember that the resulting annual growth must be flooded shallowly in fall for best results. You can't always count on rains in time to furnish the water, so unless you are prepared to gamble, make sure a dependable water supply will be available for reflooding.

The best time for freshwater drawdowns varies on the region and site, and may require experimentation. As a general rule, the later the better; waiting to remove water until early July, or even early August, often floods out undesirable competing plants, and still leaves time for rapid-growing millet and smartweed. Late drawdowns in breeding areas also give broods time to reach flight age before the water is pulled out from under them.

Seeding is frequently unnecessary. More often than not, smartweed and wild millet seeds already are present and need only the encouragement of a well-timed drawdown to germinate. You can encourage smartweed growth in many instances by burning and then lightly disking (or by disking alone) old vegetation, but this requires earlier-than-usual drainage. Where adequate natural stands don't develop, seeds of millet and smartweed usually can be gathered in the wild and broadcast on exposed mudflats, at the water's edge, or in shallow water less than an inch deep. These seeds are hard to find commercially, although with enough inquiries you may turn up a source. Japanese millet, a commercially grown variety, works well when seeded this way, and is obtainable from most seed dealers.

Where you can't control water levels, it is sometimes possible to create millet stands by broadcasting seed on bottoms or shorelines exposed during natural dry periods.

Creating openings in vegetation-choked wetlands, as described earlier, can be as effective in attracting migrant and wintering waterfowl as it is in encouraging breeding-season use. Waterfowl respond to edge in all seasons.

New wetland areas can be designed specifically to attract waterfowl during migration or in winter. Two types have proved especially effective for puddle ducks, primarily mallards—the so-called "shallow-field" and "green-tree" impoundments. Both hinge upon furnishing an abundance of shallowly flooded food. Both may be eligible for cost-sharing by state conservation departments or ASCS and SCS offices, and construction designs and details usually are available from the same agencies.

The principle of the shallow field rests on fall flooding of an annual grain crop planted earlier in the year. The site should be as flat as possible, and the soil type and texture capable of cultivation and growing a good grain crop, yet able to hold water. A water-control structure, through which the field can be drained thoroughly enough to permit cultivation, is essential.

Most sites selected are flat, lowland cropfields with heavy soils. A low, permanent dike (sufficient to retain a foot or so of water) is constructed around the perimeter with a bulldozer or other earth moving equipment. The control structure is located in the dike at the lowest point in the field. Grading may be necessary to ensure that all parts of the field will be drained when the structure is open.

A dependable source of water for fall flooding is important. This may be a permanent pond or impoundment, a stream, a tidewater creek, or a well. (Check to be sure state and local laws permit diversion of natural waters.) Water may be pumped from these sources or better still, for reasons of economy, fed by gravity into the field. The water source should be close at hand and plentiful; it takes a great deal of water to saturate and flood a dry field, even if for only a few inches. If you gamble on fall rains and run-off as a source, you risk disappointment.

Resident mallards move into shallowly flooded millet in a wet-field impoundment well before the first flights of migrants arrive.

Canada geese and a variety of puddle ducks work over a shallowly flooded millet field.

Even an acre or two, properly located, planted, and flooded, can pull in good numbers of birds. In the long haul, size may depend more on available water for flooding than anything else. Several smaller units of 2 to 4 acres each, for example, near or adjacent to one another, often are better than one big field. They can be flooded in rotation to keep fresh food available over a long period. One or more in the series can be maintained in water for several years, permitting growth of aquatic plants to attract waterfowl not drawn to flooded grain, or for development as a breeding and production area. If large enough and located first in the series, and on higher ground, the permanent unit can also serve as the source for flooding lower fields by gravity flow.

Plant shallow fields in spring or summer, depending on the region and the maturity date of the crop. To avoid loss to blackbirds, it is usually best to plant so that the crop matures as late as possible without risking loss to frost.

A number of grains will do the job, but millets are used most often since they mature rapidly and tolerate fairly heavy soils. Browntop millet matures in about sixty days and produces heavy yields. Prepare the field for browntop by plowing and disking, and either plant the seed with a grain drill, ½ to 1 inch deep, or broadcast it and drag to cover the seed. Use 20 pounds to the acre, and fertilize well (500 pounds of 5–10–10 fertilizer or the equivalent per acre frequently is recommended). Plant in late June in northern states, early July in the South—even August in the deep South.

Browntop requires dry soil; it won't tolerate standing in water while growing. Japanese millet, also a fine duck food, will take wet soil and even shallow flooding during growing season. It requires sixty to a hundred days to mature, and its seeds deteriorate a bit faster underwater than browntop. Planting details and time are as for browntop. Pearl ("cattail") millet sometimes is used; it is good in dry years or on very dry sites, but tends to become too leafy and tall on moist soils. Field corn, combine grain sorghums, and buckwheat are among other crops for shallow fields. Corn generally takes longer to mature than most grains, and the field must be well drained and fertile. If your intention is hunting, under federal regulations you cannot knock down corn—or any of these crops—to make them more accessible. But you don't need to; ducks will reach the corn ears. You can leave unplanted strips to create some open water, if you wish. Buckwheat matures very quickly, but yields less than millets or corn and the seed rots rapidly when flooded, as do peas and beans. Use buckwheat as a last resort if planting is delayed too late for other crops.

Although it is late winter, and most of the millet has long before been eaten by early arrivals, this shallow wet-field impoundment still harbors many mallards.

In fall, when the grain is mature and the seed set and hard, flood the field just before or as waterfowl arrive. One to 12 inches of water is ideal. Exceeding 14 to 15 inches means that dabblers can't feed on grain on the bottom. If the field is not level, flood gradually so birds can work the low spots first before the water gets too deep. If blackbirds become a nuisance, you can alleviate the problem by earlier flooding. Drain for replanting in spring—as late as possible to allow waterfowl use.

Using a similar principle, rice fields, or any lowland cropfield that can be flooded without harm, can be flooded after normal harvesting, making waste grain available to waterfowl.

The green tree "reservoir"—the second popular impoundment constructed to attract waterfowl—requires a good stand of oaks and/or other trees producing crops of nuts or fruit attractive to ducks. Oaks with small acorns, such as pin and willow oaks, are best. Blue beech and gums work well also. As with the shallow field, a low dike, to hold 1 to 12 inches of water, a control structure, and an adequate water source are needed. Flood in October, and drain in February or March before tree growth begins. Numerous studies show that winter flooding actually improves growth of commercial hardwoods, so the trees will prosper as long as water is removed on time.

Mallards, black ducks, and wood ducks are attracted to green-tree floodings, often in great numbers. The fabulous mallard hunting of the Stuttgart, Arkansas, region is based in large part on flooded pin-oak bottomlands. Further inducements can be added by cultivating and seeding clearings in the woodland to millet, and by some selective cutting to release the most productive tree species.

MANAGING UPLANDS FOR WATERFOWL

We have mentioned the need for retention or establishment of well-vegetated upland areas around breeding-ground marshes and potholes. Management of surrounding land to provide cover for ground-nesting birds is vital, which means there can be no burning or mowing and little or no grazing except if needed to maintain suitable grass. Recent experience indicates that heavy stands of native prairie bunchgrasses may be among the most effective cover for upland-nesting species.

For geese, in particular, uplands on production areas are important beyond just nesting needs. Young geese obtain most of their food by grazing on fresh greens, near water. Maintaining tender shoots of grasses and herbs requires periodic mowing, which ob-

Crop residues remaining after harvest are a staple winter food for Canada geese and other waterfowl.

viously can be detrimental to duck nesting. So the safest practice where both geese and ground-nesting ducks occur is to establish one or more areas bordering the wetland specifically for goose "pasture," while leaving the remaining uplands for nesting. Perennial grasses and clover work well for pasture, as do spring wheat, oats or annual rye. If perennial pastures are kept clipped short, nesting use and chances of nest destruction during mowing should be minimal.

Uplands also can be managed to attract dabbling ducks and geese in migration and on wintering areas. Crop residues after harvesting, particularly cornfields, serve as a major food source for

Uplands in tall and intermediate grasses furnish nesting sites for many dabbling ducks.

144 Canada geese and mallards, as well as for blue and snow geese, pintails, and others. Again, waterfowl may not be hunted over crops knocked down or otherwise manipulated (except by flooding), contrary to standard farming practices. But you can leave untouched, standing rows of corn, which geese and ducks will often use after exhausting waste grain supplies in harvested fields. Geese will reach up to 36 inches above the ground to feed on ears of corn on the stalk.

Geese also are very fond of green vegetation in winter. Fair-sized open fields, or strips in or along harvested or standing corn, planted to annual rye or winter wheat, work very well in goose concentration areas. So do such perennial grasses as orchardgrass, redtop, fescue, timothy, and perennial rye, as well as red or ladino clover, provided they are clipped short in fall to stimulate tender new growth and create the short, sodlike condition geese prefer. For best results, lime and fertilize these feeding fields just as you would a cash crop.

Use by Canada geese of ponds and lakes for resting and loafing can be improved if at least one shoreline and adjacent upland area is seeded to one or more of the above-mentioned perennial grasses and clovers, again clipped short before the birds arrive in fall. Such shoreline areas serve as combination loafing-feeding sites, allowing the clear view of their surroundings that geese seem to need.

THE SANCTUARY PRINCIPLE

More than one landowner, manager, or sportsmen's group, after much hard work to set an attractive table for migrating or wintering waterfowl, has been frustrated and puzzled by seeing ducks or geese settle in, only to pull out again after a day or two. More often than not such behavior by birds results from failure by humans to incorporate one of the most effective of all management techniques—a sanctuary, a site free from disturbance.

Wild waterfowl will not tolerate harassment for long. Highly mobile, well able to move and explore considerable distances, and bound by no laws to stay in a given area, they will leave abundant feed and attractive water behind if disturbed too often—not just by being shot at, but as a result of being frightened by people, vehicles, or dogs.

On the other hand, an attractive site, kept free of disturbance, can become the focal point of concentrations of ducks and geese that return year after year. The sanctuary site need not be large: a 9-acre pond and a few acres of surrounding fields fenced against tres-

Disturbance-free refuge areas are highly important in waterfowl management. These birds may have to fly many miles to feed, but return to this sanctuary for open water, clear loafing areas, and—especially—peace and quiet.

pass by people and animals at Remington Farms in Maryland attracts and holds thousands of Canada geese every winter. Nor does it have to provide food. Efforts to discourage geese from wintering on northern wildlife refuges, and to hasten them south to their traditional wintering grounds, by eliminating all food sources, seem doomed to failure. As long as safety from shooting, and open water for loafing, remain, so do the birds. They manage to find food elsewhere.

Obviously, the tradition of use does not develop overnight or without effort. Migrating and wintering waterfowl see many water areas; don't expect them to single you out simply because you put up a "no disturbance" sign. Birds must first be attracted by adequate food and suitable open water. At first, special pains must be taken to avoid harassment. As years pass and the tradition becomes established, birds become more tolerant of mild disturbances, and the size of the sanctuary often can be decreased.

Those interested only in attracting waterfowl for viewing should, of course, apply the sanctuary principle throughout their holdings. Where improved hunting is the primary objective, the principle should be used on one or more sites, their size and number depending upon the acreage available. Where several ponds, shallow fields, or other impoundments exist, one unit should be kept free from all disturbance. If there is only one body of water, but sufficient uplands, it may pay to confine hunting to pass-shooting, well away from the water.

The most successful hunting clubs practice a modification of this idea in place of or in addition to maintaining a closed sanctuary. They limit hunting to two to three hours a day, or only one to two days a week. This keeps disturbance at tolerable levels, especially if the holding is large enough to permit rotation of hunting sites. This may sound like a waste—to manage a large area for waterfowl hunting and then use it so little. It depends on what you prefer—one or two good days and many total blanks, or fewer days in the blind but nearly all of them ones to remember.

Whether your goal is hunting or viewing, take extra care to avoid disturbance early in the season, as waterfowl arrive and settle in. During this period it takes much less to send birds on their way than it will later.

Remember that when you create a sanctuary, or otherwise manage land to attract waterfowl, you assume a responsibility as well if your love for wildlife is more than skin deep. Whether you are a bird-watcher or hunter, don't forget that ducks and geese must go on living even if you lose interest until next season. Where water is open, birds may use these areas through the winter; where floodings freeze, migrants will still find useful food and cover after the spring thaw.

References

Home Grown Honkers. U.S. Department of Interior, Fish and Wildlife Service, Bureau of Sport Fisheries and Wildlife, Washington, D. C. 1970.

Improved Nest Structures for Wood Ducks. Wildlife Leaflet #458. U.S. Department of Interior, Fish and Wildlife Service, Bureau of Sport Fisheries and Wildlife, Washington, D.C. 1964.

New Homes for Prairie Ducks. U.S. Department of Interior, Fish and Wildlife Service, Bureau of Sport Fisheries and Wildlife, Northern Prairie Wildlife Research Center, Jamestown, North Dakota 58401.

Neil Hotchkiss. *Common Marsh, Underwater and Floating-leaved Plants.* New York: Dover. $3.00.

J. P. Linduska, ed. *Waterfowl Tomorrow.* U.S. Department of Interior, Fish and Wildlife Service, Bureau of Sport Fisheries and Wildlife, Washington, D.C. 1964. $4.00.

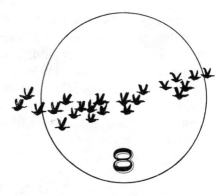

MANAGING FOR FOREST GAME

It would be nice to title this chapter "Managing for Forest Wildlife," rather than "...Forest Game"—nice, but misleading, for there has been far too little research on practical management for nongame species in woodlands and elsewhere. We know a bit about the needs of a few rare and endangered species—Kirtland's warbler requires a certain age-class of jack-pine succession in Michigan, for example—but not a great deal more.

Interest in and financial support for management of nongame wildlife may increase in the near future. In the meantime, we shall have to be satisfied with the knowledge that sound management for forest game should benefit most forest wildlife. The distinction, after all, is man-made; natural principles of edge, interspersion, and habitat diversity are fundamental to the health of wildlife populations regardless of how man "uses" those populations.

The lines between "categories" of game become more vague each year. Tree squirrels traditionally have been grouped as forest or woodland game. However, we discussed them with small farm game, because the fox and, increasingly, the gray squirrel have adapted to small woodlots, fencerow, and suburbs, and both are most susceptible to hunting and management in these settings. Yet, obviously, practices aimed at other forest species affect tree squirrels.

The whitetail deer, too, has adjusted remarkably to man and his activities; in many states he is more farm than forest game. We can be thankful for this adaptability of wildlife, and we can expect it to continue in the future. Watching for signs of the adaptation of species to man and habitat altered by man is one of the most fascinating, though least studied, of wildlife pursuits. Of course, there are limits to this adaptation. Not all species are highly flexible; few if any can be expected to adapt once habitat "alteration" proceeds to habitat destruction.

THE FOREST HABITAT

By and large, forest-dwelling species respond to land use by man, dominated by economics, in much the same manner as small game. Only the setting is different—forest and woodland rather than farmland.

The great wave of logging that swept across North America in the wake of settlement, together with year-round hunting (much of it for food or the market, rather than for sport) before modern regulations, decimated most forest game. Populations reduced by hunting could not rebuild in habitat slashed by logging and the fires that followed in the loggers' wake. As natural succession healed the landscape at varying rates, with small farms on cleared land providing "edge" and legal restrictions on hunting giving protection, forest game rebounded. Never abundant in virgin, climax forests, deer, grouse, and others established record populations as succession reached those pre-climax stages that surrounded them with ideal habitat. Assisted by transplants planned by wildlife managers, even the wild turkey, most elusive of forest game, achieved a comeback as the new forests matured.

The setting continues to change, however. Natural succession in many areas has proceeded past the point of maximum benefit to deer and many forest game species. Most of the small farms that once provided habitat diversity through the Northeast and the Great Lakes states have been abandoned. Located on land that was hopeless or, at best, marginal for grain production, they proved economically unfeasible. Under public and private ownership, many restored forest lands in the United States are now managed primarily for timber production, and directed toward speeding up succession to produce bigger sawlogs faster. A similar pattern holds in much of the South; small farms have been abandoned or bought out, and large uniform holdings, for grazing and timber production, are on the increase.

As a result, game numbers are declining in many forested regions. The cause is not hunting, which is now carefully regulated. Rather, it is the deterioration of habitat quality, variety, and edge as the result of natural succession and human activity. The thrust of modern tree farming is toward bigger, faster, and more profitable yields. This is achieved by: (1) harvesting (and replanting) large acreages at one time, to take advantage of big, modern equipment and to minimize labor costs—hence large-scale clear-cutting; (2) eliminating natural succession (in order to reduce the time necessary to replace sawlog timber) by planting tree seed or seedlings immediately after logging; (3) reducing competition by removing brush, "weed-trees," and less profitable or slow-growing timber (mast-producing oaks and other deciduous trees in many cases); (4) minimizing "lost" space by planting all clearings to merchantable timber; and (5) discouraging wildlife species that browse on tree seedlings. Even fire, the primary means by which nature sets back the successional clock and creates diversity, has been drastically reduced.

This influence of land use by man, dictated by economics, is much less obvious in woodlands than on farmland to the average citizen. It takes little special training to recognize that mile after mile of clean-farmed, fall-plowed row crops offer little for wildlife other than the cornborer. But it is hard for most of us to grasp the fact that endless vistas of lush, green trees can likewise be a biological desert—especially when our wishful thinking is spurred by attractive lumber-company ads depicting cuddly wildlife supposedly thriving on tree farms.

Utopia for many tree farmers, which is fast approaching in some regions, will mean neatly aligned rows of hybrid conifers (sterile, of course, since seed production diverts energy from growth), cultivated or irrigated, free from all competition from other plants and from damage by pests (wildlife), stretching across valley and hilltop.

It will be a short-lived utopia. Why? Because this system has already been tried and found wanting. German and other European foresters achieved a similar "dream" decades ago, and found timber yields declining drastically as forest soils literally soured and died. Without a wide-spectrum nutrient enrichment from a variety of broad-leaved and coniferous trees and plants, soil organisms were depleted, soil chemistry altered, and natural nutrient recycling chains broken. Most American tree farmers ignore or dismiss this lesson; they will learn it anew. When they do, the first response doubtless will be artificial fertilizers, just as it has been in agriculture. They will assume a parallel between crop farming and tree farming that does not really exist. There is no substitute for food, so expensive supplemental fertilizers pay off in agriculture. But there are many substitutes for wood.

If you are interested in forest wildlife in general, or forest game in particular, the point is clear—don't follow the path of the all-out commercial tree farmer. If wildlife is your sole interest, this is no problem. Happily, if you seek a sound, sustained income from timber production, and want forest wildlife as well, you can achieve both goals, as many landowners have proved. In fact, compromise is almost certainly the safest economic route in the long haul.

To achieve this happy medium, one of the first objectives is to curtail or eliminate livestock grazing on wooded acres. This is especially true for broad-leaved, deciduous woodlands. There is an old saying: "Make it woodland or make it a pasture, but don't make it both." Livestock compact the soil and knock down, eat, or otherwise destroy tree seedlings and brush. They thus eliminate any chance for reproduction of marketable timber, and simultaneously destroy essential wildlife habitat.

The abiding principle of maintaining and, where possible, adding to habitat diversity still applies. Some clearings in permanent grass or other herbaceous cover are essential for forest game; a number of small, well-scattered openings are better than a large one. As a rule, such clearings should make up about 5 percent of the total acreage. Aim likewise for variety in plant succession stages. In the Northeast and North Central states, good timber and wildlife results are obtained on many holdings by cutting about a quarter of a 2000-acre woodland every twenty-five years.

For management for both timber and game (deer, turkeys, and squirrels in particular), on wooded units of about 1000 acres, Missouri's conservation department recommends the following pattern of succession. Up to 5 percent of the area must be in permanent clearings. Of the remainder, 40 percent should be sawlog-size timber, 30 percent "pole" stage trees, 20 percent saplings, and 10 percent seedlings. This pattern, which calls for logging off 10 to 20 percent of the wooded acreage every ten years, is also agreeable to Missouri state foresters on the whole although they would prefer to deal in larger blocks than 1000 acres.

A key point, in Missouri and everywhere else, is the maintenance of diversity within wooded acres. Good, natural mixtures of tree species, as well as successional stages, are fundamental to forest wildlife as well as to soil fertility and long-range timber yields. Mast-producing woody plants, particularly the oaks, are especially important. Missouri recommends maintaining some 50 percent of forest acreage in oaks and other mast-bearing trees. In pine-dominated areas of the Southeast, special care should be taken to retain oaks. Since acorn production tends to be erratic from year to year with different oak species, a mixture—with at least some trees of both black (red) and white groups—is important. Some individual trees produce more acorns than others of the same age and variety, so if oaks must be cut and space is limited, it pays to check acorn yields and save the top producers.

Lowland portions of wooded lands along streams, in river bottomlands, and the like are of particular value to wildlife. They not only add to overall forest diversity, but often contain the best and most varied trees and shrubs for wildlife food and cover—for forest game as well as wood ducks and other species. If forested land must be cleared and a choice made, it is normally best to salvage lowland and streamside areas at the expense of uplands.

RUFFED GROUSE

The ruffed grouse, sometimes called "partridge," ranges from coast to coast across forested areas of the northern United States and Canada, and extends south in the Appalachians to Georgia. As is true for most forest game, the ruffed grouse thrives best in a mixture of intermediate stages of plant succession—brush and preclimax woodland. In much grouse range, succession on logged-over or once farmed lands has proceeded past these ideal stages.

Interspersion of cover types, varied in both growth form and age, is especially important for this game bird. Flower buds and new leaves of aspen, the fruit of such shrubs and shrubby trees as the viburnums, dogwoods, and hawthorne ("thorn apples"), and tender greens from grasses and herbs are staple foods. Conifer clumps and brush tangles serve as winter and escape cover, although in much of the North grouse roost in loose snowdrifts into which they dive—in full flight—to bury themselves out of sight. Home range for grouse in many areas is about 10 to 25 acres; as a general rule the closer together key habitat ingredients occur, the greater the population density. Intensively managed areas may produce three or four broods per 100 acres in years of good weather, although this production level is seldom achieved across large acreages. Obviously, large, uniform, evenly aged stands of timber are poor grouse territories, particularly when these trees are in a dense sapling stage furnishing little ground cover.

In Minnesota and other northern areas aspen is often a key ingredient of grouse habitat. Minnesota biologists believe that aspen flower buds provide the best winter staple in this range. Aspen catkins and, for nesting females, new leaves are also important. Habitat for young broods in this region is best provided by aspen stands of suitable age and density; lowlands dominated by alders are next best.

Managing aspen for grouse requires adequate acreage in stands of all ages. Trees ten to twenty years old are used by male grouse and by pairs, for example, while stands twenty-five to thirty years of age or older furnish the best food supplies. Open groves of these older trees also are used for nesting.

Carefully planned rotation cutting obviously is critical in regions such as Minnesota, where ruffed-grouse numbers and distribution seem so closely tied to aspen. Enough stands must be allowed to reach maturity while at the same time periodic rejuvenation must be effected by well-dispersed cutting. Aspen seedlings require sunlight, so clear-cutting all vegetation usually is recommended on areas of limited size where the objective is renewal of a pure stand for grouse.

Seeding clovers along trails, fire lanes, and roadsides through forested areas has long been advocated as a management procedure for ruffed grouse and other forest game. As a means of providing habitat diversity and maintaining openings, this practice has merit, and many forest dwelling wildlife species feed on the greens so provided. However, as far as grouse are concerned, it is doubtful that such seedings are necessary or even important for production or survival. Legume seedings do tend to concentrate birds for hunters, in the same way that bicolor lespedeza attracts southern quail, which may be desirable or not, depending upon circumstances and management goals.

WOODCOCK

Grouse hunters in the eastern half of the U.S. frequently end up with a "mixed bag," adding a woodcock or "timberdoodle" along with their "partridge." The two species often share similar habitat, at least when grouse haunt the lowlands.

Unlike his frequent partner in the hunter's bag, the woodcock is migratory and thus under federal regulations. He breeds over nearly all the wooded portions of the United States and southern Canada, east of the Great Plains. Birds in the northern two thirds of this

range migrate south in fall to winter in Louisiana, Mississippi, and
adjacent states.

The woodcock is an unusual-looking bird, with a large head and eyes, extremely long bill, and pudgy appearance. A ground dweller, his plumage affords beautiful camouflage, and his always-unexpected flush and highly erratic flight make him a favorite for an increasing number of hunters.

The primary key to good woodcock habitat and to management is diet. Animal matter makes up over 90 percent of the items on a timberdoodle's menu—insects, spiders, and other invertebrates and, above all, earthworms. So closely are earthworms and woodcock associated that apparently ideal habitat, in terms of vegetation, site, and diversity, may never support these birds simply because the soil is too acid or otherwise unsuitable for worms. The effects of this same relationship sometimes plague hunters in the North. They may watch fondly over a swarm of late-lingering or migrant birds for days prior to hunting season, only to find them gone on opening morning after a hard freeze locks away earthworm supplies.

Wet meadows and moist lowlands along streams, ponds, and wooded marshes are fundamental to woodcock management for both production and hunting. The birds mate in small clearings of ⅛ to ¼ acre or so, and feed and shelter under lowland brush patches, particularly alder and gray and silky dogwood. Brush clumps on higher ground seem to be important for loafing sites. Nests are on the ground, in or at the edges of young timber or in brush.

Diversity again is important; there should be scattered clearings and an emphasis on brush successional stages, especially of alder and dogwood, in key lowland areas. If you are interested in woodcock and can work with a suitable site that has moist, earthworm-supporting lowland soils, brush thickets are not difficult to establish. Both alder and gray dogwood are available inexpensively as seedlings from many state forestry departments and private nurseries, and are easily established by the planting techniques discussed in Chapter 5.

Alders, also favored by ruffed grouse, can be seeded with good success on appropriate soils and sites. Collect seed in the fall and sow in February or March on cool, moist soils. If ground cover is dense, disking prior to seeding may be necessary; otherwise an adequate "catch" usually results without any soil preparation.

As pointed out previously, natural and planted brush becomes senile in time—tall and full of dead stems and branches (often a symptom of the passage of succession from shrubs to trees). When this happens, alder and dogwood stands can be renewed by cutting them back nearly to ground level during the dormant season. Such clear-cuts may be necessary at intervals of about twenty years. Prime brush clumps threatened by shade and competition from invading trees should be released by removing the invaders.

Woodcock are tied closely to plant succession; woodcock management requires a knowledge and manipulation of succession's clock. By and large, these birds benefit from management practices aimed at deer and ruffed grouse, which also require diversity and early to intermediate stages of plant succession.

DEER

The species and races of deer—whitetail, mule, and blacktail—range across most of North America. Literature on their biology, natural history, management, and hunting fills a good many shelves in every wildlife library. Despite all our knowledge, however, essentially deer, like the ring-necked pheasant (another library filler), have been governed much more by land-use changes and by their own innate adaptability than by any wildlife manager's efforts.

We can only hit a few highlights in this brief coverage of deer "management." And these highlights concern whitetails primarily, although many apply to most blacktail and mule deer populations as well.

Deer are creatures of plant succession. Large tracts of dense, mature forests, where shade and competition permit few shrubs or seedlings to survive as deer browse and reduce the good quality of those that do, may hold as few as two deer per square mile. The "forest primeval" is poor deer range.

The same land, fifteen to twenty years after the forest is cut and succession allowed to proceed, may harbor sixty deer per square mile. The history of forest game in the United States, which we discussed previously, applies particularly to deer, and especially to whitetails. Depleted at first by clear-cut logging and uncontrolled hunting, deer populations soared to record highs when post-logging succession converted vast acreage to prime browse, and when strict hunting regulations were introduced and enforced. Today, deer numbers (again, whitetails especially) are declining slowly in many areas. Why so, since logging continues? Because today's tree farming and lumbering too often do not allow for habitat diversity or for a lengthy brush state of succession.

Largest and healthiest deer populations occur where ample areas in intermediate stages of succession supply adequate browse

Riverside and other water-bordering low woodlands are often the most varied and valuable habitat for forest game.

and are interspersed with clearings (meadows, small marshes, or newly cut or burned openings) in grass and herbs and, especially in the North, fairly dense stands of evergreens. The latter cover type—clumps and strips of conifers—is especially useful for winter cover and year-round shelter when located near water—one more reason why lowland forest strips bordering streams and wetland areas should be preserved when uplands are logged.

Where whitetail and ruffed-grouse ranges overlap, more forest management efforts can be directed to benefit both species. For example, in northern Minnesota and similar areas, aspen stands are gradually replaced by fir and spruce in the successional process. Small stands of these conifers are helpful to both deer and grouse, but large expanses are of little use. Renewal of aspen, leaving scattered fir and spruce patches, by clear-cutting every fifty years or so is recommended. Sample rotation-cutting schemes for northern areas and Missouri were outlined previously.

To renew brushy feeding areas that are growing beyond reach of deer, or losing their vigor, utilize methods described in Chapters

4 and 5, including mowing with a rotary "chopper," and hand-cutting to remove unwanted competing plants. In the West, where vast brush-dominated deer ranges exist, a number of mechanized techniques have been developed. These include "chaining" and "cabling"—pulling 150 to 200 feet of heavy chain or cable between two caterpillar tractors, to uproot and smash undesirable vegetation and speed regrowth or, more often, to open areas for seeding. Long-range effects of some of these techniques are not fully understood. "Crushing," a brush-renewal method utilizing a bulldozer with blade lowered near the ground to shear off or smash old brush stands, is an example. Initial growth response often is good, but after three or four years there may be less desirable brush growth than before crushing.

Consult state conservation department big-game managers before attempting large-scale brush clearing or manipulation, especially on western ranges; proceed with some caution. Make sure the methods they suggest have been in use and studied long enough so that long-range effects are known.

As mentioned, clearings, openings, and small fields in grass and other herbaceous growth are important ingredients of deer range. Such plants are valuable food sources, especially in late winter and early spring. As a rule, clearings should be well dispersed, about 4 to 10 acres in size, and occupy about 5 percent of the total range. Where natural meadows are too few, clearings should be created and seeded to such early-sprouting plants as alfalfa, winter rye, and crested wheatgrass. If it is not feasible to open a clearing within forested land, strips planted to grasses and legumes along forest edges are useful, especially where smaller woodlands are involved.

An important phase of deer management is control of population size. Like many big-game species, deer can ravage their own habitat when their numbers build beyond normal carrying capacity of the range. Few large predators remain to exert natural limits on deer populations. If hunting or other means of control are not exercised, the all too frequent result is an overbrowsed forest or woodland, with virtually all vegetation destroyed below the height deer can reach. Unless an expensive artificial feeding program is pursued, most deer perish. Worse, most other wildlife species are depleted as well, and decades may pass before the habitat recovers.

A healthy herd can take vigorous "cropping," and may require it to remain healthy. Removal of 25 to 30 percent of the herd annually is considered a desirable goal on many ranges, and means does as well as bucks.

The turkey is one of the few species that do best in later stages of forest succession. Ruffed grouse, deer, woodcock, and others require considerable amounts of brush and understory vegetation; turkeys prefer open, more mature woodlands, especially in oak or oak-pine mixtures. These older stands offer tall trees for roosting as well as the most productive age-classes of oaks and other mast-bearing vegetation. Turkeys also need room to roam. Normal annual ranges of many wild flocks cover 5000 to 10,000 acres, although especially attractive and well-managed woodland tracts as small as 500 acres may occasionally serve for a flock of limited size.

For much of the year turkeys are vegetarians. Mast—especially acorns, pine nuts, pecans, beechnuts, and the fruits of flowering dogwood, blackgum, and sweetgum—is the staple winter diet. Wild turkeys will not survive or prosper where forest nut and fruit crops don't exist. Consequently, habitat management requires the preservation of prime mast-producing trees and their encouragement by release cutting to remove undesirable competitors. Attention also should be directed to planting seedlings of mast-bearing trees to establish new range or supplement existing stands.

In late summer, wild turkeys forage across forest openings to feed upon grasshoppers.

Clearings in large tracts of forest add to habitat diversity important to all forest wildlife.

Turkeys do a great deal of grazing on young, green vegetation in late winter and spring—especially on grasses and legumes. Scattered clearings an acre or more in size (4 to 10 acres if you are aiming for deer use, also) should be maintained in herbaceous vegetation. Or, where feasible, strips and small fields in or adjoining woodland should be planted to such crops or greens as barley, annual rye-grass, winter wheat, or clovers. These areas serve an important second purpose; the grasshoppers they often attract are a favored food for broods of young turkeys. If green in winter, such grazing sites are a powerful enticement, and are sometimes employed to pull flocks within hunting or viewing range.

Turkeys need water daily, so a permanent source is a necessity. In Pennsylvania and many other northern areas, turkeys seldom range far from springs and "seeps" during hard winters. In addition, throughout most of their range, turkeys nest near open water supplies. The importance of safeguarding natural water sources is obvious. Where available water is scarce or poorly distributed, the construction of carefully located small impoundments or guzzlers is well worthwhile. Here again, as for most forest wildlife, the need to preserve lowland forest areas bordering streams, lakes, and ponds is apparent. In addition to providing nesting, roosting, and loafing cover near water, lowland woods usually contain a rich variety of food producing trees and shrubs.

Unfortunately, management solely or primarily for wildlife is as yet rarely considered economically feasible on many forests under private or public ownership. Even where money is not a major consideration, too many view a forest that does not produce sawlogs as somehow wasteful and morally wrong.

Hopefully we will always be able to retain some lands that are not compelled to "produce," that can remain natural and untouched by both foresters and game managers. Hopefully, too, other wooded lands that are needed for timber production will be managed with an eye for more than simply the maximum yield of the best sawlogs—a self-defeating goal if carried to its extreme, as we have seen.

From the business aspect, timber production and forest wildlife management are mutually compatible. Reasonable returns on a sustained-yield basis can assuredly be derived under sound administration. If this is your goal, you will need to consult both foresters and forest-wildlife experts to come up with a balanced approach. What you will encounter, from both state and federal agencies, will depend on where you live. In some instances, you will find foresters and wildlifers diametrically opposed, each adamant about the priority of his own interest, with little thought for the other side. Elsewhere, the two interests and the professionals who speak for them agree on compatible goals. In any situation, listen to both sides and seek a reasonable middle road if you wish both wildlife and timber sales from your woodland.

As we have pointed out, most forest game does best in a diversified habitat, which can be created and maintained by well-planned and properly timed and rotated timber cuttings. Special attention to retention of limited, key habitat types (such as stream-bordering and lowland woods) and species (such as mature, mast-producing oaks) is critical. Think long and hard before you destroy these prime ingredients. They may have considerable immediate values as sawlogs; they are likely to have far greater long-range value to wildlife over a large area.

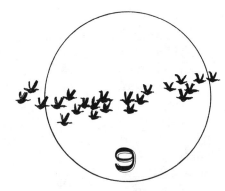

SHOOTING PRESERVES

Shooting preserves are privately owned areas, licensed by states, on which pen-reared game can be harvested under more liberal regulations (longer seasons and bigger bag limits) than apply in the wild. "Shooting preserve" is the term semi-officially adopted by most states and the preserve industry itself, but on occasion "controlled hunting area" or similar terms are used.

The first formal licensing of a private shooting preserve, as defined here, was in 1910 in New York State. However, the basic theory—the release of hand-reared game birds to guarantee plentiful hunting—was imported from England and dates back many centuries.

The shooting-preserve concept was endorsed by Aldo Leopold, father of modern game management. Leopold pointed out that game was a product of habitat, and that—for small game, at least—the landowner could do the most efficient and economical job of habitat management for game. He added that few landowners were likely to devote much time or many acres to game production without a worthwhile incentive—a return on their investment. (Significantly, these two observations—the commanding role of the landowner and his need for reimbursement—have withstood the test of time. They are true more than ever today. Unfortunately, not much more has been done to act on them in the interim than was

done when they were first expressed nearly forty years ago.) Leopold believed that the licensed shooting preserve inspired individuals and groups to manage and improve habitat and stock game
through the incentive of more liberal hunting regulations.

By and large, things have turned out this way. Today's shooting
preserves, in most states, are licensed for hunting over a five-to-
seven month season, with permission to harvest 70 to 100 percent of
the game they stock. The long season and large bag limit (in reality
restricted only by the pocketbook of the hunter), and the fact that
preserve hunters are sure to see game, have been sufficient motives
to prompt the support of private and commercial shooting preserves
across the nation.

There are two basic types of preserves. One group generally is
referred to as "private." This is misleading, in a way, since all are
privately owned, but the whole concept is riddled with misnomers,
as is evident in the combination of the opposed terms "shooting"
and "preserve." "Private" shooting preserves are operated by individuals, informal groups, or sportsmen's clubs who stock and manage the area themselves, for their own hunting enjoyment and for
guests they may invite. Costs are paid by the individual, or shared
equally among the group or club. Land may be owned, rented, or
leased.

Private preserves outnumber those in the second category—the
commercial or, again misleadingly, "public" shooting preserves.
The latter are operated for a profit, with the owner charging a fee
for shooting on the area. Commercial preserves fall into two sub-
categories—"clubs" and "daily-fee" operations. Daily-fee preserves
are open to all who are willing and able to pay the tab; clubs have a
limited number of members who pay a fixed, annual sum, plus additional charges based on the game they shoot and the use they
make of the club area.

Private and commercial preserves have certain things in common. Both must meet the requirements of state legislation (which
now exists in nearly all states) for licensing. Such legislation requires payment of a license or permit fee (ranging from $10 to $100
or more annually), suitable marking or posting of preserve boundaries, and maintenance of records. Depending upon the state, legislation may also specify a minimum and maximum number of acres
that may be licensed, as well as a minimum number of birds that
must be released.

In return for meeting these and other requirements, a preserve
license grants an extended hunting season (five to six months, from
October through March is typical) for specified game, and a liberal

bag limit. This bag limit is based on the number of birds stocked and usually upon the status of the species in the state. Where a bird exists in the wild as a game species, as do pheasants and quail in many areas, the bag limit usually is set at 70 to 80 percent of the number of birds released. Where the bird is not "normal" game (the chukar partridge in the East and Midwest, for example), preserve hunters may be permitted to harvest 100 percent of those released—if they can.

In some states licensing requirements differ between private and commercial shooting preserves. Management methods and operations also vary considerably; hence, we shall discuss the two types separately.

COMMERCIAL SHOOTING PRESERVES

A great number of so-called "small businesses" collapse, disappear, or pass into bankruptcy every year. Commercial preserves are no exception; if anything, their failure rate probably well exceeds that of the average small new business. It is not that a potential market is lacking. There are many sportsmen who can and do pay for good "put-and-take" shooting preserve hunting, and many more who would do so under the right circumstances.

The problem lies in creating those "right circumstances." A successful commercial preserve needs certain physical assets, including a suitable location, preferably within reasonable driving distance of cities large enough to furnish an adequate number of customers. Sites in regions where intensive farming or suburban growth have depleted close-to-home habitat and game have an advantage. There are exceptions, of course. Southern preserves offering good quail hunting often are far from major population centers, and are in relatively rich game country. But they are resort regions where many "Yankee" hunters vacation only to find that quail hunting on nonpreserve lands is seldom open to outsiders.

Successful commercial preserves also feature top-quality birds, good dogs and guides, and adequate, well-maintained hunting cover. Some sort of clubhouse facility is also important, though plush accommodations are not necessary. A preserve located where there is no good nearby restaurant, in which diners wearing hunting clothes will feel welcome and comfortable, should be equipped to serve at least a good lunch in clean surroundings. Similarly, a preserve far from metropolitan areas and decent motels is almost obliged to be set up to accommodate hunters overnight.

Commercial preserves catering to hunters within easy driving distance do not have to have dining or sleeping facilities, but should still provide a clean washroom and a comfortable room or small building where hunters can change clothes and relax with a drink after the hunt. Such a room or building also serves as the place where hunters "sign in," meet their guide, and buy ammunition and licenses.

All of these ingredients—suitable birds, grounds, dogs, buildings—cost money, obviously, and require a certain amount of know-how. But they are basically "mechanical"; they can be acquired. The decisive factor in any successful commercial shooting preserve is the operator himself. He must like people and have a winning personality. He must know and enjoy hunting, birds, and dogs, be willing and physically able to work hard, and have an open and inquiring mind. The best preserve operators are a combination of salesman, vaudeville showman, practical businessman, dirt farmer, and dog trainer. And it helps if they can get along with four hours of sleep a night.

If you are contemplating operating a commercial preserve, this is the kind of person you need to be, or hire. With an operator of this caliber, even a preserve that is poorly located and has marginal facilities or other strikes against it (always excepting dogs and birds, which must be good) may be successful. Without such an owner or manager, a preserve that is ideal in all other standard requirements will likely fall flat.

This chapter, and the references recommended at its close, discusses methods for successful management. But because the casualty rate is so high, let us dwell briefly on the typical failure. Our "unsuccess" story usually starts with someone who likes hunting and the outdoors, but who is working at a factory, office, or other job he doesn't much care for. He has saved a little money and owns, has just inherited, or knows where he can buy a piece of land. The acreage is small and too poor for successful farming, but it "looks great" for hunting. All his friends have assured him that they will patronize his club if he starts a commercial hunting area. It really adds up—he can be outdoors, doing something he has always liked, and make a living, too.

So he makes the plunge, and everything goes wrong. The recommended cover—sorghums, corn, etc.—he tries to plant does not grow well in that poor ground. He has decided to raise his own pheasants since they cost so much to buy full-grown (after all, his wife used to raise chickens). But, somehow, they start feather-picking and end up without tail feathers. As his first season approaches, the only responses he has had to his advertising attempts are a request from a youngster for literature for a term paper on conservation, a letter from a guy who would like to come out and work his dog but doesn't want to shoot anything, and some junk mail from feed companies. What about all those friends who were going to come out and shoot as soon as he opened? The few who remember his name throw up their hands when they hear the price. Thus, in order to have any business at all, he lowers his rates beyond what is realistic.

His old dog has a hard time locating the birds he releases, since the cover is too poor to hold the birds long. Tailless, those birds that do flush look like flying basketballs. Somehow he gets through the season. According to his books he broke even; he has not figured anything for his own or his family's time, for depreciation, or for his land investment. According to his bank, he is just broke. So he "moonlights" at another job to support his family. He learned a lot that first year, but he cannot apply it adequately because he no longer has the time or money. After one more season he gives up, wiser and a lot poorer.

The moral of this sad story should be clear. It takes much more than a love of hunting and the outdoors, a piece of marginal land, and the promises of friends to make a go of a commercial preserve. To those requirements already mentioned, add one more—sufficient savings or income to carry the undertaking through the first two or three years. Most currently successful ventures did not approach a break-even situation until their second or third year, and did not operate in the black until their third season or later.

In discussing commercial-preserve management, let us try to answer those questions asked most often by would-be operators. First is usually: "How much land do I need?" To begin with, check licensing requirements in your state; they may specify minimum and maximum acreage limitations. Within this framework, the answer depends a lot on the land itself. Properly planted, managed, and stocked, a 40-acre area can keep one party of three or four hunters busy and contented for two or three hours or a half-day's hunt. If you are going to do a good business, you will need at least 4 to 6 such areas, so spaced and/or separated by trees or terrain that parties on adjacent areas aren't breathing down one another's necks, or getting peppered by shot fallout. This calls for about 350 to 400 acres as a rough average. With intensive management and careful guiding and stocking, a good operator can get by with less, provided the land is fertile enough to grow excellent cover. Where the land or climate won't support good cover, or where extensive woodlands or difficult terrain exist, overall acreage may have to be much greater.

"Do I have to own all the land?" It is by far best if you do. You can try leasing or working out some arrangement for hunting on neighboring lands, but this is shaky unless you have a long-term, ironclad contract. About the time you have built a business that depends on that land, it is apt to be sold, or the owner may change his mind.

"What is best, a daily-fee or a club operation?" The answer to this is a look at the track record of successful preserves. Most started as daily-fee operations, taking any hunters who were willing to pay the price, and most, after several years, ended up as clubs, catering to a limited number of hunters who were willing to pay for exclusive rights. This pattern occurs not because daily-fee operations cannot be profitable—many have been and still are—but because a club normally offers the operator greater security and fewer headaches. A club provides a known minimum income and a limited number of hunters whose character, personal wishes and foibles you can get to know, and is not as vulnerable to those vagaries of weather and economy that can plague daily-fee preserves.

But it is a rare preserve operator who can start from scratch with a guaranteed clientele large enough to support a club. Hence, there is a tendency to begin by accepting all hunters, followed by a gradual transition as a body of solid "repeat" customers becomes interested in and willing to support a club.

It is likely that this pattern will continue. The needs of the casual hunter, and those who cannot affort club rates, will probably be met in the future, as in the past, by preserves in the early, daily-fee stages of evolution. Increasingly, too, state-operated public hunting grounds, charging a fee for hunting released game birds, will offer opportunities for the nonclub sportsmen.

"What and how should I charge my customers?" This is a bit complicated because there are several methods of charging for preserve shooting. Basically, hunters may pay for birds bagged, for birds released, or simply for a hunting experience. The first is preferred by most customers, at least initially, but it is the worst choice for the operator, whose fortunes fluctuate with the shooting ability and seriousness of purpose of every hunting party. If he stocks a lot of birds for a big party, many of whose members are inexperienced hunters, he can lose his shirt.

Despite the complaints you will get from some customers, who won't believe that you have released the full number of birds they have paid for, it is still far better to start out by charging for birds released. With good guides and dogs, you can get the birds up for your hunters and, from then on, the worry is theirs.

How much to charge? The national average is around $6.50 per bird shot and $5.50 per bird released for pheasants, and somewhat less for mallards, chukar partridge, and quail. It is necessary to insist on some sort of minimum; you can't turn over a hunting field for a day or half a day for two or three birds. If you charge on a birds-bagged basis, include birds knocked down and not retrieved.

There are all sorts of "package" deals, especially among clubs. All clubs charge an annual fee, payable prior to the hunting season (this is the "insurance" for at least a minimum income, referred to earlier). This fee may range from $50 to $500 a year, or more, depending on the number and desirability of facilities and attractions available. In many cases, the annual fee includes the opportunity to bag a given number of birds. A club with a $250 annual fee might, for example, allow a member to bag twenty-five pheasants, or twenty pheasants and ten ducks, without additional charge. But additional birds shot or released during the season by or for the member and his guests would be charged at normal per-bird rates.

Nearly all commercial preserves provide a bird-dressing and freezer-holding facility for hunters—and charge for it. Dressing charges average about 75 cents per bird. Charges for other services—guides and dogs, for example—vary widely. In the long run, you are far better off furnishing a guide and your own trained dogs for each party. Guides and dogs cost money, so you must either charge separately for these services or, better still, make sure your overall prices per bird shot or released are adequate to cover your costs. Some clubs furnish guides and dogs "free" but charge a guest or gun fee of $5 to $10 for each guest of a member, in addition to bird fees, and thus cover extra costs.

The prime rule in setting prices is to make sure that you are making a satisfactory profit. And figure in *all* your costs. Too many preserves have failed because the owners kidded themselves into thinking they were making money simply because their income exceeded their bird costs. Besides what you paid for the birds, add your own labor as well as that of any hired help, plus depreciation on buildings and equipment, taxes, and all related expenses.

Finally, do not expect to make a fortune. The average successful preserve operator makes only a reasonable living for himself and his family—often less money with more hard work than he would make in another job. He has to like hunting, game birds, and people to make a go of it, and be willing to accept the satisfaction derived from working with all three in place of a big income.

One immediate concern of a budding preserve operator is whether he should raise his own birds or buy them. All preserve operators in their formative years should buy their birds; most are better off buying even after they are established. True, there appear to be certain advantages to raising your own. You can produce the type of bird (as regards weight and size, coloration, etc.) you prefer; and it seems as if it would be cheaper than paying someone else. But successful game-bird propagation is a demanding and difficult art, just as is successful shooting-preserve management. You had best master your preserve operation before even contemplating running a game farm as well. It is far better to do a good job of one than a poor job of both. As far as costs are concerned, experience shows that unless a preserve operator is releasing on the order of 10,000 or more birds a season, he is better off financially to buy his birds.

There are many excellent game breeders specializing in pheasants, quail, chukar, turkey, and mallards for preserve hunting. Look and shop around—and buy from established, full-time game farms. Their operators cannot afford to sell a second-rate product. You may save a few cents buying from some here-today, gone-tomorrow backyard hobbyist, but you usually get what you pay for—in this case, often sickly, poorly feathered birds that will mean dissatisfied hunters.

Regardless of breed, good dogs are a mainstay of the shooting preserve industry.

When you find a reliable source of good birds, it is best for both you and the game farmer from whom you buy to arrange a written contract specifying age, quantity, and the price of the birds, delivery date, and delivery costs, if any. For your protection, the contract should state that the birds must be fully feathered and otherwise meet contract specifications or you have the right to reject them. Do not buy from anyone who refuses to agree to such a contract.

The percentage of commercial shooting preserves that eventually succeed financially is small indeed. One reason is that all ingredients must click. These ingredients not only include location, terrain, cover, birds, and the ability and personality of the operator, but dogs as well. Good shooting-preserve dogs must not only be willing and able to quarter cover thoroughly and locate birds, but must work in close to the handler and be excellent retrievers as well. A good ol' "meat dog" is worth ten "big-going" field-trial champions under preserve hunting conditions, and a fancy pointer that can't be bothered to track down and bring back cripples will put you in bankruptcy.

Nearly all hunting breeds have been used successfully for pheasants on preserves, from shorthairs and Brittanys to Labrador retrievers and English pointers. Quail are traditionally hunted in the wild with pointers and should so be on preserves. Chukar partridge usually respond best to flushing breeds. It is the individual dog and his ability to work under preserve conditions—not the breed or ancestry—that counts. And it counts heavily; dogs can make or break you, literally.

What perentage of the birds released can you expect to recover on a commercial preserve? The state sets the upper limit, as mentioned—usually from 70 to 80 percent up to 100 percent for some species in some states. You should aim for the 70 to 80 percent recovery area, especially if you are getting paid for birds harvested rather than released, and should be able to achieve it. Commercial preserves recovering 60 to 65 percent or less are apt to be in trouble. Low recoveries usually can be traced to problems in cover, dogs, or guides. Very high recoveries (where legal) of 90 to 100 percent are a sure sign that hunting is much too easy and artificial—as serious a problem as low recoveries.

PRIVATE PRESERVES

Shooting preserves operated for fun, with the owner footing the bill for his guests, or a group of sportsmen sharing the costs, involve many fewer problems than commercial areas. Primary management concerns center on cover (discussed later), and on securing, holding, and releasing good birds so as to enjoy reasonably good hunting through the extended season at a cost that is not overwhelming. Where the individual or group owns the land and lives on it or has a full-time tenant, there is no great difficulty. Cover can be planted, cared for, and manipulated following principles outlined here, and an inexpensive pen built and maintained in which a quantity of purchased birds can be held for periodic releases. Under these circumstances, the operator should seriously consider, manpower permitting, stocking along the lines of commercial preserves—that is, making a small initial release of pheasants and/or quail just before the hunting season, and then releasing quantities of his birds an hour or so before each hunt thereafter. No matter how good the birds or cover, the number of birds you will see and recover starts to decline from the moment of release, as they wander into inaccessible areas or off the property, or succumb to predation or weather. Despite what you have heard or may think, most birds—pheasants in particular—are as wary and "sporty" an hour after release as they will be days or even weeks later. You have everything to lose and nothing to gain by doing all or most stocking before the season's opening.

Individuals or groups who lease land for a private preserve have bigger problems. Usually lacking the manpower, money, and land to build and maintain a holding pen and make frequent small releases, they also cannot dictate the kind of habitat planting and management needed to hold birds from the one or two large releases made directly by their supplier. The low recovery and high costs per bird bagged that result have knocked out many a private preserve.

This problem often can be reduced by a little greater outlay of money and effort—costs that seem higher initially but usually average out to considerably less per bird in the bag. First, contract with the landowner to plant, leave, or maintain some good cover capable of holding and feeding the released birds. This might be only six to eight rows of corn left standing next to ditchbanks or fencerows, or several planted sorghum strips. They can be paid for in cash, in hunting privileges, in seed, or in return for labor you or your group can supply. The primary point is that the landowner receives, in cash, goods, sport, or work, an income-per-acre equivalent to what he would get for a cash crop on the same land.

Then look for a game breeder near your area who has good birds, and work out a contract to purchase birds for release several times over the season, rather than once or twice. It will cost a bit more than buying and releasing your season's quota in one or two large groups, but the return will be worth it. You can also save money by picking up the birds rather than paying for delivery.

COVER PLANTINGS AND MANAGEMENT

Variety of cover and habitat is important for wildlife in general. It is also important for shooting-preserve management, although at times for slightly different reasons. The core of habitat management on a shooting preserve is good holding cover. By this I mean cover that is attractive enough to prevent newly released birds from straying widely after release. Few preserves, commercial or private, can survive long without adequate hunting recovery of released birds. For commercial preserves, at least 70 percent of the birds released normally must be bagged; most private preserves can live with a recovery of 50 percent or more.

Time and mode of release play a part here, as we will discuss. But cover is critical. For heavily hunted commercial areas, the objective is that birds stocked for a shoot be present in the area assigned to the hunting party. Since stocking in such situations is usually done just prior to hunting, cover need only hold the birds for a matter of minutes, or an hour or two at most. Here food is relatively unimportant; the need is for plantings that furnish dense enough over-the-back cover to give confused, newly released birds a sense of security. Where heavy snow and severe winter weather is no problem, many types of plantings—tall perennial grasses, sorghums, weedy fields, and even high grain stubble—may serve the purpose. In the North, grassy areas and grain stubble may work in the fall, but heavy, sturdy cover that won't flatten under snow is needed for most of the hunting season.

Perhaps the most frequently used winter cover on northern preserves is sorghum. Short, combine grain sorghums—of varieties that will mature in shorter northern growing seasons—are stout enough to stand up under most snows. However, since they rarely bend over or lodge, they seldom furnish the kind of clumps and tangles of cover that pheasants prefer. Tall, forage sorghums such as sudan grass, and black amber and orange Waconia canes, on the other hand, may lodge and flatten completely in severe weather. A mixture of the two types—grain and forage sorghums—is usually preferable. Hunters like variety, and are accustomed to hunting in the wild in the variable cover game likes best, so do not put all your hunting areas in sorghum. If they don't already exist, establish clumps and patches of evergreens and stemmy brush, encourage the

A mixture of tall forage sorghums and short grain sorghums makes excellent cover for releasing and hunting pheasants on shooting preserves. Despite steady use and heavy snows, this strip still provides good food and cover in late winter.

sturdier native plants, such as the grass-goldenrod-aster stage of succession—common in the North—and plant switchgrass and other tall perennial bunchgrasses. You can utilize the same planting and cover maintenance methods and techniques for manipulating succession described in previous chapters.

When establishing holding cover, annual or perennial, strive for a natural look. Avoid straight lines and repetitive patterns if possible, and where the cover is to be used in particular for pheasant stocking and hunting, stay away from wide, cultivated rows, such as cleanly cultivated corn. Pheasants run like race horses in such cover. Your objective is to flush and get shots at as many of the birds you release as possible. You will go broke chasing running birds all day. So broadcast or drill your annual cover or, if you must use wide rows and cultivate, drill a 20-to-30-foot strip at right angles to the rows at intervals across the rows. Running birds reaching such denser cover usually will stop and hold for a flush. Clean-mowed "breaks," 30 to 40 feet wide, cut at intervals across hunting strips likewise tend to stop running birds. The aim, especially for pheasants, is to retain some control over where and how far the birds can go on the ground before having to flush. In huge fields, among cover strips over 40 or so feet wide, or among long, unbroken strips, a dog and hunting party of three or four can play tag for hours with crafty pheasants and seldom see a bird in the air. Or if the birds are finally cornered, they all flush at once and you may re-cover one or two out of ten.

These same basic principles of good cover in a variety of types, planted, spaced, and broken up so that stocked birds will hold and can be located and flushed, apply to lightly hunted private pre-serves as well as commercial areas. However, since the private pre-serve usually is stocked only once or a few times, instead of daily or regularly, more emphasis must be placed on long-range attractive-ness to the game. Food becomes important, and planning needs to emphasize many of the techniques described earlier in this book for managing wild game birds.

SHOOTING-PRESERVE GAME SPECIES

In recent years there has been a growing interest in big-game shooting preserves, for deer, boar, and other native and exotic spe-cies. But most preserves still operate with "the big four"—pheasants, bobwhite quail, chukar partridge, and mallard duck. An increasing number are experimenting with wild turkey. All are birds, of course, and all share the attribute of lending themselves to large-scale artificial propagation.

Year in and year out, nationwide, the ring-necked pheasant is the backbone of the preserve industry, not because he is all that easy to propagate—feather-picking ("cannibalism") and disease troubles have driven many a pheasant breeder out of business—but because he is big, colorful, and, reared properly, hardy after release. Also, the ringneck normally "goes wild" as soon as he is released, furnishing tough and sporty hunting under proper management. He is by no means "easy," but he is still the best and safest bet for nov-ice preserve operators. However, nearly all ringnecks would rather run than fly, so take the precaution of designing your cover to min-imize running opportunities. Be careful, too, of the dogs you use; an old "meat dog" learns to outwit and turn or hold pheasants, but the same birds can drive most highly trained field-trial pointers up the wall.

Bobwhite quail are at the opposite extreme. Very susceptible to disease, they should be held on wire, off the ground, in all but sandy, well-drained soils in southern climes. Worse, they are prone to tameness—to the point where they will walk up to a hunter and peck at his shoe—and poor flight performance unless reared by experts under ideal conditions. Probably not one in ten, or even one in twenty, of the game farms selling bobwhite turn out a truly good bird. If you are lucky and persistent enough to locate a source of good quail, your problems have just begun.

For one thing, it is next to impossible to duplicate a typical covey rise using only released birds. You can stock a group of eight to fifteen quail together, of course. But when dog and hunters approach, even if the group is still more or less together, the birds will flush in twos or threes or singly, not as a covey. Consequently most preserve operators release no more than three or four birds together—and hope for the best.

Yet the bobwhite is the mainstay of a few of the largest and most successful of all shooting preserves. How so? First of all, most such areas are located in prime native quail range. Their operators manage for and maintain ideal year-round bobwhite habitat where wild birds thrive and multiply and where unharvested released

The ring-necked pheasant is the backbone of the shooting preserve industry. Alternate strips of brome grass and corn look natural and "birdy," and provide the cover diversity important even for "put and take" management.

quail often survive and prosper as well. Released birds are stocked into existing wild coveys, or soon find them, and these coveys are carefully maintained. Here everything is working for the released birds, including the behavior example set by their wild brethren.

A handful of preserves beyond natural bobwhite range also feature good quail hunting, although still never the real McCoy. Their owners achieve this by combining the best of hand-reared birds with meticulous attention to cover management, dog work, and "atmosphere." These are real pros. Obviously, even in good quail country, the bobwhite is not for the amateur or novice preserve operator.

In more ways than one, the chukar partridge is the in-between preserve bird. Intermediate in size between the ringneck and the bobwhite, and better eating than either, the chukar adds variety on a preserve. But he is a real problem. Like the bobwhite, the chukar can drop dead of disease while you blink your eyes, and he is equally prone to tameness when raised in captivity. The secret to getting good hunting from them lies in a combination of good birds (like the bobwhite, produced by only a few of many breeders), suitable cover, and the right dogs. Because chukar will either freeze to a pointing dog and never flush, or walk out and stare at the hunters, or run like a pheasant, they are usually hunted by flushing dogs (Labs and the like) on preserves. Increasing in popularity as more preserve operators master the secrets of their management, chukars are well worth a try.

Last of the big four is the mallard, for whom cover—important for the upland species—takes a back seat to terrain and water. Mallards, being waterfowl, are under federal jurisdiction, unlike the state-controlled resident game that make up the other popular preserve-hunting species. To enjoy long seasons and unlimited harvests, the preserve operator who releases and hunts hand-reared mallards must control his flock rigidly, so that no wild ducks will be lured in and shot. Consequently, the location and operation of a mallard-hunting preserve are subject to tighter restrictions than preserves releasing and hunting only resident game. A site where wild waterfowl occur frequently during fall and winter cannot even be licensed for "put-and-take" mallard shooting, for example.

Even where chances are slim that wild birds will venture near, release and hunting patterns must be watched closely. To live within these restrictions, an established, workable system has been developed. There are three fundamental components, in addition to good quality birds capable of fast, sustained flight: a body of open water adequate for the flock to rest in and drink from; a covered holding pen at a suitable distance, with space and feeders sufficient for the flock; and terrain and cover between pond and pen of a nature that will force the birds to fly high and fast enough to furnish tough, sporty shooting.

The ducks are placed on the pond when they are four weeks of age or older, and fed there until they begin to fly at eight to ten weeks of age. The feeders are then moved to the holding pen in stages over a period of several days, and the birds, of course, walk or fly to the feeders, eat, and return to the pond. When the feeders are eventually placed within the holding pen, the ducks follow and can be shut into and held in the pen. Normally no water is available in the pen, so the ducks, after feeding, readily fly back to the pond when released, to drink, bathe, and loaf. Thus a daily regimen can be established. Usually feeders are filled in the late afternoon. Having learned this, the ducks leave the pond in the afternoon and fly to the pen, enter, and feed. The operator closes the gates and holds the birds overnight. If hunting is scheduled for the next day, the birds are released in small groups at intervals until hunting ends. Then all remaining birds are released to spend a day on the water. If there is no hunting scheduled, all the flock is released in the morning as customary.

From the first day that the ducks are placed on the pond, a signal of some sort should be used when feeders are filled. This may be a call, a bell, a car horn, or whatever. The sound soon becomes associated with food, and the flock will move to the feeders at the signal, helping to ensure control.

The success of a "flighted" mallard operation hinges upon the route the birds take from pen to pond. Ideally, the pen is located a half-mile or more from the pond, and on considerably higher ground, with a good stand of tall trees between. The ducks, upon release, fly straight for the pond. They are forced up to a good elevation by the trees, and gain speed by going downhill over a sufficient distance. The hunters are placed in blinds at the foot of the hill, near but not at the pond, and either in or at the edge of the trees. The blinds are constructed and placed so that shots are possible only at oncoming or sideswiping birds—not at ducks going away and never at ducks landing on the water. Blinds placed among tall trees along the flight path are the toughest of all.

Done right, this creates difficult shooting, usually much more so than that experienced in hunting wild ducks over decoys. But it lacks the element of suspense that is so much a part of waterfowl hunting and, perhaps for this reason, has never grown in popularity to the same extent as has hunting for upland game on preserves.

Yet, as good wild-duck hunting becomes increasingly difficult to find, mallards have a greater potential for preserve hunting than any species. If management techniques can be developed that would permit more natural hunting of released mallards, without harm to wild waterfowl, and restrictions relaxed as a consequence, the mallard could well replace the pheasant as the number one "put-and-take" bird—and hunting pressure on wild waterfowl might well decrease significantly as a result.

SOURCES OF HELP

Advice and assistance in planning, developing, and operating a shooting preserve, commercial or private, is available if you are willing to look, ask, and, at times, pay for it. A few state conservation departments have a staff member whose job it is to assist preserve operators, so ask your state agency if such help is available.

As is so often the case in wildlife work, county representatives of the U.S. Soil Conservation Service often can provide informative leaflets, cover-management tips, and, in some cases, cost-sharing programs for preserve development.

Private sources provide the bulk of available help. Many states have associations of preserve operators who meet and discuss common problems. Pennsylvania, Wisconsin, and Illinois are outstanding examples, but there are many more. Ask your state conservation department if your state has an active association. If so, join it; if not, join the association of the nearest state that supports one—you will be welcome. Perhaps the greatest help of all to both novice and experienced operators comes from the North American Game Breeders and Shooting Preserve Association—the national trade association. This group sponsors an annual conference featuring experts on all phases of preserve management and game-bird propagation, and publishes a monthly newsletter that is the best source of current information on these subjects, served up in highly readable fashion. Membership is nominal; contact Dr. E. L. Kozicky, Secretary, NAGBSPA, Olin, East Alton, Illinois, or John Mullin, Editor, *NAGBSPA Newsletter,* Gooselake, Iowa.

Good current literature on either preserve management or game-bird propagation is not easy to come by. By far the best for the preserve operator is *Shooting Preserve Management—the Nilo System,* written by Dr. Kozicky and John Madson and published by Winchester Press, available through the Olin Corporation, Conservation Department, East Alton, Illinois.

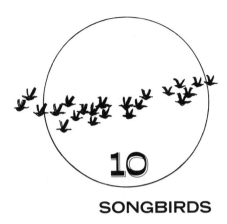

SONGBIRDS

Let's turn from game to nongame wildlife—specifically song-birds, present nearly everywhere across the continent in greater or fewer numbers and variety, and brightening the day wherever they are found.

Like any other wildlife group, songbirds must have an adequate supply of food, cover, and water (in one form or another) to survive. The principles of edge and diversity again apply. In general, the greater the number of niches or variations in habitat in a given area, the greater the number of songbird species that will be present. The population of any one of these species normally will be in propor-tion to both the quantity of suitable food, cover, and other require-ments that are present, and to the degree to which these key in-gredients are intermingled.

Songbirds have other common bonds with game species. Ac-cording to estimates, over 10 million Americans pursue the hobby of bird-watching—one of our fastest-growing forms of outdoor rec-reation. Thus design and management of parks and other public lands for the enhancement of songbird resources help fill the needs of many citizens, just as management for game species provides rec-reation for sportsmen. Private landowners and developers should take heed. The farmer who supplements his income by operating a camp ground, the full-time outdoor-recreation "entrepreneur," those who plan, build, and landscape new subdivisions, and many others who sell recreation or land will find increasing public response to and profits from providing wildlife-viewing opportunities—especially if that wildlife includes a variety of songbirds.

Songbirds differ from the game species we have discussed in that they number vastly more species and, as a result, have a much greater variety of life styles. Some are year-round residents nearly everywhere they occur. Others nest in the far north, winter in Latin America, and are present over most of the populated regions of North America only as migrants. Still others are seen by most of us as residents in summer or winter only. Some songbirds feed almost exclusively on insects, or hard seeds, or soft fruits; others consume all three with equal aplomb. Songbird nesting habitat may mean bare ground or clumps of grass, low bushes or tall trees, or tree cavities. Even size becomes critical. The smaller species have high metabolic rates. Put simply, the energy demands of their tiny bodies, to move and even to keep warm (they have a great deal of heat-losing body surface in proportion to their "mass"), are such that they must eat a large amount, and often, to keep alive. Chickadees, nuthatches, sparrows, and other small species that winter in the north must have adequate food and warm shelter close together, or they simply cannot survive a long (fourteen hours or more) northern night in subzero temperatures.

For all of these reasons, then, diversity and interspersion ("edge") are critical to songbird management, whether in a 10,000-acre park or a ¼-acre back yard.

HABITAT MANAGEMENT ON LARGE AREAS

Since the same general principles apply, the basic ideas outlined in previous chapters for the planning and development of large tracts—estates, farms, parks, and the like—for game species should be reviewed and put into effect for songbird management. Because variety in food and cover needs to be stressed even more for songbirds, emphasis should be placed on manipulating natural succession, which tends to create greater diversity than does planting. In addition, even greater care than in the case of game species must be taken to preserve and/or establish small or unusual habitat niches.

In managing woodlands, for example, maintenance of existing clearings and establishment of additional openings where few or none are present are important, as is occasional selective cutting to open up a canopy to encourage growth of desirable trees and shrubs. But any cutting must be highly selective if songbirds are your goal. Older trees, partially dead or with cavities, furnish nesting sites for a surprisingly large number of our most attractive and interesting birds, and food sources for others. Eliminate such trees and you immediately destroy a good share of what you are aiming for. As we shall discuss in more detail later, songbird variety and abundance depend in considerable part on year-round food supplies. So-called "weed-trees"—including box elder, hawthorns, the smaller elms, mulberries, and others—often furnish food supplies that, because of their high palatability or their presence in critical seasons, may be vital to local songbird abundance.

The edges of woodlands, where they adjoin cropland, pastures, or other open fields, are key areas in the management of many game species—particularly the bobwhite—as we have seen. Such borders are even more important for songbirds, especially if few clearings exist within the woodland. Borders are an edge in themselves. More important, they give access to sunlight in which many shade-intolerant shrubs and vines that offer food, shelter, and nesting sites for songbirds can prosper. Where woodlands end abruptly along a cultivated field, pasture, or similar opening, the desirable brush-vine border can be created in two ways. Abandoning cultivation in a strip of the adjoining cropland, or plowing and then fallowing a similar strip in adjoining pasture or meadow, will initiate natural plant succession. In time, the desired brushy stages normally will develop. Faster, but somewhat more costly in manpower, is selective cutting of tall trees along the edge, to reduce shade and root competition. Which course to choose depends on many things, including your own patience and budget, and which habitat ingredient you can best afford to lose—open land or woodland. If you choose to cut, remember that selectivity is mandatory. Do not remove trees that furnish choice food or nesting ingredients, especially if they are uncommon species in your woodland.

Planting trees, shrubs, and vines has a role in managing large tracts for songbirds. This is true especially where little woody vegetation exists and plant succession may take too long to fill in the missing habitat ingredients, or where natural succession may not supply certain important groups of plants, such as conifers.

In situations where planting seems desirable review the details and steps outlined in Chapter 5. These points on planning, ordering, caring for, planting, and maintaining plant materials for upland game species are relevant here as well. Later we will discuss species and groups of woody plants important for attracting songbirds to small lots, yards, and gardens. Most also are ideal for planting on large tracts.

Too often we relate songbirds only to tree and shrub habitat, forgetting that many species require grasses, forbs, or grains for nesting and for much or all of their food supply. Grassy fields are necessary to such desirable birds as the meadowlarks and several of the sparrows, for example. Well-managed pastures will suffice in many instances, but better still are ungrazed swales, meadows, and roadsides. For songbirds, grasslands usually are best when their composition is varied: several species and growth forms of grass intermingled with perennial flowers, as opposed to single-species plantings. Working with natural succession, as described in Chapter 4, is the cheapest and often the best way to achieve this diversity. Seeding mixtures of native prairie bunchgrasses—bluestems, switch grasses (whose seeds are a choice food of indigo buntings), and the like, that provide food and cover for grassland birds—is becoming increasingly popular. County SCS offices or state agricultural colleges usually can provide directions and seed-source references for establishment of native grasses.

Food patches of annual grains are perhaps not as important as for upland game birds, but some plots are still desirable for attracting and holding songbirds. This is true especially in the North, where juncos, tree sparrows, and a number of other seed-eaters can be counted upon to frequent standing grain in winter, particularly if perennial cover is nearby. As in game-bird management, the whole point of good winter grain strips and patches for songbirds is to make food available. Crops that lodge and lie flat under snow or ice are of little use. Stiff-stemmed sorghums or sunflowers, interplanted or seeded in combination with the taller millets (Japanese, German, or pearl), make excellent food patches in northern winters. Further south, where snow cover is limited, buckwheat and proso millet are choice food-patch ingredients.

Do not forget water. Many songbirds require or are attracted to open water for drinking or bathing. Others prefer the vegetation associated with wetlands as a source of food or nesting cover. Where natural marshes, ponds, or streams exist, maintain them. Where they do not, consider construction of one or more small impoundments, or even man-made guzzlers, as described in Chapter 6. State wildlife agencies and your county SCS representative can help here with plans and, at times, some cost-sharing assistance.

Interest in songbirds has resulted in the development of intensive management techniques—plantings of selected fruiting shrubs, construction of bird houses and feeders, and installation of special small watering devices—designed for small properties. The cost of using these techniques on a massive scale is too great for most individuals or public agencies owning large tracts of land. Yet such methods can be applied to a small segment or two of large acreages, as a focal point attracting birds from surrounding lands that are under more natural and less intensive management. The development of wildlife focal points should be considered more often by owners and managers of parks and outdoor recreation areas because they serve to concentrate viewing opportunities and to provide educational experiences. In this context, the following discussion on "back-yard songbird management" has possibilities for those who manage large properties.

PLANTING GARDENS AND YARDS FOR SONGBIRDS

If you are interested in trying to do something for wildlife with your own hands, but feel frustrated because you do not own a farm or ranch, don't be discouraged. You can accomplish a great deal literally in your own back yard, whether small or large, in the city or in the country.

Herein lies the magic of songbirds. Highly mobile, and with an enormous variety of habits and habitat preferences, they present the back-yard wildlife enthusiast with his best opportunities. With only a tiny yard in the city you stand a chance of attracting, feeding, and sheltering, even though briefly, small feathered migrants, as well as playing host to the increasing number of species that are adjusting to city life. With a large lot in the country or suburb you may develop surprising numbers of nesting, wintering, and year-round resident birds in addition to numerous migrants.

In favorable settings you may be surprised at what you will see some morning. Plantings and feeders in suburban yards, aimed at songbirds, have helped "suburbanize" squirrels, cottontails, racoons, and opposums. In some areas the once wary crow also is becoming adjusted to the suburbs. This trend will probably continue, and more of the larger birds and mammals may begin to rub elbows with people.

In planning and developing your lot to attract songbirds, concentrate on supplying diversity of food and cover, as we have stressed continually, but on a small, highly intensive scale. Nearly all your efforts will center on plantings and artificial devices; few yards are large enough for techniques such as the manipulation of plant succession or selective cutting to be feasible. Because every inch counts in small developments, planning becomes especially critical. Review carefully earlier chapters on mapping, planning, soil tests, plant selection, planting methods, and maintenance. Remember to plan with an eye to the future. In working with limited space, make a special attempt to learn and allow for problems that growth may bring, including shade, root competition, and the appearance of your property.

You almost certainly have more in mind than attracting birds when you plan and plant your yard. After all, this is your home, too; you want a good landscaping scheme, shade trees for summer comfort, a hedge for privacy perhaps or as a screen against an ugly view, and maybe a windbreak. But birds do not have to take second place, because this is one of the few times in life when you can have your cake and eat it, too. With a little care, you can find flowers, shrubs, and trees that are ideal for all your needs as a homeowner—landscaping, shade, privacy, screening—and that double as prime food and cover sources for many birds.

To be successful in achieving this dual goal—"birdscaping" your property—strive for as much variety in plantings as space and landscaping balance permit. Songbirds vary greatly in food requirements, as I've mentioned. Mourning doves eat nearly 100 percent plant foods—primarily small, hard seeds. Robins and cedar waxwings prefer soft fruits, although robins love earthworms and waxwings often "hawk" for flying insects. The cardinal plays few favorites—hard seeds, juicy fruits, and insects are all fair game. These are only a few examples; the bird world includes both specialists and generalists as regards feeding habits. The point is that the more kinds of food you supply, the more kinds of birds you will see.

Variety is important for other reasons. Many perennial plants vary greatly in their production of seed or fruit from year to year. The more kinds you grow, the less chance there is of a total "crop failure." Also, different plants furnish food at different times of the year; a variety of plant materials helps ensure attractive foods at all seasons.

While shrubs, trees, and vines usually dominate a bird-lover's yard, annuals should not be ignored. On larger lots, a patch of millet, buckwheat, or sorghum, or a mixture of all three, will attract and feed many wintering birds. Millets and buckwheat require little time to grow and mature, so if space is limited, try seeding them where you have pulled out radishes, green onions, or other early garden crops. You can grow three crops this way—spring vegetables, summer grain, and winter birds.

Sunflowers along the back lot-line or fence make an attractive background for your flower or vegetable garden. Left on the stalks or harvested for use in a feeder, their seeds are a delectable food for grosbeaks and many other wintering birds.

Do not be in too big a hurry to clean up your vegetable garden in fall. Seeds in the squash, gourds, pumpkins, corn, beans, and other vegetables you failed to harvest will attract and feed birds well into winter.

Annual flowers play a role, too. It is hard not to like humming-birds; to see more in your yard, consider featuring petunias, morning glories, snapdragons, and nasturtiums. Perennial flowers that are favorites of hummingbirds include columbine, beebalm, and pentstemons (among good wildflowers for garden use), along with lilies, gladiolas, and phlox.

Five principles for selecting woody plants

It is among the woody plants—vines, shrubs, and trees—that the home bird-watcher finds the greatest challenges and opportunities. In selecting woody plants for your property, and planning where to place them, begin with some general principles. First, consider how much space you have, and just how natural and "wild" a yard you and your neighbors can tolerate. There are many woody plants that are simultaneously conducive to birds and excellent for land-scaping in tidy formal or semiformal gardens, large or small. But some of the very best species for birds—the elders and wild cherries, for example—are gawky or lack attractive form, foliage, or flowers. As a rule, if you own an acre or more in a rural or semirural setting, you can well afford at least a small area set aside for naturalized, "wild" plantings. With a smaller lot in a crowded suburb, plan for a happy medium between birds and landscaping beauty.

Second, work for both food and cover, especially in the North. You can set an attractive "table" for wintering birds with well-stocked feeders and fruit-filled deciduous scrubs. But these food supplies lose much of their allure, as well as their value as survival rations, if located in bare, windswept settings.

Third, depending upon the space available and upon how your personal preference swings the balance between appeal to birds and the visual appeal of the plants in question, avoid shrubs and trees that offer little or no food to songbirds. These include coral-berry, crape myrtle, the deutzias, forsythias, hydrangeas, English holly, lilacs, mock orange, redbud, althaea, and ninebark. Most are attractive landscaping plants, and some make good escape cover for wildlife and are used to a certain extent by nesting birds. But none rate more than limited space, at best, in "birdscaping."

Fourth, you will encounter certain genera of shrubs and small trees highly touted for landscaping—the cotoneasters, viburnums, honeysuckles, and others—that exist in a huge number of species, horticultural varieties, and hybrids. In these cases learn all you can before you buy, about the different varieties, using this book, the references cited at the end of this chapter, and the numerous volumes on shrubs and trees in your local library. There are often great differences within these large groups as to the amount of fruit or seed certain varieties produce and their relative attractiveness to birds. As an extreme example, a current fad among nurserymen is the "seedless" tree or shrub. Seedless ashes, locusts, and other varieties are advertised as being less "messy" than their seed-and-fruit-bearing counterparts; they are also birdless. Other plants, such as Clavey honeysuckle, are selected by landscapers because of their growth habits, but produce little fruit. So if you hear or read that honeysuckles, cotoneasters, viburnums and other large groups of plants are "great for birds," don't rush out and buy the first variety your local nursery or garden shop displays. You could end up planting a biological desert for songbirds.

The same large groups of closely related shrubs and trees, popular among nurserymen and landscapers, often contain some varieties native to North America and others imported from Asia or Europe. With a few exceptions, your best bet is native plantings. As a rule, native species are better adapted to weather problems, more resistant to disease, and more familiar to our native birds.

The fifth principle is more complicated. We have mentioned that songbirds differ in their feeding habits—that some prefer hard seeds and some soft fruits, and that others will take both equally well. But not all fruits or seeds are equally satisfying to all fruit-eaters or seed-eaters. Fruits and seeds of different woody plants differ in their palatability to birds. Put simply, some "taste good" and others do not. A few shrubs and trees bear fruit that just never seems to be very palatable to any birds; coralberry is a case in point. More often, palatability varies with bird species. In human terms, what is cake to a cedar waxwing may be spinach to a cardinal.

Furthermore, palatability, which determines the success you will have in attracting birds, may change with the season. Some fruits, such as those of the blackberries and honeysuckles, are obviously tasty even before they are fully ripe. Others, such as those of the high-bush cranberries, don't seem to be sought after until they have been altered (possibly in texture or taste or both) by successive freezing and thawing in winter.

The fruits of still other shrubs and trees, including many of the sumacs, privets, hawthorns, and crab apples, are on the borderline.

They are "persistent" fruits, clinging to branches well into or through winter, but birds don't seek them out greedily as soon as they are ripe. In mild winters in the North they may never be eaten. But at the end of hard winters, when tastier foods have long since been devoured or buried under snow, these less palatable but nutritious fruits are taken by many birds and may well permit their survival. Every yard planted for birds should contain some shrubs or trees from this group.

A last word on palatability. If we leave out the extremes, those woody plants that never furnish edible fruits or seeds, and those whose fruits are eaten on sight, the attractiveness of most fruiting shrubs and trees is bound to depend upon local conditions. For example, if large numbers of migrating or wintering birds occur in an area where fruit and seed supplies are limited, or concentrate during an exceptionally severe winter, even barely edible fruits and seeds may all be consumed. The same foods may be ignored if fewer birds are present, if food is abundant or if weather is less severe.

So do not be too surprised if books or magazines you read seem to differ widely as to how inviting certain trees or shrubs are to songbirds. The authors may be basing most of their observations on localities where the relationship between bird numbers and food availability is unusual for one reason or another. Also, take those "hot tips" you will encounter in some nursery flyers, or newsletters from local bird clubs, with a large grain of salt. Mrs. Thornbottom may report seeing three cedar waxwings sitting in her Flowering Turkish Erckleberry bush, and this may mean much to Mrs. Thornbottom and dealers in Erckleberry bushes. To the waxwings it may mean that this was the only spot in which to rest for 50 miles (and they may never make that mistake again).

I don't mean that you cannot rely on reference books or periodical publications. I do mean that you will find, as you explore the literature on plantings for songbirds, that there are certain trees, shrubs, and vines whose value all are agreed upon. By and large, these will be native species. These are the plants that you should count on and work with. You will also encounter plants praised by one author and ignored or low-rated by others. By and large, these will be imported exotics. If space is no problem you may wish to experiment with a few. But if room is at a premium, pass them by and stick with the known winners.

Choice shrubs and trees for birdscaping

The following list of twenty species and groups of woody plants (with some alternatives for local conditions) is based upon a variety of references and upon personal experience. These twenty have been effective for "birdscaping" through the years and over a wide geographical range. Most are selected because they serve several functions well, a few because they are outstanding for a single purpose.

1. Flowering dogwood (*Cornus florida*). A beautiful small (20 to 30 feet) native flowering tree; fruit a favorite food of many birds and mammals; used on occasion for nesting. An understory forest tree that consequently does best in light shade and with some shelter from severe weather. Thrives on most soils from southern Missouri, Illinois, Ohio through West Virginia and Maryland and south. Outstanding specimen tree for yards in this range.

2. Autumn olive (*Elaeagnus umbellata*). An Asian import and one of the few exotics on the list. A tall (8 to 14 feet) bushy shrub, whose heavy crops of red berries are a choice of many birds and mammals. Occasional nesting use. Attractive foliage; takes pruning well and suitable for informal hedge or screen planting. Hardy nearly everywhere except on wet soils or in deep shade.

Heavy yields of highly palatable fruit make autumn olive a favored shrub for "birdscaping."

3. Eastern red cedar *(Juniperus virginianus).* Native "evergreen," 20 to 40 feet tall (often less), with columnar growth form. Excellent multiple-purpose plant since it combines the windbreak and view-screening shelter values of conifers with persistent berrylike fruits that are an excellent food source. Often used for nesting. Does well on most soils and sites, including dry, poor, "problem" soils.

4. American mountainash *(Sorbus americana).* Small (20 to 30 feet) native tree whose foliage and large clusters of red fruit— choice bird food—make it an outstanding specimen for tree-banks and yards. Hardy in most regions and on most soils, including dry sites. The European mountainash *(Sorbus aucaparia),* similar in appearance, may be hardier under city smog conditions. Its fruit seems to be less palatable initially and so tends to persist as an emergency, late-winter food supply.

5. Paper birch *(Betula papyrifera).* Birches make excellent medium-sized (30 to 50 feet) lawn trees because of their handsome bark and graceful form. Less well known is the fact that their seeds or buds draw many wintering birds—finches, siskins, crossbills, redpolls, and others. Often used for nesting. The native paper birch is "prettiest," with the whitest bark. The gray birch *(B. populifolia),* another native, has dingier bark but takes city smog conditions much better. And the European birch *(B. pendula),* intermediate in "whiteness," stands heat the best and so is the choice farther south.

6. Black cherry *(Prunus serotina).* A tall, native tree, too large and not really attractive enough for use in small lots, but at or near the top of any list as a food source for nearly all fruit-eating birds, and as such deserving of a place on any property where space permits. The smaller (25 to 35 feet) pin cherry *(P. pensylvanica),* another native, while not quite as pleasing to birds, offers an alternative on smaller properties. Fruits of both cherries are consumed or have fallen by autumn; they are summer drawing cards, not winter food sources.

7. American elderberry *(Sambucus canadensis).* A medium-sized (6 to 10 feet) native shrub whose fruits appeal to most fruit-eating birds in late summer and fall, but whose coarse, rampant growth form suits it best for large, "wild" gardens. The European red-berried elder *(S. racemosa),* while not quite as tempting to birds, makes a much better formed shrub for smaller lots. (Don't confuse it with the "European elder"—S.

nigra—which is much too coarse for garden use.) Elders do well on moist sites.

8. Amur honeysuckle *(Lonicera maacki)*. A medium-sized (8 to 15 feet) bushy shrub, with abundant fruits highly enticing to birds. One of the best shrubs for nesting. Fruit, foliage, and growth form suitable for landscaping in smaller yards, especially as a screen or informal hedge (takes severe pruning well). Hardy on most sites and soils. The preferred bush honeysuckle for "bird-scaping" since its fruits appear later and persist longer than those of Tatarian and other honeysuckles.

Amur honeysuckle holds its attractive red berries much longer into fall than does tatarian honeysuckle.

9. Downy (or shadblow) serviceberry *(Amelanchier arborea; A. canadensis)*. Small (10 to 20 feet) native tree, whose fruits appear in early summer, and are favored by many birds. Pretty white flowers in early spring. Does well in most ordinary garden soils. Suitable for small lots but perhaps best used as an understory woodland tree in larger, "wild" gardens.

10. Blackberries and raspberries *(Rubus species)*. Small, thorny bushes, with numerous native species and cultivated varieties. Included here—even though hardly useful for landscaping—because they are probably the most popular of all fruiting plants

to birds in summer, although the fruits rarely persist into winter. Furnish excellent escape cover and good nesting sites.
Space should be given to a berry patch on any large property;
even smaller gardens may spare a back corner for this purpose.
Choose varieties adapted to your climate that will produce good
fruit for you as well as for the birds.

11. Gray dogwood (Cornus racemosa). A medium-sized (6 to 10
    feet) bush, among the best of the several native shrub dog-
    woods. White fruits, an asset in landscaping and excellent for
    birds, produced earlier than most dogwoods. Some nesting use.
    Extremely versatile, making an excellent hedge (responding
    well to shearing and pruning), resisting city smog, and thriving
    in sun or shade, on wet or dry sites.

12. Alternate-leaved dogwood (Cornus alternifolia). Tall (8 to 12
    feet) native shrub, somewhat gawky and so best used in larger
    or "wild" gardens. Fruit perhaps the most attractive to birds of
    all the shrub dogwoods. Does well on most sites and soils.

13. Red osier (Cornus stolonifera). Another good native shrub dog-
    wood (5 to 8 feet). Used by birds somewhat less for fruit and
    somwhat more for nesting than are the species above. Does well
    on most sites and soils, but prefers moist areas. Red stems in
    winter are of special interest for landscaping in northern yards.

14. Flowering crab apples (Malus species). Flowering trees number-
    ing twenty-five species plus scores of horticultural varieties.
    With the exception of the shrubby Sargent crab (4 to 6 feet),
    they range from 15 to 40 feet in height. Outstanding for speci-
    men plantings and focal points on small lots because of their
    colorful fruit and masses of flowers (white, pink, or red, depend-
    ing mn variety) in spring. Fruits usually persist well into and
    through winter and so—while a top choice of only a few birds—
    furnish ample supplies of excellent survival or emergency food
    for many species. In severe winters this fruit may collect flocks
    of such desirable birds as red crossbills, evening and pine gros-
    beaks, and waxwings. Since there is some debate as to which
    varieties are best for birds, pick several locally adapted varie-
    ties in the flower and fruit colors you prefer. Combining out-
    standing landscaping beauty, hardiness on most sites and ordi-
    nary soils, and persistent fruit in quantity for winter birds,
    flowering crabs should be represented in every yard.

15. Washington haw or "thorn" (Crataegus phaenopyrum). A
    thorny, medium-sized (20 to 30 feet) native tree with features

and advantages for birds and for landscaping similar to those of the flowering crab apples, plus greater nesting value and more striking fall leaf color. Clusters of white flowers and red fruit; hardy on nearly all sites and soils. A fine specimen lawn tree for "birdscaping."

16. American cranberrybush or highbush cranberry *(Viburnum trilobum)*. Medium-sized (8 to 12 feet) native shrub useful in landscaping for its autumn leaf color and clusters of red fruit held well into or through winter. Fruit a good to excellent winter food for many birds. Best in moist soils. European cranberrybush *(V. opulus)* is easier to obtain commercially but is less hardy in most areas, with the possible exception of smog-plagued cities.

17. Arrowwood *(Viburnum dentatum)*. Medium-sized (10 to 15 feet), many-stemmed native shrub, outstanding for massed plantings, backgrounds, or screens, with abundant clusters of blue berries against brilliant red leaves in fall. Does well on most soils and sites, including problem city areas. Fruit receives good use by birds. Some nesting use.

18. Blackhaw *(Viburnum prunifolium)*. Medium-sized (10 to 15 feet) shrub or (when pruned to one "trunk") small tree. Brilliant red foilage in fall and blue-black fruit make it a desirable landscaping plant, useful as a single specimen or massed. Bird values and use the same as arrowwood. Blackhaw and other native viburnums tend to be ignored by many nurserymen, landscape architects, and homeowners in their race to come up with new exotic viburnums or horticultural varieties. This is too bad, because the natives—although sometimes their flowers are less showy—usually display equally or more colorful fall foliage and larger quantities of showy fruit, tend to be hardier, and seem to be preferred by birds.

19. Cotoneasters *(Cotoneaster species)*. Prostrate to tall (12 to 16 feet) exotic shrubs frequently used in landscaping because of their foliage (often glossy, sometimes evergreen or nearly so) and colorful berries. Fruit is a choice food of a few birds, a fair emergency food for others. Somewhat overrated in landscaping (they are prone to insects and disease) compared to many less frequently used native shrubs, the cotoneasters are mentioned here because they are readily available commercially in a variety of growth forms.

20. Common hackberry *(Celtis occidentalis)*. Medium to tall (60 to 100 feet) native tree, frequently used for nesting, and with fruits that are a favorite among a wide variety of birds. Possibly the best tall shade tree for yards from a bird's-eye view. Resistant to city smog and thriving on dry soils, but sujbect to "witches broom" (an infection producing clusters of twigs) and various leaf-disfiguring problems that—while seldom harmful—render it unsightly at times. A near must for large-property "bird-scaping"; selection as the primary shade tree on small lots should weigh advantages and disadvantages carefully. The smaller (30 to 70 feet) sugar hackberry *(C. laevigata)* is less prone to disfiguration, but it is also less popular among birds and is not as hardy.

This "top twenty" list holds up for much of the United States. In the Far West, additions or substitutions that should be considered include the native buckthorns (used much more in the West by birds than are their native or exotic counterparts in the East) and manzanitas, and the California peppertree, a South American species widely used for landscaping on the Pacific Coast and an excellent food source for birds. In the deep South, the native Southern magnolia *(Magnolia grandiflora)* is perhaps first choice as an outstanding large shade tree, combining top ratings for birds and beauty. Some hollies—not hardy in the North—make excellent food and cover plantings in southern gardens. American holly *(Ilex opaca)*, Chinese holly *(I. cornuta)*, and winterberry *(I. decidua)* are good; English holly *(I. aquifolium)* has colorful fruits, but they are seldom used by birds.

Obviously there are other common trees and shrubs attractive to people and birds besides those listed here. Among species generally rated high for "birdscaping" are the privets, barberries, and pyracanthas. All make excellent hedge plants. Their persistent fruits are often used by waxwings, mockingbirds, and some finches but apparently are unpalatable to many other birds, although they may serve as last-resort survival foods.

The native sumacs have persistent, nutritious fruit in quantity and provide superb fall color. Smooth sumac *(Rhus globra)* is perhaps most inviting to songbirds, but some individual plants do not bear fruit. The same is true of staghorn sumac *(R. typhina)*—it is more colorful in the garden but less of a drawing card for birds. Both are best when massed in large naturalized or wild gardens, where they thrive on dry, poor soils; neither serves well for screens, for single specimens, or on small lots.

Silky dogwood, Tatarian honeysuckle, Russian olive, and maple-leaf viburnum are handsome plants, of value to songbirds. All however, are closely related to species on the "top twenty" list that have superior "birdscaping" attributes.

Some shrubs and trees often acclaimed for garden plantings have—in my opinion, at least—drawbacks serious enough to give them a secondary role. The mulberries, for example, frequently are touted as a must. Coarse, unlovely trees, often spreading rampantly from bird-borne seeds, and requiring both male and female trees to produce fruit, mulberries offer nothing that the wild cherries, serviceberries, and others can't provide equally well and with a more pleasing appearance. The yews (Taxus species) sometimes are highly rated for birds. There is no question that they are handsome evergreens for landscaping, yet fruit crops, while relished by some birds, usually are disappintingly sporadic and sparse, even when care is taken to plant both male and female specimens. The box-elder (Acer negundo), a coarse, messy, bug-ridden tree, often is recommended because its seeds attract evening and pine grosbeaks; most native ashes (Fraxinus species) are equally appetizing to the same birds and are infinitely preferable in the yard. Blueberries, cranberries, and some other natives of the North tend to be too selective as to soil or site requirements for general use, although they should be considered by "birdscapers" whose property offers suitable conditions.

Vines

Woody vines are instrumental in landscaping—beautifying fences, patio dividers, and walls. Some can serve to encourage birds as well. The fruits of native and cultivated grapes, in their numerous species and varieties, are as choice a food for songbirds as they are for game birds. Grape vines provide nesting sites for a few species. Excellent when used "in the wild" on large properties, or cultivated for human consumption, grapes are rarely employed in landscaping since they are coarse in appearance, although some make good screens. Those best combining appeal to people and birds are the native fox (Vitis labrusca) and riverbank (V. riparia) grapes, and the introduced "gloryvine" (V. coignetiae)—fastest-growing and excellent as a privacy screen—and Amur grape (V. amurensis).

Virginia creeper or woodbine (Parthenocissus quinquefolia) bears fruit that is equally or more palatable to birds than that of the grapes, and is more colorful (it has bright-red leaves in fall) and less coarse as a cover for trellises and stone walls. A native to the United States, woodbine is very hardy, grows rapidly, and takes sun or shade on dry or moist sites.

Few other perennial vines offer fruit of real value or palatability to birds, although the native American bittersweet is a fair food for some species. Trumpetvine and passionflower are among the best flowering vines for attracting hummingbirds.

Shrubs and trees for special use

Plant materials are often needed for specific jobs in landscaping and lot designing. Screening back yards from unsightly views or all-too-close neighbors has become increasingly necessary in crowded cities and suburbs. Massed, screen plantings assist birds by furnishing shelter from wind, weather, and predators; choosing certain fruiting shrubs can add a bonus of tempting food. Recommended evergreens for tall "birdscaping" screens include eastern red cedar, spruces, firs, and hemlock. Pines furnish some food and nesting cover but most are not dense enough to provide either good view screens or songbird shelter. Gray dogwood, Amur honeysuckle, and autumn olive make good hedges, as do the privets, although fruits of most privets are rarely preferred bird foods.

In choosing tall shade trees for the yard, best bets are common hackberry, Chinese elm, sweetgum, oaks, maples, and ashes (except seedless varieties). All furnish food in the form of fruit, seeds, or buds, and all receive considerable nesting use.

With city smoke, soot, and smog a mounting problem, urban dwellers who seek good survival rates and good bird use from their woody plants should turn to species and varieties adapted to urban conditions. Shadbush or Allegheny serviceberry (*Amerlanchier laevis*), European mountainash, gray birch, gray dogwood, arrowwood, common and sugar hackberry, Washington haw, autumn olive, flowering crab apples, woodbine, the native sumacs, American elderberry, and European cranberry bush all tolerate city environments well, making up a remarkably varied list for urban "birdscaping."

Feeders and supplemental feeding

Setting out food for songbirds to supplement natural sources has become an extremely popular pastime for millions of Americans, possibly one of our top hobbies or winter "sports." Done properly, feeding can be a valuable assist to the survival of wintering birds as well as a source of great enjoyment and educational value to those who practice it.

Anyone who feeds wild birds must keep one fact foremost in mind; the birds attracted may prosper because of feeding, but many also may have remained farther north, or farther away from safe, natural food and cover, because of feeders. Those who feed birds bear a real responsibility. Don't fail in bad weather; that is when you are needed most. Don't leave for a long vacation in mid- or late winter without arranging for someone to keep your feeders filled. Finally, don't stop feeding too soon. Early spring, when the snow is gone and winter seems over, is often the toughest season for birds in the North; natural food supplies usually are exhausted and new supplies not yet available.

For maximum effectiveness keep certain principles in mind regardless of where, when, or how you feed. Choose a sheltered spot, out of the wind and weather (preferably in the sun, especially in the North), as in the lee of conifers, buildings, or hedges. If there are cats in your neighborhood, don't feed under overhanging branches, or closer than 8 to 10 feet from concealing vegetation.

When should you feed? All year, if you wish. Supplemental food will help birds most in critical seasons, especially late winter and early spring, or during periods of severe cold or heavy snow. But while the birds don't really need your help in summer and fall, feeding at these seasons still will draw many species for viewing. Fresh fruits, suet, and peanut butter, incidentally, seem to be the favorite foods in summer. If you can feed through the winter without interruption, start in early fall for best results.

Just scattering food on the ground is the simplest approach. While effective, ground feeding has certain drawbacks, among them competition from mice (which may then move to your house) and squirrels, as well as a greater risk of predation, and problems where snow is frequent and buries the food supply. You can ignore one "danger" sometimes cited for ground feeding—namely spoilage. As I pointed out earlier, if wild birds died from eating grains and fruits "spoiled" from lying on the ground, we would have been birdless long ago.

The best elevated feeding structure for the beginner—and basically appealing enough to birds to continue in use even after you have "advanced" to fancier devices—is a platform feeder. Easiest to build, it is also most apt to be used by birds unaccustomed to feeders. A simple, flat shelf made of wood (other materials tend to be too slippery or cold) about 2 feet square, mounted securely on a post or windowsill, or hung at least 3 or 4 feet above the ground, will attract a wide variety of birds. A low rim helps keep the food in place; a high back and sides serve the same purpose and add shelter from wind. Don't be concerned if seeds blow off, they will be picked up quickly. One tip on platform feeders—don't stint on size. The larger the surface, the more room for timid species that might otherwise be driven off by bigger, more aggressive birds.

A simple shelf feeder atop an air-conditioning unit brought these red crossbills close for window viewing. The evergreen in the right foreground shelters the feeder from wind.

Because food on open platforms can be swept away in high winds or buried under snow, "hopper" feeders are popular. They are available commercially in numerous styles, some of them architectural marvels more impressive to people than to birds. All hoppers have one basic feature in common—an enclosed storage space, where food can be kept dry and from which the food trickles out by gravity to an open feeding shelf. The big advantage of hopper feeders is that, once filled, they automatically replenish food as needed over a period of time varying with the use received.

A third basic feeder style is designed to hold suet, highly appetizing to nuthatches, woodpeckers, chickadees, brown creepers, and a host of other birds, some of which rarely visit other types of feeders. While many styles are marketed at varying prices (mostly high), you can make an effective suet feeder by fashioning a small, cylindrical basket of ½-inch-mesh hardware cloth. Filled with suet, the basket is fastened to a tree trunk or suspended by a wire from a branch. Suet "logs," made by boring holes in a piece of wood and filling them with suet, are equally useful. Beef suet is the basic ingredient, often ground and/or with other ingredients added. There are as many recipes for seed cakes as for Southern fried chicken; try them all and make up your own if you like. Just don't leave out the suet.

Beyond the basic platform, hopper, and suet designs, feeder styles are limited only by the imagination. Swinging feeders, small and suspended from a single point by wire, tend to discourage some of the more common, voracious birds such as starlings, jays, and sparrows, and so are used to hold sunflower seeds and other expensive foods enjoyed by "desirable" birds. "Weathervane" feeders

A suspended, hopper-type feeder made from parts of tin cans. A suet chunk is fastened to the base.

A suet "log"—a mixture of suet and seeds is stuffed into holes bored in a section of limb and the whole is suspended by wire from a branch. Nuthatches, chickadees, and woodpeckers, among others, enjoy this treat. Small perches are not essential.

have one open side and are so designed as to turn that side away from the wind. They have value in unprotected sites. "Trolley" feeders—usually hopper styles—are mounted on wires equipped with pulleys and located so that they are initially well away from the house. As birds become accustomed to the feeder, it is pulled closer to the house, finally ending up at a viewing window. Designs that combine basic styles are useful. A large platform or shelf, for example, with back and sides, may have a small hopper added at one side and a suet basket at the other.

The theme, obviously, is variety. Several feeders, offering different foods in different locations, draw a greater variety of birds and minimize chances that large, common, and aggressive species will crowd out the others. So start with a platform, most favored by most birds and the best way to accustom them to feeders, and work from there.

What to feed? We have mentioned suet—a must for certain birds. For seed-eaters, millets, sorghums, cracked corn, buckwheat, hemp, small grains, and sunflower seeds are all good. Most occur in bird-food packages sold commercially. You can also grow your own if you have space—especially sunflowers, whose seeds are among the most desirable and expensive. Peanut butter is excellent. Raisins, currants, nuts, cut-up apples, and other fruits are delectable but costly. Plain old bread, torn into pieces, draws a surprising

Large hoppers keep food dry and supply seed for many days without refilling. Evergreen at left provides a wind screen but will not support a climbing cat.

Hopper feeders protect food from wind and snow.

number of birds; being highly visible it makes a good invitation for your first feeding attempts.

Don't overlook grit—coarse sand or finely crushed oyster shells, commercially available from poultry supply houses and pet shops—which is essential to seed-eating birds. Supply it in feeders along with standard foods.

Squirrels, while fun to watch, can be a problem at feeders, driving away birds and consuming volumes of food at one sitting. To minimize squirrel competition, protect post-mounted feeders by fastening a wide smooth metal band around the post. Suspended feeders can be protected by metal cones, 30 inches in diameter, around the wire above the feeder. Place all feeders at least 5 feet above the ground and well away from overhanging branches to discourage bushy-tailed acrobats. And feed the squirrels elsewhere; a wire basket of corn on the cob, fastened to a tree, will keep them happy and less apt to explore your bird feeders.

Housing for songbirds

There is evidence that American Indians used gourds to provide purple martins, and perhaps other birds, with nesting space long before Columbus reached our shores. Those Indians, as well as Columbus and probably the martins themselves, would be amazed at what the ingenuity of modern man has since devised. Birdhouses, like feeders, now come in an almost endless variety of designs.

The reason is that the purple martin is only one of dozens of desirable species of birds which normally nest in cavities provided by hollow trees or stumps in nature, but which accept suitable man-made "cavities." Bluebirds, chickadees, nuthatches, woodpeckers, and wrens are but part of a list that includes many owls and such waterfowl as the goldeneyes and wood duck. Furnishing suitable artificial nesting sites can be an effective complement to nesting cover supplied by plantings, and the only way to persuade certain species to nest where natural cavities don't exist.

The simplest basic birdhouse is a wooden box, with a roof sloping to the front. Constructed so as to have interior measurements 5 inches square and 8 inches high, with a ½-inch round entrance hole placed 6 inches above the floor, such a box will serve for a number of species. The size and entrance diameter of the basic design can be altered to accommodate most hole nesters. (Several of the references listed at the conclusion of this chapter detail specific measurements for various species.) Wood makes the best box material, and cypress the best durable wood. Use non-corroding screws for lasting, tight construction.

Durable wooden songbird "house" is fastened together with screws for tighter construction and easier maintenance.

Basic wooden nestbox, for woodpeckers and other large birds.

Regardless of box size or target species, provide ventilation by drilling two or more ¼-inch holes in the sides of the box, just below the roof (holes drilled lower will create drafts, chilling young birds). Allow for drainage by drilling similar holes in the floor. Equip the top, bottom, front, or one side with hinges or securely fastened hooks for easy removal, to permit cleaning out debris (and any parasites) in fall.

As described elsewhere for wood-duck nestboxes, deep-bodied boxes (for woodpeckers, for instance) should be provided with hardware-cloth "ladders" leading down inside from the entrance to assist young birds leaving the nest. Boxes for certain species, including wood ducks, woodpeckers, and chickadees, should have sawdust and fine wood shavings added as nest material.

Robins, phoebes, some swallows, and certain other birds, while not hole-nesters, seek out semi-sheltered locations and will use man-made nesting "shelves" just as they use the eaves of buildings. Most shelves are 7- or 8-inch-square platforms, securely fastened beneath the overhang of building roofs and eaves, or provided with sides and a sloping roof and fastened to trees or buildings well above the ground.

Certain rules apply to all birdhouses. Where cats or other predators cause problems, place houses on posts and protect them by means of wide metal bands or collars, or utilize protective devices as described in Chapter 6. Face nest structures away from prevailing winds, and get them up well in advance of the nesting season—by March 1 in the North. Finally, except for martins and a few other colonial nesters, don't crowd a lot of boxes designed for one species into a small area. Most birds are "territorial," the males de- fend a home area against others of the same species, so all but one of your nests are apt to go empty. As with plantings and feeders, variety is the major factor in attracting birds with nesting structures.

Water

Don't overlook provision of water as a prime means of aiding and luring songbirds. While not all birds require water for drinking (some can subsist on juicy fruits), nearly all enjoy it and many will seek it out for bathing.

Birdbaths are available in a multitude of styles and sizes from commercial sources. If you are handy and have time, you can make your own. Concrete is the best material since it is less slippery than metal or plastic. Small in-ground pools, again best made of concrete, are increasingly popular, serving both to bring birds and as landscaping features. Whether elevated or in the ground, water containers or pools for birds should be shallow, with gradually sloping bottoms (grading from ½ inch at the edge to 3 or 4 inches at the center, for example).

Keep watering spots clean and full, and employ the same precautions against cats and other predators that you take with feeders—place baths and pools well away from overhanging branches or thick cover.

Dripping, falling, or sprayed water attracts many more birds than does still water. Moreover, water is especially valuable to birds in below-freezing weather. If you have the time, fill your birdbath several times a day with hot water in winter. If you have the money and not much time, buy one of the effective and relatively inexpensive electric warmers available from poultry and livestock supply dealers. They are used to keep stock tanks and chicken waterers ice-free, but they will do the same job for a birdbath.

SOURCES OF HELP

While conservation departments are not a major source of advice or literature for songbird management as yet, many are becoming aware of and responsive to the need for research, management, and educational efforts on behalf of nongame wildlife. Consult your state agency; it may be among those beginning to provide helpful publications.

The U.S. Department of Interior's Fish and Wildlife Service and the Department of Agriculture's Soil Conservation Service both have useful, brief publications, some of which are listed below.

There are a number of bird and bird-watching clubs in every state—very likely one near where you live—whose members may offer advice and tips. Many of these clubs are affiliated with state Audubon societies that in turn are linked with the National Audubon Society. The national society publishes *Audubon,* a fine magazine, and is deeply involved in major ecological issues, conservation education, and reserarch. However, for practical help on songbird management, especially for beginners, the publications of state Audubon chapters are often more useful.

Financial assistance from public agencies is rarely available for small, private projects, but should be investigated where public lands or major private developments are concerned. The same is true for shrubs, trees, and other plant materials from state forestry or conservation departments. Such materials usually cannot legally be used for home landscaping. There are exceptions, however, so at least explore this possibility with your conservation department.

Because both gardening and birding are so popular, local libraries normally feature many good books on both subjects. Careful browsing should turn up some references pertaining directly to songbird management, in addition to those listed below, as well as books giving greater detail on the characteristics, site requirements, and hardiness of the shrubs, trees, and vines we have discussed here.

References

Verne E. Davison. *Attracting Birds: from the Prairies to the Atlantic.* New York: Thomas Y. Crowell Co., 1967. 252 pp.

A. C. Partin, H. S. Zim, and A. L. Nelson. *American Wildlife and Plants.* Reprint. New York: Dover Publications, Inc., 1961. 500 pp.

John K. Terres. *Songbirds in Your Garden.* New York: Thomas Y. Crowell Co., 1968. 156 pp.

Pamphlets available from the Superintendent of Documents, U.S. Government Printing Office, Washington, D.C. 20402:

Invite Birds to Your Home. U.S. Dept. of Agriculture, Soil Conservation Service. 20¢. (Also available from county SCS offices.)

Homes for Birds. U.S. Dept. of Interior, Fish and Wildlife Service. Conservation Bulletin #14. 20¢.

Attracting Birds. U.S. Dept. of Interior, Fish and Wildlife Service. Conservation Bulletin #1. 15¢.

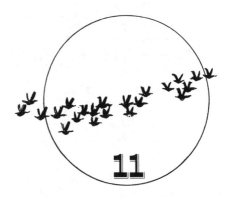

THE HUMAN ELEMENT

T here is an old saying in the wildlife management profession: "Our biggest problems are with people, not wildlife."

The world's plants and animals have always lived with natural catastrophes, from forest fires, floods, tornadoes, earthquakes, and drought to glaciation and massive volcanic activity. Most species survived, adapted, recovered, and increased in the face of such adversity.

The advent of man as the dominant life form has produced catastrophes of new dimensions for living things, not always as immediately visible or dramatic as those of nature, but often more deadly. Many influences of man on his own environment and that of wildlife seem irreversible—at least at present. Floods subside, fires burn out, droughts are broken, and living communities recover. But the man-made semideserts of Asia Minor, North Africa, and southern Europe remain, as do pollution-choked lakes and streams and concrete-covered prairies. True, nature has a great capacity for recovery. Most, if not all, man-made scars would heal in time, if man were to disappear from the face of the earth. But concerned people seek a solution short of the elimination of mankind—a solution that would permit recovery from past catastrophes and prevent others in the future by means compatible to both man and nature.

An impossible dream? We are talking about problems that encompass our entire environment, not just wildlife. Yet, perhaps, the
difficulties faced by wildlife, which is our "environmental barometer," and a possible solution to those difficulties may shed light
upon whether the dream is possible.

Is wildlife in danger from direct overuse? Wild animals today
are "used" primarily for outdoor recreation in North America. This
recreation takes two main forms—sport hunting of game species,
and "watching" game and nongame animals as a serious hobby or
as an interesting addition to back-yard or vacation scenery.

Sport hunting is a "consumptive" use, involving killing and removal of animals. As such it has come under increasing attack from
"nonconsumptive" users—the "watchers." Is this attack justified? Is
sport hunting a threat to wildlife? Not when conducted legitimately,
under current, scientifically based regulations established by state
and federal agencies. Decades of research and hundreds of millions
of dollars—nearly all of it from sportsmen's pockets—have been in-
vested to build a body of facts, a system of refuges, detailed management programs, and a corps of experts to ensure that game species can both prosper and promote hunting recreation. Would that
the same funding had been available from the nonconsumptive use
and users of wildlife, to help ensure the welfare of nongame species!

No, current threats to American wildlife do not come from
hunting. They stem directly or indirectly from loss or alteration of
habitat—of the soil, water, vegetation and natural communities—that
make up the environment of wildlife and man.

Habitat loss may be abrupt, direct, and obvious, as when indus-
trial complexes, subdivisions, and highways replace grassland or
woodland, at time almost overnight, or when drainage transforms a
marsh into a dry cropfield, or channelization destroys a stream and
its fringe of lowland forest. These are the wildlife habitat losses that
are most dramatic, that consequently receive the greatest publicity
and, recently, the strongest public reactions in protest.

Other types of habitat destruction are often gradual, or so mas-
ked by changes in vegetation that the casual viewer, unless witness-
ing the changes, is unaware of any problem. A shifting crop and
land use pattern in agriculture is one case in point. Throughout
much of North America's best farmland, recent years have witnessed an accelerating trend toward larger farms, bigger fields,
more row crops, less pasture and hay, and greater emphasis on fall
plowing. To the average tourist passing through rural landscapes in
spring and summer, nothing has changed; the fields are still green

with crops. (He might wonder a bit in passing the same way in winter, and seeing only snow blackened by windblown topsoil.) To wildlife there is a difference, and a critical one. The fencerows between small fields, the odd corners of cover, the small woodlots and pastures, and even the hay and small-grain fields, where shelter, nesting cover, and food once could be found for most of the year, are now rare or nonexistent.

On marginal farmlands in the lower Midwest—southern Iowa and Illinois, for example—farmers are still clearing hardwood woodlots to create pasture on steep hillsides. If the resulting pasture is well managed, the green of grass replaces the green of oak trees, and the passerby detects no change unless he witnessed the actual cutting and bulldozing. Sadly, however, the same shortsighted greed that led to the destruction of the woodlot almost inevitably leads to overgrazing and raw scars of erosion—clues to what has happened.

Other examples of subtle and not-so-subtle habitat change are all too numerous. Overgrazing on private or—under the permit system—public rangeland in the West normally does not proceed to the final stage of creating a barren desert. Instead, one set of greenery replaces another as a varied native, perennial plant community succumbs to a flora reduced in variety and often dominated by exotic annual weeds and grasses. The deliberate replacement of varied, natural forests by single-species tree farms creates a somewhat similar situation.

These areas of America are still "green" at most seasons. But in each instance a complex, highly varied natural community of plants and animals, including and supporting those species both sportsmen and wildlife watchers value most, has been replaced by a highly simplified plant community, supporting a sparse animal population largely composed of species of little recreational value.

Pollution of air, water, and soil alters wildlife habitat and environment, as well as affecting animals directly. Pollution and related contamination by pesticides and herbicides are widely publicized, and have been reviewed repeatedly in other books and publications. We shall not dwell on them here, other than to emphasize their net result as one more danger to wildlife and wildlife habitat.

Still another threat, once largely ignored but now becoming apparent, is a loss in the quality of wildlife habitat and wildlife-related recreation, as a result of too many "users." This problem first appeared after World War II in hunting, where large numbers of both hunters and game were concentrated in the same locality, as on stocked public hunting grounds, or waterfowl migration stops, near cities. Hunters crowded shoulder to shoulder in situations highly unpleasant for themselves and for the wildlife they sought—hardly a "quality" recreational experience. Fishermen experienced similar problems on popular waters.

New regulations governing numbers, spacing, and open hours for publicly owned hunting lands have helped considerably to improve hunting quality in such problem areas. But the same crowding now plagues many nonconsuming users of wildlife—particularly the casual watchers who visit popular parks and refuges in part because of the animals they feature. A classic case is Yellowstone Park, where wildlife-viewing opportunities, particularly for the famous bears but also for bison and elk, were an attraction equaling or exceeding Old Faithful. Today's average visitor has little chance of seeing a bear; those that once frequented roadsides have been trapped and removed since their presence created impossible traffic jams. Nor are other large mammals any longer so easily viewed. Constantly disturbed by hundreds of people, each seeking to run closer than the next in order to get an unobstructed camera field, few elk, bison, deer, or antelope now venture near roads.

The disturbance of wildlife and the loss of opportunity to view undisturbed wildlife away from a babbling mass of humanity are obvious and serious signs of deterioration in the quality of this recreational experience. The crush of humanity into areas supposedly set aside for wildlife and nature has even more permanent effects. Longer vacations, fewer workdays, and more money, coupled with the boom in off-the-road vehicles—dunebuggies, snowmobiles, and their innumerable exhaust-belching, ear-deafening cousins—have enabled millions more Americans to venture into once remote areas. Here their sheer numbers, and their vehicles, create direct destruction of wildlife habitat. Soil compaction from the unrelenting tread of human feet has become a major cause of tree loss in heavily used forests. The passage of a single snowmobile compacting snow over dormant, sensitive forest-floor wildflowers may delay their ability to sprout in spring until after emerging tree leaves blot out the life-giving sun.

These are direct losses of key habitat ingredients. There are others consequent upon the crush of human hordes in "wild" lands. Roads must be widened to handle the traffic, camp grounds enlarged to hold the mobs "camping out" (on asphalt 3 feet away from adjoining campers), sanitary facilities and commissaries expanded—all at the direct expense of wildlife habitat.

One cannot blame the tourists themselves for this problem or even, as is popular in elite wilderness circles, question their ability to enjoy the outdoors. Experience in nature is relative, as are all human experiences. We can hardly fault people for being satisfied with a situation when they have never known or been educated to expect anything better. The fault lies in a failure to instill an understanding and appreciation of the natural world—"ecology," if you will—in more of mankind. It lies, too, in the failure (with a very few recent exceptions) of those who know better, and who have the power to institute administrative and management changes, to alter the situation. The trend in many public recreation areas, of which Yellowstone is a prime example, to speed with great efficiency the passage of visitors by methods that eliminate the reason for which those same visitors have come, is worse than absurdity. It is total abdication of responsibility.

Incidentally, this is—in my mind—an overriding reason for the complete protection of wilderness areas, keeping them inviolate from vehicles, concessions, and the like. Until we can create, through education, an appreciation of the quality of a true natural experience in the minds of people, and until those who administer our public lands can demonstrate a greatly improved sense of responsibility for the resources with which they are charged, only rigidly drawn and enforced "hands-off" legislation will save the best wild lands. At present neither the average layman in search of wildland recreation nor the average administrator in charge of providing it can be trusted.

Such scenes are becoming rare as "people pressure" on our National Parks, and park management measures in response, destroy the very features that attract the visitors.

We must acquire and cultivate an ecological conscience if future generations are to see—and appreciate—wildlife as part of the community of all life.

Oddly, still another threat stems from those who love and understand, or profess to love and understand, wildlife but who spend most of their effort battling with one another. These battles have become particularly virulent recently with the attack of antihunting organizations against hunting and hunters. The assault is based on two premises—that hunting is destroying game populations and that killing living things is morally wrong. The first charge simply is without foundation, for North America in any event. Yet it is propounded, in the face of overwhelming scientific evidence to the contrary, by highly vocal antihunters who choose to ignore or call false any evidence, no matter how convincing, that does not support their position. The second premise—that hunting should end because killing is "wrong"—is an interesting moral point, though hardly a real issue at this stage of civilization. It might carry some weight if those who proposed it were at least vegetarians. None are, to my knowledge.

This controversy and others that arise between sportsmen and bird-watchers, hunters and antihunters, preservationists and conservationists, threaten wildlife's future. They tend to shake public confidence in those national organizations and agencies, public and private, whose voices, votes, and money have long been the primary and, at times, the only moving force behind wildlife conservation. Well-publicized ravings by a few uninformed or self-seeking individuals have a dangerous way of overwhelming less dramatically presented facts.

Equally serious is the tendency for such disputes to splinter and set against one another groups and individuals sincerely concerned about wildlife—already a minority in our population. The majority of Americans are urbanites who have, at most, no more than a casual interest in wildlife, much less an understanding of wildlife as a barometer of their own environment. If conservationists, real or so-called, continue to squander their time in petty squabbles, they and the resource they profess to cherish will soon drown in the waves of apathy spreading from the urban majority.

What can you do? Seek facts, become informed by studying all sides of debates on wildlife, and don't be stampeded by hysteria or by controversy-crazed media. Join and support organizations such as the National Wildlife Federation, the National Audubon Society, and the Izaak Walton League of America, whose long records of service on all natural-resource issues speak quietly but eloquently. Think twice before backing new, strident, single-issue groups. Some may prove sincere and reliable. Let them so prove. In the meantime there are already more than enough time-tested organizations that need your support.

Work for cooperation and understanding between concerned individuals and groups. Through them, become informed about and take a stand on legislation. Many of the greatest crimes against wild-life habitat and the future of the environment we share with wild-life have been perpetrated by federal legislation and public agencies. Programs and policies that tolerate, induce, and even en-courage soil erosion, habitat destruction on farmland, rangeland, and forests, wetland drainage, stream destruction, pollution, and countless other needless atrocities are still proposed and voted for by the people you elect to public office. Even worse, these same pro-grams frequently are carried out on public land—your land—and paid for with public funds—your tax dollars. Don't believe that your letters and votes don't count; they are the only things that matter to most politicians.

Work, too, toward the establishment of a soundly based eco-logical conservation curriculum in every public school system, be-ginning at the early elementary level. Those who respond to this proposal by stating that "the kids are already overworked" and that there is "no time," should pause to reconsider priorities. Instilling an understanding of an appreciation for environmental con-servation is becoming essential simply for survival. As such it can well supersede many subjects that are trivial by comparison—not simply be offered as an optional token course.

Where shall we find all of the teachers needed? A good place to start would be among the host of young graduates of natural resource and wildlife ecology departments of universities who have little hope of employment in the crowded field of wildlife management and research.

The goal which these measures, among others, may hope to achieve is the development in man of what Aldo Leopold termed an "ecological conscience." Partly intuitive, partly learned through educational processes, partly gained from experiences in the outdoors, ecological conscience represents an attitude of understanding and responsibility for the natural world and man's role therein. This attitude seems to be lacking in some individuals who have all the advantages of education and experience. Even if we are able to provide appropriate opportunities for education and outdoor experiences for most Americans—a mammoth task in itself—can we hope for an appropriate understanding and response? It would seem that we have little choice but to try.

Federal agencies

Agricultural Stabilization and Conservation Service, U.S. Dept. of Agriculture, Washington, D.C. 20250 (and ASCS offices in most county seats)

Extension Service, U.S. Dept. of Agriculture, Washington, D.C. 20250 (extension agents at state land-grant universities; county extension agents with offices in most county seats)

Fish and Wildlife Service, Dept. of Interior, Washington, D.C. 20240; regional offices as below:

   Pacific Region: 1500 Plaza Bldg., 1500 N.E. Irving St., Portland, Ore. 97208

   Southwest Region: Federal Bldg., 500 Gold Ave., SW, Albuquerque, N.M. 87103

   North Central Region: Federal Bldg., Ft. Snelling, Twin Cities, Minn. 55111

   Southeast Region: Peachtree St., 7th Bldg., Atlanta, Ga. 30323

   Northeast Region: U.S. Post Office & Courthouse, Boston, Mass. 02109

Soil Conservation Service, U.S. Dept. of Agriculture, Washington, D.C. 20250 (SCS offices in most state capitals and county seats)

State agencies

Alabama: Dept. of Conservation and Natural Resources, 64 N. Union St., Montgomery 36104

Alaska: Dept. of Fish and Game, Subport Bldg., Juneau 99801; Dept. of Natural Resources, Goldstein Bldg., Juneau 99801

Arizona: Game and Fish Dept., 2222 W. Greenway, Phoenix 85023

Arkansas: Game and Fish Commission, Game and Fish Comm. Bldg., Little Rock 72201

California: Dept. of Fish and Game, 1416 Ninth St., Sacramento 95814; Dept. of Conservation, same address

Colorado: Division of Game, Fish and Parks, Dept. of Natural Resources, 6060 Broadway, Denver 80216

Connecticut: Board of Fisheries and Game, State Office Bldg., Hartford 06115

Delaware: Division of Fish and Wildlife, Dept. of Natural Resources, Tathall Bldg., Legislative Ave. and D St., Dover 19901

Florida: Division of Game and Freshwater Fish, Dept. of Natural Resources, 620 South Meridian, Tallahassee 32304

Georgia: State Game and Fish Commission, Trinity-Washington Bldg., 270 Washington St., S.W., Atlanta 30334

Hawaii: Division of Fish and Game, Dept. of Land and Natural Resources, 1179 Punchbowl St., Honolulu 96813

Idaho: Fish and Game Dept., Box 25, Boise 83707

Illinois: Dept. of Conservation, 102 State Office Bldg., Springfield 62706

Indiana: Dept. of Natural Resources, 608 State Office Bldg., Indianapolis 46204

Iowa: State Conservation Commission, State Office Bldg., 300 4th St., Des Moines 50319

Kansas: Forestry, Fish and Game Commission, Box 1028, Pratt 67124

Kentucky: Dept. of Fish and Wildlife Resources, State Office Bldg. Annex, Frankfort 40601

Louisiana: Wildlife and Fisheries Commission, 400 Royal St., New Orleans 70130

Maine: Dept. of Inland Fisheries and Game, State Office Bldg., Augusta 04330

Maryland: Fish and Wildlife Administration, State Office Bldg., Annapolis 21401

Massachusetts: Division of Fisheries and Game, 100 Cambridge St., Boston 02202

Michigan: Dept. of Natural Resources, Mason Bldg., Lansing 48926

Minnesota: Dept. of Natural Resources, 301 Centennial Bldg., St. Paul 55101

Mississippi: Game and Fish Commission, Box 451, Jackson 39205

Missouri: Dept. of Conservation, P.O. Box 180, Jefferson City 65101

Montana: Fish and Game Dept., Helena 59601

Nebraska: Game and Parks Commission, P.O. Box 30370, Lincoln 68503

Nevada: Dept. of Fish and Game, Box 10678, Reno 89510

New Hampshire: Fish and Game Dept., 34 Bridge St., Concord 03301

New Jersey: Division of Fish, Game and Shellfisheries, Dept. of Environmental Protection, Box 1390, Trenton 08625

New Mexico: Dept. of Game and Fish, State Capitol, Santa Fe 87501

New York: Division of Environmental Management, Dept. of Environmental Conservation, 50 Wolf Rd., Albany 12201

North Carolina: Wildlife Resources Commission, Box 2919, Raleigh 27602

North Dakota: State Game and Fish Dept., 2121 Lovett Ave., Bismarck 58501

Ohio: Division of Wildlife, Dept. of Natural Resources, 1500 Dublin Rd., Columbus 43212

Oklahoma: Dept. of Wildlife Conservation, P.O. Box 53465, Oklahoma City 73105

Oregon: State Game Commission, Box 3503, Portland 97208

Pennsylvania: Game Commission, P.O. Box 1567, Harrisburg 17120

Rhode Island: Dept. of Natural Resources, 83 Park St., Providence 02903

South Carolina: Wildlife Resources Dept., Box 167, Columbia 29202

South Dakota: Dept. of Game, Fish and Parks, State Office Bldg., Pierre 57501

Tennessee: Game and Fish Commission, P.O. Box 40747, Ellington Agricultural Center, Nashville 37220

Texas: Parks and Wildlife Dept., Reagan Bldg., Austin 78701

Utah: Wildlife Resources Division, Dept. of Natural Resources, 1596 W. N. Temple, Salt Lake City 84114

Vermont: Fish and Game Dept., Agency of Environmental Conservation, Montpelier 05602

Virginia: Commission of Game and Inland Fisheries, Box 11104, Richmond 23230

Washington: Dept. of Game, 600 N. Capitol Way, Olympia 98504

West Virginia: Dept. of Natural Resources, 1800 Washington St. East, Charleston 25305

Wisconsin: Division of Forestry, Wildlife and Recreation, Dept. of Natural Resources, Box 450, Madison 53701

Wyoming: Game and Fish Commission, Box 1589, Cheyenne 82001

(Note: Only state agencies primarily concerned with wildlife management are listed; most states also have divisions or departments of forestry that can often supply useful information on plant materials, planting methods, etc.)

National organizations

The Izaak Walton League of America, 1800 North Kent St., Suite 806, Arlington, Va. 22209

National Audubon Society, 950 Third Ave., N.Y., N.Y. 10022

National Wildlife Federation, 1412 16th St., N.W., Washington, D.C. 20036

North American Game Breeders and Shooting Preserve Association, John M. Mullin (Information Officer), Arrowhead Club, Gooselake, Iowa 52750

The Wildlife Society, Suite S–176, 3900 Wisconsin Ave., N.W., Washington, D.C. 20016